MW01025601

FATE &
FREEDOM

To - Florence

Best Wishes,

KTKnight

1619-2019

FATE & FREEDOM

BOOK II: THE TURNING TIDES

K. I. Knight

First Freedom Publishing

First Freedom Publishing, LLC

Fate & Freedom
Book II: The Turning Tides

ISBN 978-0-9908365-6-8

Library of Congress Control Number 2016911831

Copyright © 2017 by K. I. Knight

All rights reserved by the copyright holder. No part of this book may be used or reproduced in any form or by any electronic or mechanical means, including information storage and retrieval systems, without permission in writing from the author.

www.firstfreedompublishing.com

Book Design by Pro Production Graphic Services
Jacket Design by SJulien.com

Printed in the United States of America

First Edition

FOR THE ANCESTORS

CONTENTS

Contents

Contents

ACKNOWLEDGMENTS

could not have created a book of such vast historical scope without the input and expertise of others.

On my production team, I want to thank:

Chris Angermann (*www.bardolfandcompany.com*) for his guidance, advice, and numerous other contributions.

Sharon Julien of Sharon Julien Web Design (*www.sjulien.com*), who has a great eye for producing a beautiful series of covers.

Bob Land (*boblandedits.blogspot.com*), editor extraordinaire, with the finishing touches.

Richard C. Moore (*www.ship-paintings.com*) whose beautiful works of maritime art and other paintings grace the collections of many museums, for the lovely cover images for the series.

Rosanne Schloss, creative director of Pro Production Graphic Services (*www.proproductiongs.com*) for the interior design and layout.

I also want to express my appreciation to Victoria Lee and Daniel Y. Cooper for lending their likeness to Margaret's and John's images on the cover, photographed by Michelle Brown Photography (*www.michellebrownphotography.com*).

A heartfelt thank-you to my husband, Tom, and my children James, Jesse, and Jessica, for putting up with me for the many years during which I was preoccupied with this project.

ix

Acknowledgments

And finally, I want to thank my parents, Willis G. Hall and June G. Hall, for their ongoing support and for reminding me that there is nothing unachievable if you just believe.

THE SAGA CONTINUES...

FATE & FREEDOM

BOOK II: THE TURNING TIDES

PART ONE

NEW BEGINNINGS

1

MARGARET

Jamestown—February 1624

It is a brisk, blustery, gray winter day when Margaret returns to Jamestown. Sitting on the hard wooden bench in the rear of a rowboat, she shivers from the chilly gusts of wind piercing her linen gown and pulls the woolen shawl tighter around her shoulders. She watches the two rowers pulling hard on the oars, sweat pouring from their straining faces. They are making good time heading up the James River, the skiff bouncing on the lapping waves.

Margaret is glad to finally leave behind the area of Warrosquoake and Bennett's Welcome, the plantation where she has worked for nearly two years. Of the more than 100 Puritan settlers who arrived there from England with high expectations, fewer than 30 remain, and they are in a sorry state—a small, disheartened group of survivors whose gaunt, haunted faces tell an ill-fated story. First, the brutal Indian massacre of 1622 devastated their ranks, then the pestilence took further, cruel toll, and the harsh winters and starvation did the rest.

Some of the men have left, seeking employment elsewhere. Even the Reverend William Bennett, sole remaining member on Virginia soil of the family that owns the land, is about to relocate to another plantation. It won't be an easy transition. His wife, Catherine, is about to give birth to their first child, and moving is always filled with anxiety. Those left behind will be a mere outpost of indentured servants of the Bennett family, along with a handful of soldiers stationed at the fort overlooking the south bank of the river. Led by Lieutenant Shepherd, the redcoats are there to protect the lingering settlers against Indian attacks and to give advance warning of any incursion by enemy ships, since England and Spain are at war.

Margaret had been waiting at Bennett's Welcome for her summons to Jamestown ever since the previous fall when John Chew, a successful merchant, asked her to join his household. She had met him at Warrosquoake after he was appointed to settle the estate of Robert Bennett. Margaret had hoped that Mr. Chew would convey her to his home himself in his pinnace—he visited the plantation often enough—but he always left without her. She had almost given up when, this morning, without warning, one of his servants had arrived in a skiff to collect her and take her upriver.

"I'm Walter Hazelton," said the stocky, pimply faced young man dressed in brown breeches, a woolen overcoat, and a Monmouth cap. "Master Chew has sent me. He would have come himself, but there are important visitors in Jamestown, so he dispatched me instead."

Seeing Margaret's puzzled expression, he elaborated, "There is a Royal Commission come from England, sent by King James himself, to report on the affairs in our colony. Its president, John Harvey, is staying at the house, and we can use the extra help."

That explanation didn't make any more sense to Margaret, but she nodded and went in search of the Reverend Bennett. With Walter in tow, she found him sitting on a log behind the main house, reading his Bible. His dark brows were furrowed in concentration.

When he finally looked up, Margaret curtsied and said, "I have come to take my leave, sir. Master Chew's servant here is to take me to him in Jamestown."

Unsmiling, the Puritan minister fixed his stern eyes on her and said, "Very well."

Then he turned to Walter and asked, "When will I receive the payment for my two years' service here, as promised?"

Walter shrugged awkwardly and said, "Don't know anything about that, Reverend Sir. You'll have to settle that with Master Chew himself."

As Bennett turned his back on him in frustration, Margaret headed to the cookhouse to say her good-byes to Humphrey. The cook looked at her affectionately and gave her some corn bread wrapped in a small linen cloth for the journey.

Then she went to the cottage where Anthony and Mary were staying. Although she had seen less of them since they'd gotten married, they were her best friends at Warrosquoake. Unlike Margaret, they had spent time working on a plantation in Bermuda before coming to Virginia, but all three grew close because they liked each other and could share good memories of Africa, not to mention unpleasant encounters with the Earl of Warwick in England.

In the aftermath of the Indian massacre when help from other parts of Virginia arrived, Margaret had also become friendly with two other Africans, Frances and her son, Peter, who had been at Bennett's Welcome for several months. They and Margaret had spent a harrowing time together in the bowels of a Spanish slave ship, the *San Juan Bautista*, that took them from Africa to the New World. Their journey made them kindred spirits, *malungu*—survivors of a traumatic transatlantic voyage.

It had been a happy time for Margaret because she finally had someone she could confide in and ask questions of a personal nature. But Frances and her son had to go back to Floridew, the plantation from which they had come. After that, Mary had become a good friend, but it wasn't the same; and Anthony, her husband, was like an older brother, who checked on Margaret from time to time to make sure she was all right. He did like to talk and often shared his plans for the future with her, of becoming a landowner and having a plantation of his own.

Margaret marvels at how he has managed to keep his tenacious dream for freedom and independence alive despite all the difficulties that have befallen them. At age 14, new experiences still overwhelm her, and she copes with them by reacting and doing what's demanded of her, rather than holding on to a vision of a future of her own making. While she is looking forward to entering the household of the wealthy Jamestown merchant until the terms of her indenture are fulfilled—by her reckoning, she has five years of service left—she has no dreams or plans for what might happen beyond that time. She'll have to ask Captain Jope about it the next time he comes to visit.

Having learned more than she wished to know about loss and how fleeting life can be, Margaret embraced Mary and Anthony as if she would never see them again. Walking up the hill from their cottage, she looked back several times in order to imprint the image of them waving after her deep in her memory.

She would have liked to say good-bye to Lieutenant Shepherd, too. He always treated her with kindness, appreciation, and respect after she nursed his men during the pestilence that decimated the colony. But he was away on a scouting mission. Perhaps she would see him in Jamestown sometime.

Now, sitting in the bobbing rowboat, the smell of the fresh breeze reminds her of being on the open seas in the *White Lion*, and she wonders how Captain Jope and John are faring. She doesn't have much opportunity to reflect, though, because Walter is quite a chatterbox. Holding onto the rudder in back, he tells her all about the staff at Master Chew's house and the eminent visitors there. "All the burgesses are in town because of the Royal Commission," he remarks self-importantly.

Margaret pays careful attention, hoping to glean some foreknowledge of the workings of the Chew household to make it easier for her to fit it.

It is early afternoon by the time they approach Hogg Island. Sheltered from the wind blowing downriver, the two rowers lift the dripping oars from the water to take a break. Margaret shares her corn bread with them and receives gruff thank-yous and nods of gratitude.

When they resume rowing and round the tip of the island, gliding past wetlands and forested patches of land, Walter suddenly points and says, "That's our plantation there."

Squinting, Margaret sees a dock and a large wooden storage shed in the distance. There is no one on shore, although the place does not look abandoned. Farther inland, she can make out the thatched roof of a house and smoke curling in the air from the chimney. For a moment, Margaret is taken aback. She expected to go to Jamestown, not stop here.

Unaware of her concern, Walter prattles on. "There are three servants working the place, George Gooding, John Vaughn, and Thomas Winard, not that their names would mean anything to you." He adds with a conspiratorial smile, "Bit primitive, the surroundings, if you ask me. Master Chew would like to settle there, but her ladyship won't have it. She prefers the comfort of their house in Jamestown, and I don't blame her."

Margaret doesn't know what to make of his comment, having just spent a year and a half in just such "primitive surroundings," but she says nothing.

Walter adjusts the rudder to guide the boat away from the shallows. Up ahead on the north side of the river, they catch sight of the bell tower of the church, the highest point in Jamestown. Knowing the end of their journey is near, the two rowers pull the oars with renewed efforts, and the boat cuts swiftly through the waves.

When Margaret sees the tall masts of several sailing vessels come into view, her heart beats faster. Could one of them be her captain's ship? The last time he and John visited was a mere half year ago. Is it possible that they are back so soon? But as the skiff gets closer, she realizes that the hulls of the anchored ships with their quarterdecks riding high above the water are too bulky to be the sleek *White Lion*.

Disappointed, Margaret turns her attention to the large townhouses coming into view above the embankment along the way to the fort and main part of town. More have been built since the last time she was here, a year and a half earlier. She remembers that the area was called "Merchants' Row" because of all the wealthy traders living there.

Walter points to a large, two-story building with dark red exterior walls and a tiled roof. "That's Master Chew's—the first redbrick house built in Jamestown!" he says proudly.

As Margaret admires the place where she will spend her time from now on, she recognizes a large, wooden frame edifice a few houses farther down. It is the governor's mansion where she lived during her previous sojourn in Jamestown when Bennett's Welcome had been evacuated after the Indian massacre. A pang of anxiety shoots through her. Will Governor Wyatt remember her and the time she witnessed his abject desperation when he prayed to God on his knees for guidance because he had lost faith in his ability to lead the beleaguered colony? Being overheard by Margaret, a servant no less, had embarrassed him, and he was not a forgiving man.

The skiff travels into the harbor and reaches the dock, bumping up against one of the wood pilings. When the rowers manage to steady it, Walter helps Margaret climb up the ladder. As she steps onto the pier, she confronts a noisy hubbub of activity—sailors and dockworkers shouting to one another as they unload crates, sacks, and barrels from a tall merchant galleon. The men appear better fed and more energetic than she remembers. Gone are their worried looks and fearful expressions when they expected the Indians to attack again at any moment.

The road from the harbor to Merchants' Row is muddy from the late winter rains, and the smell of the horse dung takes Margaret back to the stables at Aldwarke in England, where she and John spent two years before she came to Virginia. She walks carefully on the wooden planks laid along one side so that the wealthy citizens and their wives don't besmirch their shoes and dresses on the way to church and into town.

As they get closer to Mr. Chew's house, Margaret realizes that it is made of small, red clay bricks. She also notices a chimney running up the side and a separate cookhouse out back. Walter leaps up the steps to the large oak front door and bangs the iron knocker several times.

Before long, a man dressed in livery opens it. He looks to be in his thirties and has a pinched face with thin lips and a hawklike nose. Looking imperiously down on the arrivals from the stoop, he asks, "Yes?"

Walter grins and replies, "Here she is!" Then he offers a mock salute to Margaret, says, "See you around, and good luck," and walks jauntily toward the backyard.

Before she can respond, the older man says, "You must be Margaret, I am William Winifred, the head butler. Please come on in."

As Margaret climbs the three steps and enters the dark vestibule, he continues, "Wait here, and I'll let Master Chew know of your arrival."

Margaret looks around the musty entry hall. There is a polished mahogany sideboard with a white marble statue of a small winged angel and a wall hanging depicting a hunting scene. Again, she is reminded of the mansion at Aldwarke and Aunt Isabel, the lady of the house who treated her so well. Margaret feels a stab of sadness remembering that Aunt Isabel died just a year ago. She hears her words, "You must overcome your fear," echo in her mind.

Just then the door to the living room opens, and the butler beckons to her. As she enters the drawing room, John Chew comes toward her. His lively eyes take in her appearance, her simple dress and drawn face. He smiles kindly and says, "Welcome to my house, Margaret. I trust you had a good trip upriver."

Margaret nods and glances around the room. It is more lavish than she imagined, filled with fancier furnishings than she has seen in a long time. She feels the warmth emanating from the log fire crackling in the stone hearth. An elegant-looking woman with penetrating brown eyes, thin lips, and coiffed hair leans languidly against the dark green cushion of an upholstered sofa with gold fringe lining the bottom. She is wearing a red gown with gold embroidery and strands of pearls sewn onto the pleated shoulders. Margaret has not encountered such extravagant apparel since she met Lady Frances Wray in England.

A young boy with chestnut-colored hair, who looks to be seven or eight, stands next to her and regards Margaret with undisguised interest. Wearing a dark green doublet and matching breeches he looks like a little man, the spitting image of John Chew. His younger brother, whose cheeks are still pudgy with baby fat, is dressed in a grayish gown and appears to be preoccupied with the tassels on one of the sofa cushions.

John Chew makes the introductions. "This is Sarah, my wife, and my children, John Jr. and Nathaniel."

When Margaret curtsies, Mrs. Chew greets her with an amiable smile and says, "Welcome, Margaret. We are pleased to have you in our home. Children, say hello to Margaret."

Nathaniel, fascinated by the cushion, ignores her, but John Jr. bows smartly.

Mrs. Chew gestures to a young woman standing off to one side. She wears a white bonnet and purple gown and worries the fingers of the hands folded in front of her. A small frown creases her forehead.

"This is Ann Waterman, my personal maid," Mrs. Chew explains. "You'll be sharing sleeping quarters and will have plenty of opportunity to get to know each other."

Ann smiles tentatively and mumbles, "Welcome."

Margaret is about to say something in reply when Mr. Chew interjects quickly, "Well, that's settled." He rings a bell and, when the butler appears, says, "William, why don't you take Margaret to the kitchen to meet the cook and the others? Get her comfortable and prepare her for tonight. We have a full house for supper."

William bows and holds the door for Margaret. As they reach the hallway that leads to the rear of the house, Chew catches up to them and says, "A word, Margaret."

He takes her out of earshot of William and continues more softly, "I had hoped to talk to you in private before you met my family. My wife wishes to keep Ann as her personal maidservant. She has grown accustomed to her. I'm sure you understand. You will help in the kitchen and serve at dinners. Your familiarity with those tasks should make it easy for you to fit right in."

"Anything you wish, sir," Margaret replies meekly, hiding her disappointment. "I am at your service."

"I knew I could count on you," says Chew, relieved, and returns to the drawing room.

When he has closed the door, William looks at her imperiously with narrowing eyes. "I suppose this is your only dress," he says with barely hidden disdain.

"Yes, why?"

"Well, we will have to make do with it for tonight and get you a new one tomorrow. It is hardly acceptable, is it?"

Margaret nods, chagrined. As she follows him down the hall, she thinks, *At least I'll be safe here.*

* * *

That evening, wearing a white apron over her gown, Margaret enters the living room carrying a trencher filled with diced pieces of roasted turkey, deer, and rabbit. William, dressed in butler livery, gestures where to put it down on the long oak table that sits in the middle of the dining room. The aroma from the meat dishes, porridge, and corn pones fills the air. Because Mr. Chew is hosting special guests, the meal is more sumptuous than a normal supper.

As Margaret approaches her new master, who is sitting at one end, he nods to her and smiles encouragingly. Although William prepared her well, Margaret feels a bit unsure of herself and is pleased that he trusts her to be a server for his important guests on her first day at his house. At the other end of the table, she sees Mistress

Chew whispering to an older man sitting next to her. He chuckles and bows his head appreciatively toward her.

As William replenishes the wineglasses at the table, he gestures for Margaret to stay, and she withdraws to one side, hidden from general view, waiting, observing and listening to the conversation. The room, lit by several flickering candelabras on the table, is cozy and dark around the edges. The atmosphere is genial, but she can sense a tension beneath the cultured exchanges.

The man sitting prominently on the other side of the table, close to Chew, must be John Harvey, the person everyone has been talking about. The president of the Royal Commission is older than his host, closer to Captain Jope's age. His fashionable mustache and pointed beard soften the hard set of his mouth. What Margaret notices most are his dark eyes, which flit ceaselessly about, taking in everything about his fellow diners. He seems wound very tightly, and when he smiles in response to a comment, his eyes remain cold and humorless.

Taking a sip of his wine, he smacks his lips in appreciation and addresses Chew in a reedy voice. "I must say I am impressed with your home and table, John. From what I have seen so far of Jamestown and environs, it hardly looks like the derelict place I was led to expect."

Chew acknowledges the compliment with a practiced smile. "I thank you for those kind words, John," he responds expansively. "Having traveled to England recently, I know what fantastical notions people there have of our colony, but they have exaggerated our plight beyond reason."

"Yes, we have recovered quite well from the Indian massacre and the plague last year," says a beefy man next to him, poking his teeth with a fork. "My plantation is producing more tobacco than ever before."

Margaret is surprised. She is well aware that Bennett's Welcome would tell a different story, but she knows better than to interrupt the gathering with her account of what a devastated and forsaken place she left behind.

Harvey's nasal voice pierces her reverie. "I've been here for three days now," he says, "and I have yet to see one of the red heathen savages I've heard so much about. If I didn't know any better, I'd think they were a mere figment of imagination."

He is rewarded with laughter all around, but Margaret can tell that there is a guarded quality to the general mirth.

"We'll be sure to take you to an Appomatuck village, then," says the man opposite Harvey, who has his back to Margaret. "They've been our sometime allies in our ongoing struggle against Opechancanough and his Powhatans, although you can't trust any of them not to betray you."

An icy chill seizes her heart as Margaret recognizes a familiar voice. She heard it more than a year ago in the stable of the house two doors down. It belongs to Governor Wyatt, the man she surprised and reprimanded for his loss of faith.

Margaret feels her heart thumping in her chest and wants nothing more than to escape from the room when William gestures her to start helping collect the supper plates. The men with their backs to her and Mistress Chew pay no attention as she reaches for the dishes and takes them to a sideboard. She receives the same disregard from Harvey and the two burgesses next to him.

But when she glances up, Francis Wyatt is staring at her from across the table. In an instant, his shocked expression turns to loathing. His furious eyes glisten and bore into her. The flickering candlelight makes his face look like the mask of an angry demon. Transfixed and unable to break away, Margaret holds his gaze. The tension mounting inside her feels almost unbearable when Wyatt looks away and reaches for his glass of wine. He takes a sip and turns to Chew, engaging him in conversation as if nothing has happened. The encounter has been so brief that none of the other guests at the table have taken notice.

Margaret expels the breath she's been holding and sways momentarily. She forces herself to finish collecting the dinner plates, and by the time she distributes the dessert dishes, she has herself fully under control. Still, the rest of the meal seems to take forever, and she feels relief only when the supper finally breaks up and the men adjourn to the drawing room to smoke.

She is happy to spend the rest of the evening in the kitchen, washing and cleaning up. By the time she gets to bed in the room upstairs, she is too tired to talk to Ann and collapses exhausted onto the straw mattress next to her.

Still, Wyatt's wrathful stare, his eyes flickering with hatred, haunts her. Gradually his angry face intermingles with her frightful vision of Captain Jope's lionlike visage when she first set eyes on him in the hold of the Spanish slave ship, as well as the bloodthirsty grimaces of the Imbangala cannibals who captured and enslaved her and John in Africa.

Perhaps not so safe, after all, she thinks regretfully before finally drifting off to sleep.

2

JOPE AND JOHN

Tavistock–Portsmouth—Early March 1624

Following their last ocean crossing, it has been a longer than usual sojourn at the home of Jope and Mary in Tavistock, and John is getting restless. He wonders if he and the captain will ever leave and go to sea again. After the belated christening of Jope's daughter, Margaret, in the fall, when Mary was already pregnant again, the captain kept postponing shipping out, claiming that he wanted to be there for the birth of his second child.

But even after Joane arrived and was baptized, he continued to find reasons to extend his stay. Gareth, the *White Lion's* first mate, who is responsible for keeping the ship in good order in Plymouth Harbor, has sent several letters begging Jope to return or at least provide him with a firm date of departure. Apparently, some of the regular crew members have become disgruntled and impatient, and are looking to hire onto other merchant and privateering vessels. Still, Jope shows no sign of getting ready to leave.

For John the extended break has been pleasant enough. Although he has not ventured out alone into Tavistock, he has participated in family gatherings, attended church services, and spent time reading the modest collection of books in the drawing room. Jope takes time every afternoon to talk with him about his studies and to make sure he continues to practice his writing.

John enjoys feeding the hogs and goats, and tending to the horses more. He likes the physical work and close proximity to living creatures. The pungent smells of slop, hay, and manure bring back fond memories of Aldwarke's stables, too.

If Mary still worries about the authorities discovering that she and Jope are harboring an African, she does not let on. It seems that the ruse the captain concocted to explain John's presence in England has satisfied her and put her sufficiently at ease.

Jope conceived of it on their last trans-Atlantic voyage, when the *White Lion* brought tobacco from Bermuda to Vlissingen in the Netherlands. While anchored in the port, unloading the large hogsheads filled with cured tobacco leaves and taking on goods for England, John joined Jope on his visit to the town hall and maritime offices to obtain the proper documents for their departure.

As they walked on the cobblestoned Walstraat, John marveled at the brightly colored façades of the merchant houses with their angular, stepped gables. Jope, always ready uses the opportunity to improve the education of his charge, talked about the time he spent two years in the Calvinist seminary there and the strategic importance of the town, both for trade and military purposes, through the rest of Holland.

Suddenly he stopped and said, "We should give you a Dutch surname and claim I took you on as a cabin boy here. That will forestall any untoward questions when we get back to England."

John nodded eagerly, pleased with the prospect of no longer having to sneak about in Plymouth and hide aboard the *White Lion* while the captain stayed with Mary.

"What shall we call you then?"

John shrugged, his Dutch vocabulary limited to just a few words he had picked up on their past trips.

As they passed a smithy where a nut-brown mare with a flaxen mane was being fitted with horseshoes, John stopped to watch, fascinated by the ringing clangs when the blacksmith's hammer struck the anvil, the metal sparks flying from the red-hot iron to the stone-covered ground, and the acrid smell of the scorched hooves.

Watching his young companion stare enraptured, an idea formed in Jope's mind.

When they resumed their walk, he said, "How about 'Graween' for a surname?" He added, teasing, "It would be appropriate. It means 'gravel hard as granite'—like your head!"

John said the name several times, tasting it on his tongue, "John Graween, John Graween, John Graween—I like the sound of it."

Jope clapped him on the shoulder. "Good. Then it's settled."

"What would it be in English?"

"John Growan."

"I like that, too."

On the way back to England aboard the *White Lion*, Jope taught the youngster a few Dutch phrases to lend authenticity to the claim in case someone questioned his background more closely.

When Jope arrived in Tavistock with John in tow, Mary got upset. Even after he explained the scheme to her, she was still reluctant; but when her father and uncle both gave their blessing, she was happy to acquiesce. She likes John as much as she did Margaret during her brief time with them—after all, she and Jope named their firstborn daughter after her. So Mary was pleased to be able to welcome John into her home with open arms.

As she watches him she notes how much the 11-year-old boy has grown since the last time she saw him. Although physically still a youngster, he seems much older than his age. She imagines that his experiences at sea and in the rough-and-tumble port cities of the Caribbean under Jope's tutelage have forced him to mature quickly.

Mary appreciates John's serious-minded, thoughtful demeanor and desire to please. The maids, grooms, and other household staff like him, too. Agnes, the nursemaid who takes care of the babies, has taken a special shine to him. Under their special attention and teasing, John relaxes a bit, and soon a playful, boyish streak emerges from beneath the guise of the solemn youth trying hard to act like an adult.

After an extended time on land, Jope mellows, too. He no longer walks with the rolling gait of an old salt. But while he enjoys Mary's company, especially after the birth of Joane, he often seems distracted. He worries about how to support her and his growing family. He knows he is not getting any younger and wants to make sure they are secure in case something happens to him.

A visit to Launceton, the home of his older brother, Joseph, brings matters to a head.

Unaware of the captain's ruminations, John is excited to go on a trip to a new place. On the Saturday of the outing, he is up and ready at dawn. After breakfast he watches the footman put two heated bricks onto a metal-lined spot of the floor of the carriage. By the time he, Mary, and the captain set out, dressed in their Sunday best, the interior feels toasty despite the bracing wind outside, and the 10-mile journey through the snow-covered countryside passes quickly. When they arrive at Joseph's mansion on the outskirts of town, John is amazed. Not since Aldwarke has he seen such a magnificent estate. He had no idea that Captain Jope comes from such a wealthy family.

Joseph greets them in the vaulted entrance hall. John marvels how different their host looks from Jope. If it wasn't for the same piercing blue eyes, you'd never imagine they were brothers. Jope's leathery face is tanned, lean, and hard-edged from years of spending time in the sun and salt air on the decks of the *White Lion*. Joseph, by comparison, is pale as chalk, and his features are soft and pudgy.

When he takes them into the high-ceilinged drawing room, where his wife and children are waiting by the large hearth, John is amazed at the understated opulence. There are wall hangings and busts on the sideboards, and while the family is not dressed ostentatiously, the quality of the clothing fabrics says more than any extravagant jewelry would.

On the surface, everything is congenial as they sit down to a lavish five-course dinner, served by three liveried servants. The men converse about the latest news from London, including the mounting woes of the Virginia Company now that it has come under royal scrutiny. The women chat about their children, plans for their spring gardens, and the newest French fashions that have made their way to Cornwall.

After the meal, John excuses himself and explores the house on his own. In one wing he discovers a library where a wall is stacked floor to ceiling with books. The room smells of dust, leather, and tobacco smoke. He walks around the carpets, then crouches on the floor next to the bookcases, close to a fabric-covered screen, where the biggest tomes are stashed. He reads the embossed leather backs and pulls out a large atlas. Sitting on the floor, he looks through it until he finds a colorful map of the New World. As he tries to figure out where Margaret and Jamestown are located, he becomes engrossed and doesn't hear the footsteps of people coming into the room.

Then he hears the door being shut and Jope's suspicious voice: "What is it you wish to talk to me about away from our wives?"

Hidden by a large chair, John scrabbles behind the dark blue screen and peeks around the edge of one of the panels. He sees Jope in profile standing off to one side of the room, looking uncomfortable and tense. Joseph takes his time removing a clay pipe from a stand on the sideboard and filling it with tobacco from a silver box. When he offers it to Jope and is met with refusal, he lights it with a candle for himself. He takes one of the armchairs and gestures for his brother to sit in another. Jope refuses to join him.

Joseph sighs, takes a deep puff, and expels a cloud of smoke into the air. "I'll come straight to the point, John," he ventures, although he does not look at Jope. "I have been very patient, but it's been five years and I have yet to see any evidence of the fortune you promised."

Jope's lips tighten, and his face flushes pink. "I know," he acknowledges. "I've been taking a safer, more predictable course of action for reliable gain."

Scratching his beard with a fleshy finger, Joseph says, "A pure-bred hunting hound will never make a good sheepdog. The *White Lion* was not meant to be a merchant ship. It was designed for warfare, privateering, and stalking prey!"

As Jope starts to pace, he approaches the screen. John cowers and holds his breath. He hopes the captain doesn't notice the open book lying on the floor.

He is saved from discovery when Joseph says, "You're not getting any younger, and your two daughters will need a dowry before you know it!"

Wheeling back, his blue eyes flashing, Jope retorts angrily, "You don't have to tell me my business, Joseph. I will take care of my family on my own!"

As he moves closer, a flicker of fear passes over Joseph's face. He holds up a hand in a conciliatory gesture. "I don't mean to offend, but it is my business, too."

He rises, goes to the sideboard, cleans out the pipe, and puts it away. Then he faces Jope and says, "I will give you another year, two at the most, but I must see results."

"Or . . . ?" Jope challenges.

They lock eyes and Joseph looks away first. He leaves the room without another word. Jope stares after him, rubs his temple as if he has a headache, runs his fingers through his hair, and kneads his neck.

Then he says, softly, "You can come out now, John."

Embarrassed, the boy emerges from behind the screen and stands up awkwardly, looking at his feet.

"Wish you hadn't witnessed that, but no matter. Just don't tell Mary," says Jope with an edge in his voice.

John nods and says, "You can count on me."

Then he picks up the book and slides it in its proper place on the shelf. He joins the captain, and they leave the library together.

When the families say their good-byes later that afternoon, Jope and Joseph act amicably, as if nothing bothersome has occurred between them. But on the way home, Jope is pensive, and Mary glances at him worriedly from time to time, wondering what has dampened his mood.

Later that evening after they've gone to bed, Jope doesn't blow out the candle on his nightstand right away and stares at the ceiling.

Mary puts her hand on his muscular chest and asks, "What's wrong?"

For a moment he considers whether to tell her what is on his mind, but decides against it. He turns to her, smooths her brow, and says, "Nothing. Nothing for you to fret about."

Then he blows out the candle and reaches for her.

The next afternoon, Jope and John go for their daily walk in the woods behind the meadows in back of the house. The air is cool and moist, and the ground, still wet from an early spring thunderstorm, squishes beneath their boots.

When they reach the moss-covered boulder where they usually turn back, Jope stops and says, "We'll be leaving soon to go out to sea. This time we'll leave off trading and try our hands at privateering again. We'll go on the hunt for Spanish ships."

John's heart leaps with joy. At last he'll be able to have adventures like Margaret in Jamestown.

Noting his young disciple's unbridled enthusiasm, Jope warns gravely, "There will be danger, more perilous than anything we've experienced in the time you've been aboard the *White Lion*. You could stay here, where you'll be safe."

But John is too excited to pay attention. "Will I get to wear a sword like you?" he asks eagerly.

Jope realizes that John hasn't heard a word after his first announcement and bursts out laughing. It is the first time in weeks that Jope has shown any signs of genuine amusement.

"I am serious," says John, miffed.

"I know you are, but a sword would be too heavy for you, so a dirk will have to suffice for now."

John thinks about it and accepts the inevitable without it diminishing his enthusiasm.

As they return to the house in a cheerful mood, they encounter Mary. She looks at them in surprise and asks, "What have you two been up to?"

"We're going to be pirates," John crows happily.

When the blood drains from her face, John realizes that Jope has not told her yet. Before he can say anything further, Mary bursts into tears, hikes up her skirts, and runs into the next room. Jope follows her slowly while John sinks into one of the armchairs. He feels guilty as he listens to the sobbing and soothing sounds that issue from behind the closed door. After a while they subside, and Mary and Jope return. Mary has recovered her poise, but her eyes are red from crying.

For the next week, a dark mood descends on the house.

On the day of their departure, the entire household assembles to see Jope and John off. Agnes and another maid, holding the babies, stand at the head of a line with the other servants. Jope blesses them all. He offers a special prayer for his daughters and kisses them on their foreheads. Mary watches him, concerned, but making the best of it.

When she bends down to hug John, she whispers in his ear, "You'll take good care of the captain for me, won't you, John?"

The boy straightens manfully and whispers back, "I promise."

She kisses him on the cheek and turns to Jope. Their good-byes are warm and affectionate.

Watching them, John thinks, *Someday I will have someone like Mary.*

* * *

As soon as they return to the *White Lion*, Jope sends word out quietly about his plans to hunt Spanish ships. He is pleased that Thomas

Osborne, his quartermaster, joins up, ready to serve. He hires an experienced navigator, Samuel Teague, who is known for his battle skills and has connections to men eager to go privateering throughout the Plymouth area. Soon, sailors come aboard to sign up. Jope interviews each of them in his cabin, and when he has decided to hire someone, he writes his name and agreed-upon compensation in his logbook.

John, polishing the woodwork in the background, watches the hiring process with great interest. He recognizes a number of men who have been loyal to Jope since the beginning of his seafaring days. But there are others, tough sailors, who proudly display scars from former sea battles. Their eyes are hard as obsidian. Suspicious as feral cats, they carry themselves with a rough-and-ready demeanor that conveys the promise of barely disguised violence. Some carry stripes on their backs from whippings they've endured. Jope asks the reason and doesn't take them on if they hesitate before answering. He presumes that it was for insubordination rather than running afoul of the port authorities for rowdy behavior on shore leave.

The ones who pass muster ignore John as too young to warrant attention or treat him with the contempt of men who have stared into the jaws of hell and recognize only fellow mates who have earned their respect.

One of them, a giant of a man with a straggly beard and muscles like knotted ropes, growls at him, "Out of my way, snipper-snapper," as he heads below to stash his bundle of belongings.

"That's Fulke. Better stay clear of him," warns Tobias, a sailor who has known John for three years. "He has a very short fuse."

John also sees a very different cargo come aboard—extra cannons, muskets, pistols, powder kegs, and barrels filled with shot. The newcomers handle the weapons with ease, polish them, and get them battle ready, leaving it to the other sailors to make the *White Lion* shipshape above deck.

John is more familiar with those preparations—repairing ropes, checking sails for wear and tear, and fixing and replacing broken tackles and pulleys. He is happiest when he can work halfway up the masts on the spars, far from the reach of the repugnant new arrivals.

As the time draws near to shipping out, the tension aboard becomes palpable. Word from the docks and other ships is that the new harbormaster from London is a stickler for rules and carries the same grudge against privateers as King James. He is known to conduct extensive searches of ships before allowing them to depart.

In anticipation, the crew has stashed some of the extra weapons in sealed barrels and hidden the powder kegs in dark corners of the hold. But there are the extra cannons and other arms harder to conceal that require careful disguising beneath canvas sails, fishing nets, and coiled ropes.

Jope, Teague, Osborne, and Gareth meet to strategize how to best pass the inspection. John watches and listens attentively. The good news is that some of the harbormaster's underlings can be counted on to turn a blind eye for a hefty bribe. The key is to distract the harbormaster when he comes aboard. Since he is known to respond to flattery and to enjoy a good glass of wine, it falls to Jope to occupy him in the captain's cabin while his three underlings get busy looking the other way.

When the day of the inspection arrives, a portly man steps onto the ship with the self-important attitude of a peacock. John, sitting on the highest spar of the main mast, watches Jope on the deck below greeting the harbormaster with effusive warmth and inviting him to his cabin. His three subordinates look around casually as if on a Sunday afternoon stroll.

Everything goes according to plan. The harbormaster returns to the deck, slightly flushed, and receives the report from his men that everything is in order. But as he looks around, a tarp flapping in the wind catches his attention. Apparently, it has not been tied down properly. He moseys toward it, his curiosity aroused. Every sailor watching holds his breath, knowing that muskets and pistols are hidden beneath the canvas, and if he pulls it back, they are done for.

Suddenly there is a high-pitched, terrified yelp from above. All eyes look up to see a small figure high up on one of the spars, swaying and frantically waving his arms. It is John, who has slipped and is desperate to regain his balance. For a moment, he seems frozen in midair, but then he loses his footing and plunges toward the deck below. A collective gasp of horror escapes the spectators.

John falls halfway down the sail when a rope catches him, and he hangs upside down by one ankle, thrashing about and shouting for help.

Jope rushes to the mast, ready to catch him, should he tumble any farther. Gareth and several sailors scramble up the ratlines to his rescue. They lash a rope around the first mate's chest and lower him toward the flailing boy. It seems like an eternity before Gareth manages to reach him.

"I got you, you're safe!" he yells as he gathers John into his arms. Even the most mean-spirited of men below cheer as the two get hauled up to safety.

Jope, visibly relieved, turns to the harbormaster, who is ashen-faced and clutching his chest. "I am sorry you had to see that, m'Lord," he says somberly. "We'll give the lad a good thrashing for being so careless when he comes down."

The plump man is breathing heavily. The spectacle of almost seeing a young boy plunge to his death has upset him more than he cares to admit. "Good thing he is safe, Captain, that's all that matters," he declares. "I hope this is not an ill omen of things to come. Godspeed on your voyage."

"I thank you for your kind words and generosity," says Jope.

The harbormaster gestures to his men, who all look a bit shaken, and they climb over the railing and down to the rowboat waiting below.

Samuel Teague looks after them, making sure they're well on their way to shore before he turns and nods to Jope.

By then, John has returned to the deck, grinning from ear to ear. He bounces up and down with excitement, brimming with energy from his ordeal, and cackles, "We showed them, didn't we, didn't we?"

Jope smiles down at him and exclaims, "Yes, we did! Well done!"

It takes the rest of the crew a moment to realize that the accident was nothing but a ruse, a bit of stagecraft to mislead the meddlesome harbormaster. When it sinks in, the sailors' consternation yields to laughter, and John receives more slaps on the shoulders than he can count. Even Fulke, who called him "snipper-snapper," nods with approval.

As Jope surveys the scene, his eyes shine with roguish delight. In one fell swoop, he has passed muster, earned the respect of the new members of his crew, and raised John's standing with them. If this is an omen, he will gladly take it as a sign of better things to come.

3

WARWICK

London—March 1624

Leaning back in his favorite armchair, the Earl of Warwick, Robert Rich, takes a deep sip of wine and scowls at his visitor. Lady Frances Wray-Rich, his father's second wife, lounging comfortably on the sofa across from him, exudes a cloud of cloyingly sweet perfume. The earl would like nothing better than to light a pipe of tobacco to dispel the penetrating scent, but Lady Frances has made it clear on a previous social call that she can't abide the smoke. Like King James, she abhors the practice of "drinking" tobacco as a vile, filthy habit.

It has been four months since Warwick's wife of 20 years died from the flux, and the rooms and hallways of his London home are still draped with the black curtains of mourning—shrouding windows, paintings, wall tapestries, and fireplaces and creating a dismal atmosphere of unrelenting gloom.

It happened so suddenly. One morning in late November, his Frances complained of a mild stomachache and nausea. By the following day she was burning with fever. Soon, she developed diarrhea and her stool turned bloody. The grim-faced doctors shook their heads apologetically. There was nothing they could do. When the news reached the earl in London, he didn't bother to take his favorite coach but rode on horseback to Leez Priory. Setting a furious pace and exchanging his mounts at the postal stations, he barely made it in time.

When he rushed to Frances's bedside, he hardly recognized her drawn and sunken face, which had turned the color of gray parchment. Warwick took her hand in his and felt her squeeze feebly in return. Her voice was only a faint murmur, and he had to bend close to her lips to understand her.

"My only regret is not seeing our daughters married," she whispered. "Especially Anne. I don't want her to become an old maid."

"Don't you worry, my dear," he said hoarsely, his throat constricting with grief.

Frances clutched his hand. "Promise me you'll find her a suitable husband!"

"You can count on me," he replied, tears welling up in his eyes.

Her face relaxed visibly and she sighed, "I always could."

Those were her last words to him. She died two hours later.

They buried her the next day in the Holy Cross churchyard in nearby Felsted. The small ceremony included only the immediate family and servants, and a few attendees from London: his butler, Alfred; his cousin Nathaniel; Captain Samuel Argall, an old friend; and, unexpectedly, Lady Frances Wray-Rich. His five children, Anne, Frances, Lucy, Robert, and Charles, stood like wooden statues by the graveside as their mother's pine coffin was lowered into the ground. Warwick exercised similar self-control even though he was bereft with sorrow.

After making arrangements for the children to be taken care of at Leez Priory, he hurried back to London and threw himself into his work. Ever since the funeral he has kept busy overseeing his diverse privateering and colonial ventures, in particular the fortunes of the New England Company and its Puritan outpost on the shores of Massachusetts. Shrouding his grief with anger, he has let his hatred for the Virginia Company and its duplicitous officers—Edwin Sandys, Nicholas Ferrar, and the Earl of Southampton—burn at fever pitch.

Now that the Privy Council has intervened and sent a Royal Commission to Jamestown to investigate claims of improprieties and neglect, the company's fate hangs in the balance. But Rich is not content to sit idly by and watch events take their natural course. Nothing short of utter destruction will satisfy his lust for revenge, and with the help of his cunning cousin, Nathaniel, he does everything in his power to tilt the outcome in that direction.

Only rarely does he think about his children and the deathbed promise he made to his wife. Much to his surprise, Lacy Frances Wray-Rich has assumed responsibility for his offspring by taking both of his older daughters under her wing. In the past, her sharp mind, rapierlike wit, and unwanted interference in his affairs has annoyed him to no end. But now he is glad that she invited Anne and young Frances for a stay at her London home, introducing them into society and pointing out all the eligible young men.

In return, he tolerates her frequent, unannounced visits when she wishes to inform him of her progress. On this occasion, she has already described several good marriage prospects for Anne and received his indulgent praise.

Now she picks at the clove-studded pomander on her gown and announces, "You know, Robert, it is time for you to start looking for a new wife, too. Say the word, and I will cast my net in the appropriate waters. But make no mistake: You, my dear, represent the biggest catch in London."

The earl is about to make an excuse and once again wrap himself in the mantle of mourning, but to be honest, he is tired of looking at the dreary drapery and living in an atmosphere of despondence and gloom. Yes, he still dresses only in black, but the fact that he has started to make sure his doublets, capes, coats, breeches, and stockings are of the finest velvet, brocade, and silk—rather than the simple woolen and linen garb preferred by most Puritans—signifies his desire to move on. The idea of forging a valuable political alliance in the process has considerable appeal as well.

So he decides to humor her. "By all means, cast away, m'Lady!"

He notes the glint of surprise in her eyes, followed by the flush of excitement of a born busybody given permission to ply her trade. But if he thinks allowing Lady Frances to play matchmaker will satisfy her desire to manage his personal affairs, he is mistaken.

Setting aside her glass of claret, she smooths a ruffle on her vermillion gown and asks, "Have you given any thought to your oldest son? It is time to bring him here, so he can receive the training to become your worthy successor."

Rich stiffens. He does not appreciate the reminder of his own mortality and replies dismissively, "There will be plenty of time for that later on."

"The boy is almost 13, Robert."

"What of it? At his age, if I saw my father once in a fortnight, I counted myself fortunate."

Lady Frances snorts in derision. "Just because your father neglected you is no reason to do the same with young Robert. Besides, you had your mother look out for you and use all her connections at court and in society on your behalf."

The earl sighs. He knows she is right, but he can't tell her that the main reason he has avoided bringing the youngster to his London house is that he reminds him too much of his dead wife. It surprises him to realize how much he still misses her.

Frances Gawdy-Hatton was 15 when Rich married her, and while he was only three years older, they were worlds apart. He was already a charismatic nobleman with considerable experience of the world, and she was a pretty, shy, sheltered lass. Their union had been arranged by Rich's mother, Penelope Devereux, who thought the girl would be a good match for her son.

Unfortunately, her grandfather, Sir Francis Gawdy, an important justice on the King's Bench, disapproved. He had been a judge for a number of major trials, including the one that led to Sir Walter Raleigh's imprisonment in the Tower and ultimate beheading on the scaffold, and he had nothing but contempt for the Rich family. He considered them a brood of ambitious privateers—"bloody pirates," he called them—and refused to have anything to do with his daughter after the wedding. Warwick was just as happy when he died a year after his marriage.

But Frances was devastated. She had held out hope that her grandfather would reconcile with her. Soon after, she lost both her parents to disease, and she became morbidly worried about the health of her children and her husband's well-being. When Rich traveled in secret to Holland this past summer to fight a duel with Lord Cavendish, she had been nearly hysterical at his disappearance.

Warwick understands that Frances was loyal to him to a fault, and since he values loyalty above all else, he knows he must honor her memory. So he sighs again, gulps down the remainder of his wine, and says, "Have Robert sent to me. I will install him here and involve him more in my affairs."

Lady Frances nods, demurely. "Thank you, Robert. It is the right thing to do."

The earl doesn't believe for a moment that her meek expression is genuine, but he gets up and extends his hand to her. "And now that you've had your way with me, Madam, let me get back to my business," he says gallantly.

Lady Frances rises with his help, acknowledges his pleasantry with a gracious nod, turns dramatically, and sweeps from the room.

As Rich sniffs the air in her wake, grimacing, Alfred enters and heads for the cupboard to prepare a pipe of tobacco. He knows his master well enough not to say anything after a visit from Lady Frances until the earl himself decides to speak.

Warwick pours himself another glass of wine and settles in his armchair, brooding. Accepting the clay pipe and lit taper, he says, "Open the windows, Alfred. We must clear the air."

"Yes, m'Lord." Hurrying to comply, Alfred adds, "Your cousin is waiting outside."

"Good, send him in. And get the servants to ready a bedroom upstairs. Young Master Robert is going to come and stay with us."

"Very good, m'Lord," Alfred says without evincing any surprise. "I'll let the cook know as well."

He unlatches the wooden shutters and pulls the lead-paned windows open. The spring air outside is chilly, but not unpleasant. Sounds of horses' hoofs and carriage wheels clattering on the cobblestones and coachmen shouting warnings to pedestrians waft into the room from the street below.

Alfred returns to Rich's side and offers to refill his wineglass. Warwick shakes his head and expels a billowing cloud of smoke. He is pleased that the rich tobacco aroma eclipses all remnants of Lady Frances's visit.

"If that will be all, m'Lord . . . ?" Alfred lets the question hang in the air, and when he receives no reply, makes for a quick exit.

Almost immediately Nathaniel Rich enters.

"I hope you've brought me some good news," Warwick calls out to him. Then he notices another man who has followed him into the room.

"You know Captain Smith, m'Lord," says Nathaniel. "I have taken the liberty to invite him this morning."

"Of course. You are welcome in my home, Captain Smith."

An older man with a pointed white beard and distinct military bearing steps forward and bows deeply. "Thank you, m'Lord."

Warwick, examining him with interest, notes the lively eyes peering out from under bushy eyebrows. He remembers Smith from the last meetings of the Virginia Company he attended. The old warrior is an adventurer and author who has the reputation of beating his drum most loudly for himself, but he spoke with the authority of someone who had worked and fought hard to preserve the Jamestown Colony against all onslaughts in its early days. Captured by Indians, he was saved from horrific torture and death only by the intercession of Pocahontas, the young daughter of the chief. Captain Argall, who took part in many of his exploits, has always spoken highly of him.

More recently, Smith was the only voice warning against the treachery and danger of the heathen Indians, but none of the arrogant company leaders—Sandys, Cavendish, and Ferrar—would listen until it was too late and the ghastly massacre decimated Jamestown. Now the captain is suffering the exile of so many oracles whose forecasts proved all too accurate and caused embarrassment to those in power. If Warwick remembers right, Nathaniel mentioned at some point that Smith demanded money the company owed him but that his claim fell on deaf ears.

Before he can ask his cousin why he brought Smith here, Nathaniel says, "Sandys and Southampton have gone to court to challenge the Privy Council's right to interfere in the affairs of a private stock-holding enterprise and to send an investigating commission to Jamestown."

In an instant, Warwick leaps from his chair, startling Smith, who is unfamiliar with the earl's temperamental outbursts. "I knew that those scheming miscreants would not sit still," he shouts and starts to pace furiously.

Before he can work himself into a lather, Nathaniel interjects, "That is why I brought Captain Smith here today. I think he can be of help to us."

Warwick stops and looks at the captain, intrigued.

Nathaniel continues, "He has the ear of Sir Thomas Smythe, whose influence reaches all the way to the King's bedchamber."

"Smythe has grievances like mine," Smith says eagerly. "Ever since Sandys scuttled the magazine ship's monopoly of supplying goods to the colony, he and his merchant faction have lost their opportunity to make easy money. He would be just as happy to see the Virginia Company cast on the rocks!"

A look passes between the earl and his cousin.

"May I offer you a glass of wine, Captain?" Warwick asks as Nathaniel brings two glasses from the cupboard.

"Don't mind if I do. Thank you, m'Lord," says Smith.

Warwick takes the decanter and pours. "What can you do to help make sure the Virginia Company keeps heading onto the shoals of certain ruin?"

Smith draws himself up to his full height. "I have firsthand knowledge of gross mismanagement both on the part of the leading board members here and their cronies in Jamestown, and I can get that intelligence to the right people at court," he says.

Taking one of the glasses from Nathaniel, Warwick offers it to Smith. "And why would you do that for us, Captain?" he asks, with the beginning of a smile twitching at the corners of his mouth.

Smith's eyes dart to Nathaniel, who comes to his rescue. "Captain Smith has written a book, *The General History of Virginia, New England, and the Somers Islands*, and his account of the current company leadership is anything but flattering."

Warwick purses his lips. "But how can that help us? It takes months to publish a book."

"Yes, it does," says Nathaniel, smoothly. "But the manuscript is finished. If we help with the cost of printing, the good captain will not have to raise the funds himself and can use his time to serve our cause and spread the word of Sandys's misdeeds."

It takes Warwick only a moment to evaluate the implications. "And it will serve as a severe antidote if the Royal Commission's findings are too sympathetic."

Smith, eager to put the seal on the matter, says, "I would be honored to dedicate the book to you, m'Lord."

A sly grin blossoms on Warwick's face. "Oh, don't do that, Captain. I would prefer to remain in the background." He raises his wineglass and offers a toast. "To the demise of the Virginia Company!"

London—March 1624

The three conspirators clink glasses, and each takes a gulp of wine. Warwick watches in amusement as Smith smacks his lips in appreciation and finds that social blunder unexpectedly appropriate. He vows to do the same when he finally hears the news of the wrack and ruin of the Virginia Company.

4

SETTLING IN

Jamestown—March 1624

It doesn't take Margaret long to settle into Mr. Chew's household. The other domestic servants and Walter, who works in the merchant's store and takes his meals with the rest of the help, quickly get over any doubts they had about her when they realize that she pulls her weight without complaining. When they ask about what happened at Warrosquoake during the Indian massacre and the pestilence, Margaret keeps her responses brief and general, and they soon lose interest.

So long as the Royal Commissioners remain in Jamestown, the wealthy merchants and burgesses continue to wine and dine them in high style. At Mr. Chew's residence, that requires all hands on deck around the house and in the kitchen almost every day. Thomas, the cook, soon appreciates Margaret's skill in preparing a variety of meat and vegetable dishes. She, in turn, likes his easygoing manner and good humor in the face of the busy schedule and frequent last-minute demands for extra food to accommodate additional supper guests. After outfitting her with a better quality gown, William continues to treat Margaret with condescension, although even he admits to being impressed at how easily she remembers the quirks and tastes of visitors the next time she serves them.

Margaret finds the conversations around the supper table fascinating, and she enjoys the spirited give-and-take among the members of the household. Walter, it turns out, is a gifted mimic whose imitations of John Harvey's highbrow pronouncements in a high-pitched, nasal voice has them all in stitches.

Only Ann remains shy and apathetic. Although she readily answers any questions Margaret asks her in the quiet of their room at night, she rarely volunteers any opinions of her own. Of course, she has her hands full taking care of Mrs. Chew and her children. The mistress of the house is demanding, difficult to satisfy, and intent on getting her way. Her morning toilette takes longer than anyone Margaret has ever met. Even a single strand of hair out of place is enough to put her into a bad temper for the rest of the day.

In short order, Margaret meets all the eminent personages living on Merchants' Row, as well as the other notables in town. Dr. Pott lives just three houses down the street, next to Governor Wyatt.

Abraham Piercey, the cape merchant and wealthiest man in the colony, occupies the house next door with his two daughters, Elizabeth and Mary. Margaret remembers him from the time when she and John first arrived with Captain Jope at Point Comfort at the mouth of the James River and Piercey negotiated the trade of the Africans aboard the *White Lion* for food. At first she is surprised how much older he looks, with streaks of gray in his hair and beard and deep worry lines etched in his forehead. But when she asks Thomas about it, he mentions that Piercey is still mourning the loss of his wife, who arrived from England a short while ago, only to succumb to sudden illness. Still, the merchant's eyes are as shrewd and observant as ever. The first time he comes to supper, Margaret worries that he might remember her and is glad when sees no hint of recognition on his part. She doesn't want to have to answer questions about her past before Virginia. Captain Jope's warnings to keep mum about her time in England still ring in her ears.

Another merchant frequenting Chew's table is Captain Richard Stephens. Having arrived with four servants just a year earlier, he is still a relative newcomer in Jamestown, but he has already built a house farther out on Merchants' Row and purchased 15 adjacent acres. Barely 30, he is handsome and energetic, a young man with a short temper, impatient to make his mark. He has had dealings with the Bennett family in England and often confers with Mr. Chew in his role of executor of Robert Bennett's will. As a recent stockholder in the Virginia Company, he wants to improve life in the colony and is looking for the best place to build a smelting oven, which is much needed since the iron works fell into disrepair during the plague. Because he is a bachelor, Jamestown's eligible young ladies all but swoon in his presence. Mrs. Chew is always pleased to see him because he never fails to treat her with gallantry. Another reason for his popularity at social events is that one of his servants is a distiller by trade, and his jugs of homebrewed ale and liquor are always welcome.

The first time George Yeardley comes to supper, Margaret pays special attention. She knows he is the owner of Floridew, the largest and most successful plantation in the colony. Many of the Africans who came with her from the Spanish slave ship ended up there, including her friend Frances with her young son, Peter. Margaret would love to know how they are faring, but Yeardley never mentions them. Like many of the aristocrats who visit Mr. Chew's house, he treats Margaret as if she were part of the furniture. Although disappointed, Margaret doesn't let on that it bothers her.

She is pleased that Governor Wyatt rarely attends the supper gatherings. As head of the colony, he is occupied with settling property disputes, meting out punishment to religious offenders—people who fail to attend church on Sundays or curse in public—and making sure that Jamestown and its environs are well defended. With the coming of spring, there are rumors of renewed Indian attacks, and Wyatt gives orders that all buildings on outlying plantations be palisaded as a protective measure.

Margaret is glad that Mr. Chew's house is one of the newer homes located farther east on Merchants' Row. Except for an occasional visit, Wyatt has no reason to head in that direction. She is always wary when she passes his mansion on her way into town and moves past quickly, hoping he won't step outside at that very moment. On the rare occasion she does run into him on the street, when he walks to Jamestown's church to hold court there or meet with the burgesses, she hurries by, her heart beating faster, and avoids meeting his eyes.

Many of the homes along Merchants' Row have large backyards and sizeable, adjacent property to keep poultry, goats, pigs, and cattle for fresh meat, milk, and eggs. Margaret is pleased to take care of the hens because it allows her to be outside in the warm spring weather. She is also glad that Mr. Chew has encouraged Thomas to utilize both her culinary and shopping skills to the utmost. When she first accompanied the cook to the dockside tables and market square in town to buy food, not only did she choose the best fresh venison, fish, and oysters, she also bartered well. Since then, Thomas is happy to send Margaret off in the morning, sometimes with Walter to help her carry her purchases, while he gets an early start on preparing the big midday dinner for the household.

Thomas also supports Margaret when she asks to take over caring for the garden. When she first saw the overgrown plot covered with withered weeds next to the house, she was appalled.

"It's so small . . . and unkempt," she exclaimed involuntarily.

Word got back to Mrs. Chew, who was stung enough by her comment to seek Margaret out and explain haughtily, "One of our servants, John Vaughn, planted those rows early this spring, but then my husband sent him back across the river to the plantation."

Margaret knows well enough not to argue but decides that Mistress Chew lacks the Puritan virtues that Aunt Isabel instilled in her and has little grasp on how to manage a household.

"I understand," she says. "I am happy to volunteer to take it over."

Mrs. Chew remains dubious, but her husband, remembering what Margaret accomplished at Bennett's Welcome, gives his blessing. So Margaret has even more opportunities to spend time out of doors. In the morning, she gets up before everyone else to scour the woods surrounding Jamestown for herbs, mushrooms, tubers, and flowers. Walking among pink spring beauties, delicate sprigs of bloodroot, and yellow trout lilies gives her pleasure, and she feels comforted by nature the way she did during her time at Warrosquoake.

Soon the burgeoning garden starts to attract passersby. Whenever Ann takes John Jr. and Nathaniel for a walk and they see Margaret pulling up weeds or planting seeds, they beg and plead to be able to go over and watch. Margaret is always happy to explain what she is doing. At some point Piercey's daughters make an appearance. They both wear satin dresses with ruffled sleeves, and their blond hair is decked out in curls. Margaret has seen them watching her from their windows next door, but they have never introduced themselves, although the younger girl, Mary, has waved to her once or twice from a distance. Elizabeth, who is Margaret's age and has not paid her any attention, looks bored, as if she is just humoring her sister.

Mary asks curiously, "What are you doing?"

Before Margaret can answer, Elizabeth chimes in sarcastically, "Digging for earthworms?"

Margaret brushes the dirt from her hands, stands up, curtsies, and says, "I'm preparing a garden. In a month or two, there will be lady slippers, blue bells, hyssop, thyme, and rosemary, and they have a wonderful, fresh smell." She smiles and adds, "My name is Margaret, by the way."

"I'm Mary," says the nine-year-old, curtsying in return. "And her name is Elizabeth."

A look of annoyance registers on her older sister's face. Then Elizabeth says condescendingly, "You're just a servant here, aren't you? My father has workers on his plantation who have dark skin like you."

Margaret's ears prick up. "Oh? Who might they be?"

"Why would I know their names? We hardly ever go there."

Hiding her disappointment, Margaret says, "When the garden is in bloom, I'll be glad to share its bounty with you."

Mary rewards her with a smile, but Elizabeth affects boredom.

"Come, Mary, we must get back to our embroidery," she says, turning her back on Margaret and stalking off without saying good-bye.

Margaret nods kindly to Mary, knowing full well that the girl would like to stay and perhaps even help. But when she returns to pulling up weeds, she feels a pang of anguish in her chest. It hurts to be treated like an outsider. She wonders if she will ever again find a place where she feels like she belongs.

*　*　*

Talking with vendors, workers, and other servants during her shopping trips, Margaret quickly discovers that Jamestown is very much like Pungo, the African village where she grew up in the Kingdom of Ndongo—rife with news, rumors, and the latest gossip. Many servants, especially those in households of noteworthy settlers, keep their eyes and ears open and often know about important happenings and events long before their masters and mistresses. Mr. Chew is smart enough to understand this and often asks what news Margaret has heard on the docks and at the market square. So she is pleased to surprise Chew with the news, gleaned from a servant of Governor Wyatt's, that John Harvey has purchased a property farther down Merchants' Row and plans to build a house there for himself.

As it happens, Harvey, the president of the Royal Commission, who has taken up quarters in town, is a guest at supper that night. Mr. Chew informs the other two merchants in attendance, Piercey and Stephens, of what he has learned beforehand. Knowing of Harvey's fondness for alcoholic spirits, Stephens brings with him two jugs of homebrewed liquor to liven up the occasion and loosen his tongue. Pleading a headache, Mrs. Chew absents herself so that the members of the supper gathering can indulge in coarser, more boisterous language than if ladies were present. Margaret, serving roast pork, squirrel stew, corn pones, beets, and carrots, is accorded no such consideration.

Captain Ralph Hamor, in town for a few days from his home on Hogg Island, fits right in. Margaret remembers him as the commander of the ship that brought her and the other survivors of the Indian massacre from Bennett's Welcome to Jamestown. One of the original settlers of the Virginia Colony, he has come to town to testify on his own behalf in a land dispute. Apparently, he cleared a large area for planting tobacco only to have his neighbor, Ralph Evers, lay claim to the property.

With several glasses of Stephens's hearty brew under his belt, he slaps the table and shouts, "Gadzooks, I put up a barn! Why would I do that if I didn't know it was my land?" As his face flushes red, he hiccups and looks around the table for support.

Chew, who has a plantation on Hogg Island, too, and doesn't want to get into the middle of a quarrel between his neighbors, nods sagely without saying anything.

Conversation inevitably turns to the state of affairs in Virginia and the ever present threat of Indian raids. When Piercey suggests that Governor Wyatt is doing a fine job, Harvey surprises everyone at the table.

"A place like Virginia needs a military man to lead, not a man versed merely in religion and commerce," he insists. Raising his finger to drive home his point, he continues, "A soldier would make short shrift of the heathen savages and teach 'em who is master."

A look passes between Piercey and Chew.

Hamor's eyes brighten. "That's well said, by God's blood." He slaps the table again, this time so hard that some of the pewter mugs bounce, startling everyone, including Margaret and William, the head butler, who is normally unflappable. "Maybe that's what I should do about the bastard who is trying to poach my land—teach him who is master of Hogg Island!"

It falls to Mr. Chew, as host, to divert the conversation to more important matters. Turning to Harvey, he says, "Speaking of property, there are rumors you have purchased a parcel down the street. Could it be that you like our Virginia climate so much that you are planning to stay?"

If he means to put Harvey on the spot, he does not succeed. The head of the Royal Commission smiles and, in his reedy voice, says, "Why, it's no secret! Wyatt has known since this morning when I filed the papers." He takes another swig of liquor and goes on. "I'll freely admit, I have come to like it here. This place is the cradle of the future, and I mean to claim a stake in it!"

Stephens nods eagerly. "There certainly is more opportunity here than in England."

Piercey shares another glance with Mr. Chew before spearing a piece of roast pork with his knife and casually inquiring, "Does that mean we can count on a favorable report from the commission to His Majesty, the King?"

There is a moment of awkward silence before Harvey's snorting laugh pierces the air. "Why, Abraham, you old fox. James Wyatt asked me the very same thing this morning."

Unruffled, Piercey stops chewing. "And what did you tell him?"

Harvey considers for a moment, then leans forward. "I didn't. So what I'm going to say to you now must be kept in strictest confidence."

While the others around the table nod sagely, Margaret perks up her ears and leans forward. Standing by the sideboard behind him, she is barely visible in the dim candlelight.

Meanwhile, Harvey continues imperiously, "The commission will attest to the fact that you are all, understandably, unhappy with the management of the Virginia Company in London, but that things here are not nearly as bad as people have been led to believe."

The other men at the table relax, pleased, but before they can express their satisfaction, Harvey adds, "Of course, none of that will matter."

Puzzled, Hamor asks, "What do you mean?"

A brief smile flits across Harvey's thin-lipped face. He looks around the table, savoring the moment, before explaining, "The King made his decision long before the commission left London. He doesn't require our testimony. The demise of the Virginia Company is a foregone conclusion."

Piercey expels his breath with force. This is disastrous news, and he has been dreading it more than any of his peers. As cape merchant and representative of the company, he has the most to lose.

There is a glum silence around the table as Harvey's words sink in.

Mr. Chew tries to lighten the mood. "The colony will always need purveyors of goods and transport," he says.

Stephens joins in halfheartedly, "The winds of change surely will bring new prospects." But he sounds doubtful, perhaps thinking that he will lose his considerable stake in the company.

They all look to Piercey, their leader, to say something to buoy their spirits, but he frowns at the plate before him, lost in thought.

So it falls to Harvey to end the lull in conversation. "The future is in tobacco, there no doubt!"

"Well said," Hamor agrees and takes a deep draft of Stephen's brew.

With that, the discussion turns to other matters, but the cloud that has descended on the gathering refuses to lift, and the supper guests soon make their excuses.

As they rise, Mr. Chew puts his hand on Piercey's arm, signaling him to wait until the others have left. Alone with him in the entrance hall, he says, "You were right all along. John Harvey is a wolf in sheep's clothing—an agent of the King himself, sent to take over the colony. We must be prepared and consider what is in our best interest."

"Yes, there is much to digest here, besides your excellent meal, John," says Piercey, having recovered some of his humor.

Chew puts his hand on his arm again. "Let's speak of this anon, before I ship out for England."

Piercey nods. "I am at your service." Then he sniffs the chilly evening air and opines, "It smells like rain."

While William shuts the front door behind him, Mr. Chew finds Margaret, who is gathering dishes in the dining room. Seeing his serious expression, she stops and looks at him with concern.

"Not a word of this to anyone, Margaret, not even my wife," he insists. "Not until I say so."

She nods, wide-eyed. "Of course, master."

* * *

Mr. Chew needn't have worried. Within days another event occurs that has everyone in Jamestown wagging their tongues. At another boisterous evening gathering, Richard Stephens and a young gentleman named George Harrison nearly come to blows arguing about one of Jamestown's eligible young ladies. Like many who have too much to drink, they trade insults, words they later wish they hadn't uttered but cannot take back. Harrison challenges Stephens to a duel, and before any older and wiser heads in Jamestown can intervene, they square off with pistols early the next morning in a field outside of the palisades. Lieutenant Shepherd, who happens to be in town and acts as one of Stephens's seconds, later describes the encounter to Margaret in detail.

After standing back-to-back with pistols aimed in the air, both men marched off 10 paces, turned, and leveled their weapons at one another. Harrison fired first but missed. Then Stephens took careful aim and discharged his pistol. Instantly, Harrison cried out and toppled to the ground, his right leg shattered below the knee. He was bleeding badly and would have died on the spot if his second had not used his belt as a tourniquet. The seconds and two other men from the small crowd that had gathered to watch carried him to the home of Christopher Best, the town surgeon, who tended to the wound.

The duel becomes the topic of conversation on everyone's lips. The general view, frequently expressed in discussion at Mr. Chew's suppers, is that while there is nothing wrong with young men settling a disagreement with fisticuffs, using anything involving deadly weapons is conduct unbecoming to a gentleman. Margaret shares that view, although many of the male servants in town don't, gleefully talking about the spilling of blood as good sport. At some point, Margaret overhears Elizabeth Piercey talking about the victor of the duel in glowing words and realizes that not only is she excited by the idea of two men fighting over a young, comely woman, but she is quite attracted to Stephens herself.

In the meantime, most of the town notables express a great deal of public outrage over the incident. With King James himself known to be vehemently opposed to dueling, they have little choice. Governor Wyatt issues a decree that proclaims in no uncertain terms that any such future altercation will be met with the severest of penalties. No punishment is meted out to Stephens, however, indicating his high standing in Jamestown society, although he looks suitably remorseful for some time whenever he appears in public.

At first it seems that Harrison might recover, but then the wound becomes infected and starts to fester. Neither the surgeon nor Dr. Pott can do anything for him. After languishing in bed for two weeks, the young man knows the end is near. He makes his will, leaving his estate and seven servants to his brother, and his furniture and clothing to the woman who has taken care of him. He asks to be buried in the churchyard in Jamestown, and his wishes are granted upon his death.

In the afternoon after the funeral, Margaret is working on a flowerbed in her garden when a shadow falls across the dark brown earth. Looking up, she catches sight of Lieutenant Shepherd, who has made a point to seek her out. She is pleased to see him, and his warm smile tells her that he is, too. With his light brown mustache and curly locks, he looks handsome as ever and better nourished than the last time they encountered each other.

"How are you faring?" he asks.

"Well," she says, as she stands up, and adds teasingly, "It looks like Anthony and Mary are taking good care of you."

Shepherd laughs. "Yes, they and the remaining handful of settlers keep Warrosquoake going while waiting for John Chew to settle Robert Bennett's estate." He bends closer and continues, "There are rumors that when he's done, young Richard Bennett, Edward Bennett's nephew, will come from England to determine what to do with the plantation."

He talks about other matters for a while: the ever-present danger of Indians, the daily routine at the fort where he is still garrisoned, and of course, the duel. Margaret keeps her counsel, listens, and asks an occasional question. When Shepherd takes his leave, she is surprised that nearly an hour has passed. Although she has enjoyed talking with him, she can't help wondering why he sought her out.

The following morning, Mr. Chew announces to everyone in the household that he will ship out to London in two weeks' time.

5

WARWICK'S REVENGE

London—May–June 1624

The four-horse carriage carrying the Earl of Warwick, his son Robert, and his cousin Nathaniel clatters over cobblestone streets on its way to Billingsgate, London's largest harbor on the Thames River. Rich usually doesn't visit the ships in his fleet. He lets Nathaniel handle communications with his vessels or insists that his sea captains come to his residence. But on this occasion he is killing several birds with one stone. While he has a number of urgent matters to discuss with his fleet commander, he also intends the outing to further the education of young Robert. Since Warwick promised Lady Frances Wray-Rich to involve his firstborn son more in his affairs, the lad has taken up residence in town, along with his private tutor and personal servant. Today, he will get a firsthand look at the family's maritime ventures. Perhaps being out of doors and in the hurly-burly of London's busiest harbor will rouse his interest and bring him out of his shell.

The earl has not been impressed with the 13-year-old so far. The boy possesses none of the lively curiosity and quickness of mind Warwick remembers having at that age, when his mother, Penelope, took him under her wing and introduced him at court. Young Robert isn't dull, but he seems to have no head for business, and his questions betray an unexceptional mind. The best thing that can be said for him is that he has a streak of stubbornness, although when he pouts he reminds Rich too much of his departed wife, who was not particularly worldly either. The earl muses that urbanity may not be a requisite for a woman, but it is essential for the heir of the Warwick fortune.

Today Rich feels magnanimous, however. He is still basking in the rapturous glow that descended on him when the Virginia Company breathed its last.

On May 24 the court of common pleas bench rejected the suit Edwin Sandys brought on behalf of the company and revoked its charter. King James wasted no time asserting his prerogative and made Virginia a Crown colony once again.

Rich wishes he had been present at the final quarter court of the company when the Earl of Southampton, in his role as president, had to recite the justices' and James's decrees out loud. Fortunately, his cousin Nathaniel was there and gave him a detailed account of the proceedings.

Southampton read the damning documents word for word in a measured, subdued voice while Treasurer Nicholas Ferrar and the other board members looked on stoically. Edwin Sandys tried to maintain his composure, but at one point his cheek started to twitch uncontrollably and he lowered his head in despair. Like the others, he had been hoping against hope that the court would hold in their favor and stave off the demise of the company.

Everyone knew that the King declaring Virginia a Crown colony meant they all lost their investment, every penny of it—a considerable sum for many stockholders. Warwick himself lost several thousand pounds, but that sum took barely a flea's bite out of his prodigious fortune. Many of the smaller shareholders, however, saw their hopes of repayment dashed and were understandably furious. Their angry shouts, incited further by Nathaniel Rich's faction, echoed loudly in the great hall of Southampton's palace. They were joined by the furious outbursts of the group of merchants who were eager to blame Sandys and the other officers for the debacle.

"Tell me again about Sandys," Warwick had whispered happily when Nathaniel reported from the meeting. Understanding his cousin's desire to gloat—just how personal Rich's enmity toward Sandys was—the attorney obliged, embellishing the tale even further. He mentioned Lord Cavendish banging on the hilt of his sword in frustration and Captain Brewster, another of Rich's nemeses, pulling at his bushy hair in impotent fury. Then he talked about Sandys's quivering lips when confronted with the news that the monarch had already appointed a board of governors and put at its head none other than Thomas Smythe, the very man Sandys had dethroned five years earlier.

Flushed with anger, Sandys tried to regain control of the meeting. "We will petition Parliament to deny King James's grievous overreaching," he shouted above the fray.

But even as an effort to save face, it was merely clutching at straws. The following week, James sent a letter to the Speaker of the House of Commons, informing its members in no uncertain terms that they had no business interfering in the King's business, scotching that final feeble effort to overturn the verdict for good.

When the Royal Commission, recently returned from Virginia, released the report of its findings two weeks later, it almost came as an afterthought. Less critical about the day-to-day affairs of the colony than everyone had expected, it nonetheless added fuel to the accusations of incompetence, neglect, and self-enrichment on the part of the company's officers. Most damaging was the litany of complaints by the settlers and plantation owners, all good, upstanding Englishmen, that their many pleas for more people, more provisions, and more weapons had all fallen on deaf ears.

When he heard that news, Warwick said to Nathaniel, "We must hurry the publication of Captain Smith's *General History of Virginia*. I want the destruction of Sandys's reputation to be complete!"

Nathaniel bowed and smiled. "I have already set it in motion, m'Lord!"

Riding in his carriage, Warwick smirks in anticipation of dragging Sandys's name further through the mud. But when he sees his son looking out the window at the rundown homes lining the streets on the way to the pier, it occurs to him that while revenge has been sweet, it is time to put it behind him—time to build again, not just destroy.

While Virginia may no longer be in play, his holdings in Bermuda are thriving, and the Plymouth Company of Massachusetts continues to do well after a shaky beginning four years earlier. Warwick knows how important it is to get its charter renewed, especially now that James will use Virginia's status as a Crown colony to encroach on its territory.

There is also the matter of deciding on a suitable wife. Lady Frances has been busy supplying him with candidates, all with an eye toward creating valuable social and political alliances. None have met with Warwick's approval so far, however. They aim too much at gaining greater access to the royal court. Rich wants as little as possible to do with King James, his wastrel son Charles, or his sycophantic favorite, the Duke of Buckingham. For the earl, there are only two causes that matter—defeating the Spanish Catholics, whom he considers incarnations of the devil, and furthering the Puritan cause at home and abroad in the New World.

He feels hopeful that his meeting with Lady Frances earlier in the day is a sign that things are looking up. At first Warwick was annoyed that she interrupted his morning working hours, threatening to ruin the rest of the day. To forestall her cloying fragrance spreading throughout his study, he suggested that they take a walk in the gardens of his townhome. To his surprise, Lady Frances readily agreed. Once they were outside, strolling along the graveled path, she gushed that the rosebushes on both sides had started to grow new leaves and buds already, and Warwick was pleased that the smell of spring flowers in the air diluted the miasma of her perfumed aura.

While the agreeable surroundings did not lend themselves to candor, Warwick decided to be blunt anyway. "These women won't do, Madame," he complained. "The court is the last place where I want to waste more time. You must find me someone more befitting my needs."

If Frances was offended—she had put a great deal of work into this project already—she didn't let it show. Sitting down on a stone bench, she picked a wayward sprig that had landed in a fold of her vermillion silk gown and said, "It so happens, m'Lord, that I have another prospect, a woman so well esteemed, so well bred, and so sensible, she will surely suit your purpose."

When Rich looked at her expectantly, she affected interest in the twig and twirled it between her slender thumb and forefinger—her revenge for his impatience.

Warwick sighed and decided to play the game. "It gives you pleasure to put me on tenterhooks, m'Lady. Well, here I am, stretched like a helpless cloth flapping in the breeze. Do rescue me, I beg of you."

Mollified, Frances relented. "Very well, Robert. It so happens that William Halliday, the alderman, died earlier this morning. I just found out by accident. By this afternoon all London will know."

Warwick stifled a laugh. "Nothing happens by accident with you, Lady Frances," he said smoothly. "Your spy network is rumored to be better than the Privy Council's." When she bowed in acknowledgment, he continued, "Isn't his wife—err, widow—the daughter of Sir Henry Rowe?"

"Yes," Frances cooed happily. "The mayor of London is well-connected at court and, above all, a good Puritan." She touched Warwick's arm with her gloved hand. "Susan Halliday's children are grown, and she is wise in the ways of the world. We will just have to let the requisite period of mourning pass, and she is yours."

Warwick had met the lady on a number of occasions, and she struck him as a sensible woman—calm, poised, and elegant—a perfect match for him.

He bowed slightly. "Madame, I am, as always, in your debt."

Lady Frances, realizing that he had made his decision, bestowed a resplendent smile on him and said, "I will begin to lay the groundwork for cementing your union."

The carriage lurches forward and stops abruptly, jolting Warwick from his ruminations back to the present. They have reached their destination. As the earl steps onto the cobblestones, he takes in the change in atmosphere from farther inland. There is more moisture in the air, along with the smell of fish and garbage in the water. He looks up at the galleon docked at the pier. It is a magnificent vessel, with three masts reaching high into the blue sky. Warwick imagines what an exhilarating sight it must be when her sails strain against the wind and she cuts through the waves at full speed.

Pointing to the bow where the name "Warwick" is etched in the wooden plank and bestowing a benign smile on his son, he says, "I named it in our honor."

"You mean after yourself," young Robert says officiously.

Rich feels too magnanimous to upbraid him, but he can't help sighing inwardly. The lad has no sense of humor and no subtlety whatsoever. On top of it, he doesn't seem to understand the importance of his family name.

The sound of a shrill boat whistle from the upper deck captures his attention. "They are ready for us," he comments and bends toward his son. "Don't be put off by the captain's coarse manner. The man is a very competent sailor and has more shrewdness in him than meets the eye."

Then Warwick carefully negotiates the wooden planks angled upward from the dock to the ship, with young Robert and Nathaniel in tow. The gangway creaks and bends under their combined weight. Rich is relieved when he steps onto the main deck without mishap. Waiting for him is a barrel of a man holding a plumed hat by his side. Captain Daniel Elfrith is even more rotund than the last time Rich met with him.

He grins from ear to ear, bows deeply, and says, "Bugger my eyes, m'Lord, it is a grand honor to see you aboard your ship."

The sailors lined up behind him bow as one, as does a stocky, younger man in a captain's doublet with his sword at his side.

Warwick acknowledges them with a nod of his own, then turns back to Elfrith to introduce Nathaniel and Robert. "Thank you,

Captain. You know my cousin already, and this is my eldest son. He is staying with me in London."

Elfrith raises his bushy eyebrows and winks at the youngster. "Never too young to learn the ropes, I always say." Then he gestures to the man behind him. "Allow me to introduce Captain Bullard, m'Lord. He was my first mate until last year and now helms your ship, the *Lancelot*." He points to a nearby vessel where dockhands and sailors are busy loading supplies aboard.

The sturdy young man steps forward and bows. When he straightens, he holds Warwick's gaze longer than appropriate.

Elfrith, noting Warwick's surprise, quickly interjects, "What Captain Bullard lacks in manners and civility he makes up for in fierce loyalty to your cause, by God's blood."

Rich looks at Bullard with interest. "Is that so? Captain Elfrith well knows that I value loyalty above all else."

The young captain takes his cue and draws himself up further. "My Lord, I sail for the glory of England and the House of Warwick."

Rich takes measure of the man. Bullard can't be much older than 30, but his features are already grim and etched with cruelty. He reminds the earl of a vicious brute, with none of the craftiness Elfrith hides beneath his blustery exterior—a blunt but potent tool, useful as an enforcer so long as someone else holds the reins and guides him.

Warwick nods to Elfrith, "If the rest of your new captains show half the promise, you have done very well in your recruiting, Daniel."

"Thank you, m'Lord," Elfrith beams and adds, "Won't you join me in the cabin?"

Bullard takes the lead, followed by Warwick, his son, and Nathaniel Rich, with Elfrith bringing up the rear. For a moment the earl considers sending Bullard away, but it would be seen as an insult. Besides, Elfrith is likely to share anything they talk about with him afterward anyway. Letting him be part of the planning will appeal to Bullard's sense of self-importance.

The cabin is spacious and well illuminated by the sunlight coming through the windows. When they all take their seats at the table,

Warwick starts right in. "We been pleased with your success since the incident with the *San Juan Bautista*, Captain, and we wish to expand your mission."

He glances at Nathaniel Rich, who takes up the narrative. "The Africans that you brought to Virginia and Bermuda with the Dutchman have been an unexpected blessing. They are good for the plantations—hard workers, well versed in the cultivation of tobacco and livestock. We need more of them, and quickly. There is a dearth of suitable Englishmen willing to indenture themselves for a acceptable period of time."

Bullard looks mystified, but Elfrith understands the implications right away. "You want us to raid Spanish ships not only for gold and finery, but for their slaves as well," he says. "Zooterkins, if that isn't a piece of work, eh, Bullard?"

Warwick confirms, "That is exactly what I want. You can tell my other captains those are my orders when you meet with them."

Elfrith scratches his beard thoughtfully. "We can do that, m'Lord. But as the raid with the Dutchman showed, it is better to sail in consort. Makes it easier to bring the Spanish frigates to heel. And if there is a battle, I'll take odds on two to one any day."

"By all means, Captain. Far be it from me to tell you your business." Rich shares another glance with Nathaniel before he continues, "There is something else I wish you to pursue personally, but this must stay among us."

"By God's blood, the grave could not be more silent, m'Lord."

Bullard speaks up. "You can count on me, m'Lord."

Once again, Nathaniel picks up the thread. "Our Catholic monarch is determined to advance the pope's cause and make life miserable for good Puritan men and women in England. With Virginia once again a royal colony, we have only a few spots in the New World where they can find refuge and build their communities."

Warwick stares at Elfrith with passionate intensity and says, "I want you to go exploring. Look for good places to establish new homes for Puritans, like the Plymouth Colony in New England. There must be islands and stretches of land not yet conquered by England or Spain where we can settle our people and turn a good profit in the bargain."

Elfrith glances at Bullard. He knows this goes beyond his disciple's ken, but he grasps Warwick's purpose with growing excitement. "We are honored you grace us with your confidence, m'Lord. I promise we will do you proud."

Rich signals Nathaniel, who produces a leather purse and puts it on the table.

"Please distribute this among the crew, and good speed when you ship out."

As Elfrith and Bullard thank him, Warwick notices young Robert looking on dubiously and realizes he will require a great deal of explanation to understand all that transpired.

As they exit the cabin, the sailors are still standing at attention.

Elfrith whispers into Warwick's ear from behind, "The lads would sure appreciate a good word from you, m'Lord."

Aware of his role as a leader of men, Rich strides down the line with Robert at his side. He asks one bearded sailor where he hails from, another who is still growing his first facial hair if he has a sweetheart on land, and a third whose cheek has a gash from a saber blow how many voyages he has under his belt. He hardly registers the stammered replies, but sees the effect his words have—the special glow and pride of underlings who receive recognition from their superiors.

As they reach the end of the line, Elfrith gives a signal and the sailors shout as one, "Three cheers for the Earl of Warwick! Long may he prosper! Hurray! Hurray! Hurray!"

Surprised, Rich nods to Elfrith in appreciation. But what surprises him even more and warms his heart is that young Robert looks up to him with glowing eyes for the first time since he came to London.

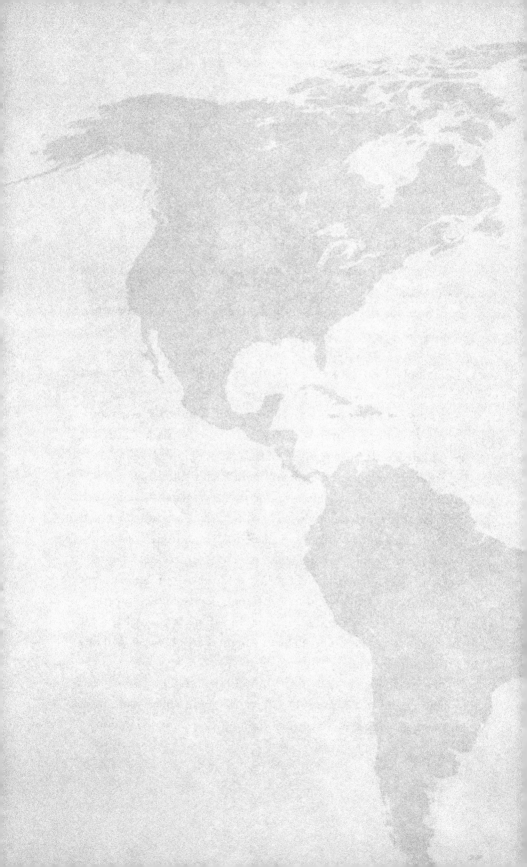

6

RIPPLES IN VIRGINIA

Jamestown—Summer 1624

The first rumors of the Virginia Company's demise reach the colony by merchant ship in mid-June, long before official letters from the Earl of Southampton and Edward Sandys to Governor Wyatt and Abraham Piercey arrive. While the news causes considerable consternation among many inhabitants of Jamestown and the surrounding plantations, most of the burgesses and merchants take it in stride. Forewarned by John Harvey, they have taken measures to protect themselves against any adverse ripples from the sea change that has taken place in England.

John Hamor, who lost his case against his neighbor but was awarded 200 acres of land on Hogg Island in compensation for his "improvement" efforts, is content with the settlement. The additional property allows him to increase his tobacco crop yield, which is what he wanted to accomplish all along.

Abraham Piercey decides to invest his mercantile fortune in tobacco production as well. To add to Piercey's Toile, his large plantation far inland from the coast on the Appomattox River, he arranges to purchase Floridew from George Yeardley. The sale is the talk of Jamestown. By adding to his holdings the most productive plantation on the James River, Piercey will more than double his property, making him the largest landowner in Virginia.

Margaret notes the increase in activity in Piercey's residence next door—various tradesmen and people she hasn't seen before coming for meetings with the merchant. With Mr. Chew in England there are no more evening banquets, and supper has returned to the more Spartan fare of egg dishes and leftovers from the midday dinner. As a result, Margaret has more time to tend to the garden, and it soon becomes a showpiece in the neighborhood. Butterflies and bees flit among the blossoming flowers and fertile patches of dark green herbs and ferns. Many a passerby stops to admire the riot of color. Mary Piercey visits frequently when Margaret is weeding or pruning, asking her the name of various plants. Even Elizabeth, prodded by her younger sister, grudgingly acknowledges that it is "a pretty piece of greenery."

One morning, while replanting some seedlings, Margaret notices an unfamiliar young man emerge from Piercey's house. He has dark brown hair spilling from beneath his Monmouth cap and the beginnings of a beard. His dark breeches and simple woolen coat mark him as a servant. Unexpectedly, he doesn't head into town, but comes over to her and looks at the garden with curiosity. Margaret notes his full lips and his sharp, blue eyes, which seem to take in everything at once and unsettle her for a moment, reminding her of Captain Jope.

"Is that hyssop?" he asks, pointing at a purple-fingered flower.

Startled, Margaret rises and replies, "Yes. I am surprised you know it."

"My name is John Upton," he says, smiling. "I come from Piercey's Toile, and I have seen the African workers there use it to brew a potation for indigestion."

Margaret feels her heart beating faster. "I am Margaret," she says. "Margaret Cornish."

She wants to ask the names of the Africans at his plantation. Some of them must have come to Jamestown with her on the *White Lion*, but she doesn't get the chance to find out.

Upton responds quickly, "It's good to meet you, Margaret Cornish. I've come to town because Master Piercey wants me to become the overseer of the plantation he's buying."

"Floridew," Margaret whispers.

"Yes. Have you been there?"

"I have friends there," Margaret volunteers, "although I haven't seen them for some time."

Upton looks at her with renewed interest. "I'm sure they're good workers. The Africans I've met know more about tobacco and cattle than the rest of the English workers combined."

Margaret feels her skin prickle with excitement. "Would you give them a message from me when you see them? Their names are Frances and Peter—her young son. Tell them I am well."

In response to her earnest eagerness, Upton says seriously, "I'll be glad to look for them when I get there and pass on your words."

"Thank you kindly, sir."

Upton acknowledges the title with a humorous bow. Bending closer to her, he smiles and says, "No need to be so formal, Margaret. I am an indentured worker like you, although I don't aim to be one for long."

Margaret looks at him, surprised.

Taking a step back, he indicates the lush foliage and multi-hued flowers with a sweep of his hand and says, "You must tell me more about your garden sometime, how you manage to make it so beautiful."

"I'll be glad to tell you what I know," Margaret says.

He tips his cap to her and heads into town, striding purposefully down the row of houses. Margaret looks after him for some time. She can't quite make out what she feels about the encounter, but she liked him and enjoyed having attention paid to her.

The encounter brings a moment of sunshine into an otherwise dreary existence for Margaret. Ever since Mr. Chew left for England to finally settle Robert Bennett's estate, his wife has shown her true colors. Nothing seems to please her, and she nags and criticizes everyone in the household.

One afternoon while Margaret is darning a hole in John Jr.'s doublet, Mrs. Chew tears it from her hands without even glancing at it and exclaims, "Your sewing skills are atrocious!"

After tasting a rabbit stew spiced with sage and rosemary from the garden, she scrunches up her nose and carps, "Your cooking is unpalatable. This swill is not fit for pigs!"

At first, Margaret is hurt and bewildered. Aunt Isabel at Aldwarke always complimented her stitches, and she never received a single complaint at Bennett's Welcome about her dishes. Soon she realizes that Mrs. Chew has harsh words for everybody in the household. Nor does it escape her that her mistress, despite her vicious tongue, has no difficulty gorging herself on Margaret's bread rounds and puddings.

For a while Margaret thinks Mistress Chew's foul temper is due to her being with child. Her belly is beginning to show, the morning bouts of nausea make her understandably miserable, and her taste buds are affected, too. But the other servants assure Margaret that she always behaves like a virago when her husband is away. She resents being in Virginia, which she considers a hopeless backwater, and would like nothing better than to return to England and live in London.

Sure enough, when the morning sickness finally passes for good, nothing changes in her shrewish behavior. Even her two sons avoid her, preferring to spend as much time as possible with their tutor out of doors. Ann, who has to serve Mrs. Chew hand and foot, catches the brunt of her tongue-lashing, as well as considerable physical abuse. It explains why she is so troubled and withdrawn. Margaret winces when she hears the slaps and hears the girl cry out. She can't imagine what she would do if Mrs. Chew treated her that way. At least she can escape the poisonous atmosphere whenever she tends to her garden or goes shopping in Jamestown.

But Mrs. Chew does not limit her scolding to the household. She dispenses her venom on everyone in town, especially the wives and daughters of burgesses and other merchants. She calls the two Piercey girls stuck-up ninnies and criticizes the appearance of the women she sees at church on Sundays—their modest dresses and hairstyles. Margaret, hearing her hold court to Ann in a loud voice within earshot of other servants, worries that if someone complains about her to the authorities, Mrs. Chew could get the dunking stool in punishment.

Fortunately, the keepers of public order are otherwise preoccupied. Royal envoys finally arrive late in July, bearing a letter to the colonists from King James himself. The missive states that their affairs have been taken into "His Majesty's pious and princely care" and "to go on cheerfully in the work they have at hand." At the public meeting in Jamestown where the envoys read it out loud, they also announce the dismissal of Francis Wyatt as governor.

The other big news from the Royal Court makes its rounds by rumor and innuendo. John Harvey is to receive a knighthood for his service to the Crown with the official ceremony to take place upon his return to England. This development bears out Piercey's contention that Harvey has been an agent of King James all along, notwithstanding the fact that he gave them all early warnings of things to come and seems to have a genuine interest in Virginia's success. His house on Merchants' Row is almost finished.

Although there are rumors that Harvey is to take over as governor, the envoys do not replace Wyatt immediately. Perhaps the royal spy has let them know that, as an inexperienced newcomer, he would encounter considerable resistance. Wyatt is popular, despite his overweening pride, because he has managed the colony's affairs well and has even brought gradual improvement to its finances.

Just how important it is for Virginia to have a steady hand at the helm becomes clear when an army of 800 Pamunkey Indians and their allies under their leader, Otiotan, threatens to attack a group of settlers on the south side of the river. Lieutenant Shepherd organizes the defense, but the best he can muster for battle is a militia of 60 armed men. Things do not look good for the settlers, even if their rifles give them some advantage. The enormous force of Indian bowmen is sure to slaughter them quickly. Against overwhelming odds, Lieutenant Shepherd saves the day by creating a diversion. He sends a small contingent of his men to the unguarded Pamunkey village, where they burn the fields and destroy whatever stores of corn they find. News of the devastation spreads confusion and despair among the Indian warriors. The Pamunkey had planted large areas of land, promising the neighboring tribes a portion of the crop in return for their joining in the raid. Facing another winter of starvation and hoping to salvage what they can, the Indians hurriedly disband, and the attack never materializes.

Still, it is a close call, and everyone in Jamestown breathes a sigh of relief when another ship arrives a month later with word to cancel the King's original order and reinstate Wyatt as governor. Apparently, Thomas Smythe, who heads the new Royal Commission, values him as a good administrator and persuaded King James to keep him in office.

* * *

Early one afternoon, after finishing the main dinner of the day, as Margaret takes a basket filled with dirty linen to wash by the river, she sees a well-dressed man walking up the road. She recognizes him as a sea captain by his clothes and the way his body sways from side to side as if he was aboard a ship. Although he looks vaguely familiar, Margaret doesn't recognize him. As he passes, he tips his hat to her, then gives her another, more penetrating glance before going to the entrance of Mr. Chew's house and knocking on the door. Margaret watches him being admitted by William, the head butler, and heads to the river, paying him no more thoughts.

But half an hour later, when she is spreading out the scrubbed sheets, towels, and napkins on the grassy riverbank to bleach and dry in the sun, he stands above on the side of the road and clears his throat. Surprised, Margaret rises and waits until he walks down to her. He is about the same age as Captain Jope, but not as handsome. His eyes are hazel colored, and his dark brown beard does not cover the large wart high up on his cheek.

He peers carefully at her and says uncertainly, "Margaret? It is you, isn't it? They told me your name at the house."

Margaret replies cautiously, "Yes, that is my name."

Breaking out in a smile, the man says, "You don't remember me. I am William Ewen. I was at Point Comfort when you first came to Virginia five years ago. I came to look in on John Chew, but I understand he is away in England."

Not knowing what to say, Margaret simply nods. She has a dim recollection of the three men who came aboard the *White Lion* to discuss with Captain Jope and his obese friend who liked to curse—Elfrith was his name—how to cover up their privateering and connection to the Earl of Warwick.

"I'm sorry, but I don't recall, sir," she says.

Undeterred, Ewen plows ahead. "I own a plantation across the river, but spend most of my time in London now. In fact, two of the Africans that came with you live there now. Their names are Michael and Katherine. Another, Matthew, joined them last year."

Margaret searches his face, trying to understand why he has approached her and bothers to take the time explaining himself to her. There is something likeable about him, though, a kind twinkle in his eyes.

"Have you seen Captain Jope?" she asks unbidden.

Ewen considers. "No, but if I do, I'll tell him what a fine young woman you've become." Seeing her react with discomfort, he adds, "I don't mean to keep you from your work. I really just wanted to say hello."

Margaret is glad that he doesn't ask her about her time in Virginia and before. She would hate to have to make up stories to account for her sojourn in England.

After a few more exchanges, he departs, wishing her well. Margaret watches him climb up the bank and forgets about him as soon as he disappears behind the crest, not imagining for a moment how influential he would prove to be in her future.

* * *

As the sale for Floridew nears completion, Margaret follows every bit of news with great interest, especially when it becomes clear that Yeardley has exempted a number of workers from the deal, bringing them to his Jamestown residence and his plantation on Hogg Island. The group includes eight Africans—three men and five women—purchased from Captain Jope five years earlier. The fact that Yeardley decided to hold on to them is an indication of how much he values them and their abilities.

Margaret awaits their arrival with eager anticipation. A number of *malungu* who shared the hellish voyage from Angola across the Atlantic Ocean with her will live just down the street. She wonders if any of them will remember her.

She meets the first newcomer on her early morning walk into town, basket in hand. A sinewy man about 10 years older than her, he is sweeping off the stoop of the Yeardley house. When he looks up, she notes his thin face with high cheekbones, but doesn't recognize him.

Surprised to see her, he stops and stares at her inquiringly. "My name is Emmanuel Driggers," he introduces himself.

When Margaret says her name, he looks mystified. Then recognition dawns on his face, and he breaks out in a smile. "I remember you now," he says excitedly. "You and that young boy were close to that pirate captain who rescued us. Frances told us she met you again when she went to help out at that plantation downriver after the Indian massacre."

Margaret nods eagerly. "Yes, Bennett's Welcome. Can you tell me what happened to Frances and her son, Peter? Are they here?"

Driggers shakes his head sadly. "No, I'm afraid not."

For a moment her heart contracts in a fit of pain and she prays that nothing terrible has befallen them. "Are they all right?" she asks, bracing herself, and feels relief come over her when he nods. More calmly, she continues, "I am so glad. What has happened to them?"

Looking down at the bristles of the broom, his face clouds for a moment and he says softly, "As a provision of the sale, we had to go with our original masters. Frances and Peter first were at Piercey's Toile. They and five other Africans came to Floridew only because they needed a safe place after the Indian massacre, and so they stayed behind. It's really a shame."

Margaret, sensing his emotion, wonders if there is more and waits for him to continue. When he doesn't, she asks tentatively, "But she's doing well?"

"Oh yes, she's a fine woman, and Peter is a good boy."

Margaret breaks out into a smile. "That is good news."

Driggers gives her a curious look and asks, "By the way, what happened to the boy who was with you? Is he here, too?"

Margaret takes a moment to consider. There is no guile in Driggers's face, nor any hidden meaning in his question. But she decides to be careful nonetheless and says, "No. I don't know what happened to him."

She is loath to utter a falsehood, even if it is a half-truth. After all, she hasn't seen John in over a year. Realizing that time is passing and she needs to get to the fishermen's tables to barter for their best catch, she puts her hand on Driggers's arm and says, "It's good to meet you, Emmanuel, but I've got to run. I do hope we will talk further anon."

He looks at her with his kind eyes and says, "I'm sure we will, Margaret. I'm sure we will."

As she hurries to the docks, a feeling of joy sweeps over her. She hopes she can connect with the other *malungu* as easily and can hardly wait for her next encounter with Driggers.

But before that opportunity arises, a momentous event intervenes. A few days later while taking breakfast in bed, Mrs. Chew complains of "disquiet" in her belly. Ann does her best to make her comfortable, but as she carries the empty dishes to the kitchen, a torrent of invective from her mistress follows her downstairs. Passing Margaret, she sighs in weary vexation.

Suddenly, a piercing scream from upstairs echoes through the house, followed by an outburst of, "Oh no! No, no, no, no!"

Ann hurriedly puts the tray on a side table, hikes up her skirts, and dashes up the stairs. Margaret follows in her wake. Bursting into the room they come upon Mistress Chew. Her ashen face is contorted in a grimace of horror, and her eyes keep darting frantically to her silk nightgown, which is soaked with a dark red stain in the middle. The air is heavy with the smell of blood.

When Ann starts to sway as if she's going to pass out, Margaret grabs her by the shoulders, fixes on her panicked eyes with a penetrating stare, and says urgently, "She's losing her child! Fetch Dr. Pott! Then take care of the boys!"

By the time Ann reacts, Margaret has started to peel the gown from Mrs. Chew. Seeing that the bleeding has stopped, she silently utters a prayer of thanks. Then she removes the bloody linen sheet and replaces it with a clean one she finds in the trunk by the bed, all the while murmuring comforting words: "You'll be all right, mistress. You'll be fine. Not to worry, mistress, the doctor is on his way."

Margaret finds another nightgown and, after some struggle, manages to put in on the unnerved woman. She notices a pitcher filled with water on a table by the window and takes a small cloth, wets it, and lays it across Mrs. Chew's forehead. Her patient still looks wild-eyed, but Margaret feels some of the tension leave her body.

Suddenly, Mrs. Chew starts to cry, quietly at first, then with greater force. "John will be so disappointed," she whimpers between sobs.

Margaret renews the compress, wipes away her tears, and tries to offer words of solace. "He won't blame you. It is God's will."

Margaret is relieved when she hears footsteps in the hall. Immediately, Dr. Pott enters the room. The middle-aged man is breathing heavily from rushing to the house and climbing the stairs as fast as he could. His lips are clamped tight in anxious anticipation until a quick glance at the bed and around the room assures him that Margaret has taken care of the necessities.

"Has she stopped bleeding?" he asks.

Margaret nods.

He sits down on the other side of the bed, takes Mrs. Chew's hand, feels her pulse, and mutters to himself. "Steady, good." Then he asks her, "Do you feel any pain?"

When Mrs. Chew shakes her head, he pats her hand and says, "Good. You'll be all right. The best thing for you is to get rest now."

But the bereft woman clutches at his arm with surprising strength. "The baby! Can you save it?"

Gently disengaging himself, he sighs and looks at her sadly.

A wailing sound of anguish issues from Mrs. Chew's mouth. "How can God punish me so?" she asks with fierce intensity.

Margaret rises and says to Dr. Pott, "I know what to do for her."

As she turns to go, Mrs. Chew reaches out her hand and wails, "Don't leave me, Margaret."

Seeing the desperation in her face, Margaret says, "I'll be right back. I promise."

When she gets downstairs, all the servants are gathered, looking mortified and milling about, not knowing what to do. Margaret tells Thomas to boil some water and hurries outside. She gathers chamomile and hyssop in the garden and goes to the kitchen out back. There she mixes an infusion of the plants with milk and an egg yolk, adds a spoonful of honey, and pours the potion into a porcelain cup. Returning to the house she passes the living room where Ann is sitting with her arms around John Jr. and Nathaniel. The two boys look like frightened deer. The other servants loiter in the hallway, grim-faced and apprehensive.

William stops her and asks, "How is the mistress? Is there anything we can do?"

"She'll be fine," Margaret says firmly and heads upstairs.

She comes upon Dr. Pott talking soothingly to his patient. Mrs. Chew looks exhausted and disheveled, and still somewhat crazed.

Margaret approaches with the potion. When Mrs. Chew looks suspiciously at the cup, Margaret says, "This will help you sleep."

"What is it?" asks Dr. Pott quietly.

"A few herbs, milk, egg, and honey."

"That's all right then."

Margaret puts the cup to Mrs. Chew's lips and helps her take several sips. For once the shrewish woman does not complain of the taste. When she has drained the cup she closes her eyes and sighs. A short while later, she is sound asleep.

Arranging a blanket to cover the patient, Margaret looks up and notices Dr. Pott watching her intently.

"How old are you, Margaret?" he asks in a quiet voice.

It is an odd question under the circumstances, but she answers straightaway, "Fourteen."

"You did a good job. Well done!"

Tears well up in Margaret's eyes. It is the first time in ages that someone has paid her a compliment.

7

JOPE'S BOUNTY

The Caribbean—Summer 1624

Standing on the poop deck of the *White Lion,* Captain Jope squints at the horizon. He can just make out the sails of the Spanish caravel they've been pursuing for the past two hours. He looks at the English vessel on his starboard side cutting through the waves and sending splashes of white spray into the air. The *Nightingale* may not be as swift as his own ship, but it is capable enough to keep up and capture their quarry up ahead.

As the two corsairs race side by side, Jope nods to his counterpart on the upper deck across the gap. The young man, dressed in a dark blue uniform that distinguishes him as a captain in the Earl of Warwick's fleet, waves back and resumes pacing back and forth nervously. Caught up in the excitement of his first chase, he can't hide his enthusiasm and worry.

Jope's blue eyes sparkle with resolve, but he feels apprehension, too. Will his plan work? Will his crewmen carry out their mission after all the practice drills he's put them through? By now he trusts his men to do their best, but he knows that there are always unforeseen circumstances in a new venture, beyond anyone's control. As a good Calvinist, he has put himself in his Maker's hands, trusting that God has singled him out as one of the elect and will grant him success.

When Jope decided to become a privateer again in order to take care of his financial difficulties, he made himself a promise. Never again would he fire upon an innocent ship. It's not that he is gun shy or afraid of a good fight, but the thought of how close he came to destroying the children when he and Elfrith bombarded the *San Juan Bautista* still chills his soul.

True, the encounter with that Spanish treasure galleon had been unusual. No one could have expected a warship to carry a hold full of African slaves; nor that its captain, Don Manuel de Acuña, would be so inexperienced or arrogant to engage in hopeless combat with two superior frigates. Any seasoned mariner would have hoisted the white flag after a few face-saving exchanges of cannon fire, but the Spaniard had resisted until his ship was but a cannonball-riddled, waterlogged carcass barely able to stay afloat.

In light of that experience, sailing in consort with another attack vessel still made the most sense. But it meant having to split the bounty and Jope wanted—needed—more than that. So he had hatched a desperate and devious ploy.

It took some time to convince the men he trusts. Although Gareth was on board right away and Teague joined in soon after, Osborn, who had no prior privateering experience, kept raising objections. Jope remained patient and, after a lengthy exchange in his cabin, finally persuaded his quartermaster to go along with the plan. In some ways he welcomed the opposition because it alerted him to how difficult it would be to sway the rest of the crew, especially the sailors who had served only on trading ships.

After the men assembled around the main mast, Jope addressed them from the quarterdeck, explaining his plan with more confidence than he felt. John, dangling from one of the ratlines, watched worriedly as some of the tars became restless and started to grumble. He fingered the dagger at his waist, but he knew he wouldn't be of much help if it came to a serious tussle.

Having expected some grousing, Jope waited, hoping for the objections to run their course. But then Fulke stepped forward.

The self-appointed leader of the deck crew glowered from under his bushy eyebrows and snarled, "This will not do, Captain. It is much too dangerous. None of us signed up for this."

Before anyone had time to react, Jope leaped down the stairs from the quarterdeck and rushed at him. A flicker of fear flashed across the giant sailor's face as Jope swung his fist and connected hard with his temple. In an instant Fulke dropped to the wooden planks like a sack of flour.

Jope looked around with blazing eyes. "Anyone else have an objection?" he growled, confronting the men who had surged forward.

Gareth had his hand on his sword ready to aid his captain, but realized there was no need. The sailors all slowly backed away.

When none of them met his eyes, Jope smiled grimly and said, "Then we are all agreed?"

"Aye, Captain," came the tentative reply, first from a few sea dogs, then swelling gradually until it became a chorus of approbation.

As Jope turned to head back up to the quarterdeck, he winked at John, surprising the boy once again. He was already shocked at his captain turning into an animal-like brute, but to realize that his outburst had been an act, as much a matter of calculation as of temper, astonished him.

Later, in the privacy of his cabin, Jope drove the lesson home when he told John, "Men are emotional creatures. Always be ready to do the unexpected when reason fails, which it often does."

For the next week, Jope, with Gareth's help, had the crew go through practice drills in anticipation of executing his plan until he was satisfied they were ready.

When the *White Lion* reached the Caribbean, he started to look for a suitable consort. He wanted someone who commanded a ship for the Earl of Warwick, the only Englishman still brave enough to make raids on the Spanish fleet against explicit orders from King James. Because the stakes were high—risking having one's head chopped off, if caught—only a daredevil would participate in such a marauding venture. But Jope didn't want a weathered veteran like

Elfrith. He was on the lookout for someone who was a relative novice at buccaneering.

He was fortunate to run into just such a greenhorn in Santo Domingo while taking on fresh water and other provisions. Captain Aron Middleton of the *Nightingale* was on his first privateering voyage. Eager and impatient for action, he had the benefit of an experienced navigator, Thomas Gundrie, but his plans to sail in consort with another of Warwick's captains had fallen through when the other ship had sprung a serious leak that required going into dry dock for repair.

Middleton and his crew had been waiting for more than a week and were getting bored and restless, so when Jope invited him and Gundrie for supper in his cabin and proposed that they go hunting Spaniards together, the young captain jumped at the opportunity. The navigator was less keen to sail with a stranger but warmed up to the idea after Jope kept refilling his cup with rum and conjured up visions of treasure hoards. It also helped that Jope carried with him letters of marque from the Kingdom of Nassau, which, not being allied with Spain, provided legitimate cover for raiding Spanish galleons.

They were three days out of harbor on the open sea when a lookout in one of the *White Lion's* crow's nests shouted out, "Sails on the horizon!"

Jope felt his pulse quicken, as did every sailor aboard the *White Lion*. Within an hour, they'd drawn near enough to make out the red and gold of the Spanish flag fluttering high on the main mast of the vessel ahead. While Jope and Middleton conferred, their quarry unfurled every sail, hoping to escape its pursuers, but to no avail. The *White Lion* and *Nightingale* were the speedier ships and had been closing the distance ever since.

John, waiting on the upper deck with Jope, can hardly contain his excitement. This is his first real adventure, and the captain has entrusted him with the job of being his personal lookout in the crow's nest on the quarterdeck mast. Beaming with pride, he goes over his tasks in his mind as they get closer to the Spanish ship. He doesn't realize that Jope has entrusted him with this assignment, not only because he needs someone he can count on to provide him the necessary intelligence, but to minimize the danger to John. Until they can be sure that the Spaniard won't put up a fight and capitulates, John will stay on deck. Only then will he climb up to take his aerie perch.

The afternoon sun is still high in the cloudless sky when the two privateers catch up to the Spanish cargo galleon. Jope shouts, "Hoist the Dutch flag," and the red, white, and blue banner ascends the main mast to the cheers of his crew.

As agreed upon, Middleton takes the lead. His navigator expertly positions the *Nightingale*'s hull at an angle to the starboard side of their quarry. Suddenly a boom and cloud of smoke issue from one of the gun ports. Seconds later a cannonball lands a good 30 feet in front of the Spanish vessel, sending a tall plume of water from the ocean into the air. There is another blast. This time the missile rips through the spritsail above the bow, making a large hole tattered at the edges.

That salvo is enough to convince the Spanish captain to surrender. He hoists the white flag and strikes most of the sails, slowing his vessel's forward movement to a crawl. Victory shouts and cheers erupt from the decks and upper spars of both pursuers.

Jope takes a deep breath and nods to John, Gareth, Osborn, and Teague. While the boy scurries up the ratlines to the mizzen crow's nest, the boatswain's whistle trills and the crew springs into action. As the *Nightingale* turns fully broadside, the *White Lion* glides forward into the gap between the English privateer and the Spanish galleon and keeps pace with the conquered ship.

A handful of sailors go about their business in a calm, orderly way on the port side facing the *Nightingale*. On the starboard side, out of sight of Warwick's crew, there is a beehive of activity. A number of sailors scramble up the ratlines and shrouds to the spars. Meanwhile, Gareth and deckhands work feverishly to lower a pinnace into the water. John, perched high above, watches the boat descend so quickly that it hits the waves hard with a loud splash. He worries that it might break in half or capsize, but it rights itself. The first mate and a number of sailors, armed with swords and pistols, jump in and start rowing toward the Spanish ship, pulling at the oars with every ounce of their strength.

Jope looks up, squinting as if the sunlight bothers him, and sees John pointing one finger at him, the signal that the pinnace is well on its way. He strides to the quarterdeck balustrade and hails Captain Middleton.

As the younger man approaches the gunwale of his ship, Jope yells across, "Well done, Captain. That went without a hitch, thanks to your able cannoneers! The Earl of Warwick will be pleased!"

Middleton flushes with pride and shouts back. "Yes, it was a pair of mighty shots!"

Jope cups his hand to his ear, pretending that the sails flapping in the wind make it hard to hear and encouraging the young captain to repeat himself.

When he does, yelling louder, Jope hollers back, "Give your sharpshooting gunners my regards for their most excellent aim. We could not have done it better ourselves. Tell them they are welcome to join my crew any time!"

Middleton grins and returns, "I won't tell them that!"

"I will have a flagon of wine in their honor sent over later."

"Much appreciated!"

Jope glances up and sees John hold out two fingers. The pinnace has arrived and his men have boarded the Spanish ship.

For the next minutes, Jope keeps Middleton engaged in conversation. At some point, the young captain starts to get restless, though. He keeps looking in the direction of the Spanish galleon in irritation, obviously frustrated that the *White Lion* is obstructing his view from their prize.

"It's time to board the Spaniard," he shouts. "Will you remove your ship from the passage?"

Jope cups his ear again and looks up toward the crow's nest, hoping for the signal that his men are on their way back with the booty, but John is looking intently toward the Spanish ship.

When Middleton repeats his question, Jope calls out, "I hope you are not heading home after this, Captain. We make good consorts and will build on this success together."

Again, the younger man preens with pride. He is about to answer when Thomas Gundrie comes up behind him and whispers in his ear. Middleton seems startled and looks suspiciously at Jope. "I must again ask you to move your vessel, Captain Jope," he barks impatiently.

When Jope glances up again to the crow's nest, he sees John excitedly waving three fingers. Relieved, he breaks out into a grin and shouts back, "Why certainly, Captain. I am as eager as you to find out what treasures lurk aboard the Spaniard!"

At a prearranged signal from him to Teague and Osborn, the men on the spars and ratlines adjust a number of sails and the *White Lion* starts to glide ahead of the *Nightingale* toward the bow of the Spanish galleon. Jope walks to the starboard balustrade and watches the men in the pinnace row in that direction, too, aiming to intersect his course.

In the crow's nest above, John holds his breath. This is the trickiest maneuver of the plan, docking the pinnace on the side of the bigger caravel. Fortunately, everything goes smoothly. By the time he clambers down and takes his place by Jope's side, Gareth and the sailors are heaving two heavy wooden chests, bolts of silken fabric, and several tanned animal hides over the railing of the main deck.

With the boat secured on the hull and everyone safely aboard, Jope signals his quartermaster again to blow a two-tone trill with his whistle. Immediately, the sailors on the spars who have been watching the return of the pinnace spring into action. They unfurl every canvas, from spritsail to top gallants, and lash them fast. As sailcloth billows out in the wind, the spars and masts creak loudly and the *White Lion* lurches forward, picking up speed.

John looks back at the receding Spanish galleon with the *Nightingale* at its side. "I wish I could see Captain Middleton's face when he realizes all the treasure's gone," he crows happily.

Jope nods with satisfaction waiting for Gareth and a few sailors to bring the spoils to him while the rest of the crew gathers below, eager to find out what plunder they've taken. The captain checks the chests quickly and looks over the silk cloth and animal hides with the practiced eye of an experienced maritime trader. Then he has Garth and another man take one of the trunks to the edge of the quarterdeck so that the men below can see it.

Grabbing handfuls of coins, he shouts, "We have had a fine haul today."

He raises his arms high and opens his fists. A shower of gold doubloons, sparkling in the sun, rains down into the chest to the roar and cheering of the crowd.

Jope singles out the cook. "Mr. Stoakes, ale for everyone!"

Another cheer rises from the deck below. The rough men slap each other's backs and start to dance with one another. For many it is their first successful raid in several years. Jope is filled with joy, too. Today's action has silenced any complaints or whispered questions regarding his leadership. Cheating the *Nightingale* of its share of the bounty appeals to his men's scavenging character. He has won them over and shown them that he is one of them, yet smarter by several sea leagues.

With the chests stored in his cabin, Jope has dinner with John and Teague. The late afternoon sun sends shafts of light through windows of the stern galley, bathing the room in gold, as they enjoy their salty beef stew. Jope feels tired as the tension of the day drains from his body. It has been a most satisfying venture, and he is pleased that everything went according to plan.

"You did a fine job today," he compliments the boy.

Still elated from the adventure, John says, "Next time, I want to go on the pinnace with Gareth!"

Jope smiles at his youthful eagerness. He trades glances with Teague and offers, "We'll see. I don't know if I can spare you as lookout."

"I don't think the captain of the *Nightingale* will be too keen on telling anyone how we tricked him on his first privateering venture," says Teague.

"No. He'll be too embarrassed," Jope replies. "But eventually it will come out."

He feels a small pang of foreboding in his gut—everything went so smoothly, it was almost too easy. He asks himself if this is the right course for him, but quickly dismisses any doubt. God has blessed him. In this one raid, he has realized more profit than he could make in five trading voyages across the Atlantic.

8

NEW RESPONSIBILITIES

Jamestown and the
Atlantic Ocean—Autumn 1624

By the time early fall arrives in Jamestown with its surfeit of colorful leaves from the maples, oaks, and chestnut trees, Mrs. Chew has fully recovered from her miscarriage and taken up her household duties again. When waves of sadness wash over her unexpectedly, she tells herself that losing her child was God's will, to test her mettle, and grits her teeth until the emotions retreat. For the most part she acts as if nothing has happened, although she devotes a bit more attention to her sons. She spends an extra hour a day with them and takes them along on her walks along the river—Dr. Pott's prescription for her the last time he checked in on her.

Overseeing the household, she also resumes scolding her servants with renewed vigor. If anything, her voice grows louder than before, as if to make sure that the recipient of her tongue-lashing is shamed before everyone else. Nor does she spare Margaret her castigating venom, upbraiding her just as before. She has not uttered a word acknowledging that Margaret saved her life or thanking her for her care. Not that Margaret expects any gratitude. She feels sorry for the woman and understands that Mrs. Chew does not wish to be reminded of what happened. At the same time, she refuses to give her mistress the satisfaction of seeing her getting upset by the scolding.

That role falls to Ann, for whom Mrs. Chew reserves her most vicious barbs, yelling at her for the slightest mistake—real or imagined.

Reprimands screamed at the top of Mrs. Chew's voice, like "Clumsy cow!" "Hopeless hussy!" and "Can't you do anything right!" echo through the house, followed by a loud slap or two.

When the young woman cries out and starts to sob, Mrs. Chew shows no mercy. "Quiet! Stop your blubbering!" she yells until there is silence.

Some of the servants look at one another with exasperated glances. Others go about their work as if nothing has happened, secretly glad that they were not the object of Mistress Chew's scorn this time. Margaret hates the poisonous atmosphere and spends as much of her time as possible outside. She enjoys talking with Emmanuel Driggers when she encounters him in Jamestown on her shopping excursions. His kindness toward her acts as an antidote to Mrs. Chew's acrimony. It turns out that he is not from Ndongo at all, but was captured by Portuguese slavers in North Africa and transported to the port of Luanda before being put aboard the *San Juan Bautista* and rescued by Captain Jope. She wonders if his gentle, slightly formal manner is his own or due to coming from a different tribe and society, but she doesn't know him well enough yet to ask him about it.

Things improve somewhat when Mr. Chew returns from his trip to England. Stepping off the ship he finds out at the docks what has happened to his wife during his absence and rushes home to make sure she is all right. Then he calls on Dr. Pott to receive his assurances that she has suffered no ill consequences. For the next few days, he fusses over her like a nursemaid over a sick child, holding her hand whenever possible and whispering endearments to her.

Mrs. Chew tolerates his attentions, but what she really cherishes are the presents her husband has brought from London—a pearl necklace and a rose-colored satin gown with gold trim in the newest French fashion. They so delight her that she forgets to complain about the tarragon-flavored stew Margaret serves that evening and fails to rebuke Ann when she accidentally drops a silver hairpin during her morning ablutions.

The merchant's devotion to his wife astonishes Margaret. It is hard for her to understand how anyone could love such an unpleasant woman, especially since she does not appear to reciprocate his feeling. She knows about loveless, arranged unions and marriages of convenience, but she also has seen relationships of genuine passion—Jope and Mary, and Anthony and his Mary—where the mutual affections run deep.

When she mentions this to Driggers the next time she meets him in the marketplace, he smiles knowingly and says, "The ways of love are mysterious and surprising. You'll find out soon enough."

Confused, Margaret wants to ask him, "Have you ever loved anyone that way?" but feels too shy to take the chance.

She likes the fact that there are now more Africans in town, most of them servants in the Yeardley home. While she doesn't know any of them well, they acknowledge her because of their shared history as *malungu*. The two women, Lucy and Embeline, who are 10 years or so older than her, always greet her warmly, eager to share the most recent news and gossip. Embeline, in particular, has a loose tongue, and Margaret learns more about the quirks of George Yeardley; his wife, Temperance; and their three children, Argall, Elizabeth, and Francis, than she cares to know.

But not all their exchanges concern their masters and mistresses. At some point, Embeline looks at Margaret and says mischievously, "You're beginning to fill out. Before you know it you'll have all the young men stalking after you!"

Margaret flushes with embarrassment and feels bewildered. She wishes she knew the two women better so that she could talk openly with them, the way she did with Frances at Bennett's Welcome. She has noticed the changes happening to her body—her figure becoming rounder and her breasts growing—and she is aware of the glances of many young and older men as they pass her. In the past they hardly paid any attention to her. Now they look at her with appreciation and interest. Not sure how to respond, Margaret does her best to ignore them.

One afternoon Margaret is working in her garden, clearing wilted plants and flowers and mulching the beds in preparation for winter. It is a balmy day, one of the last before the cold weather arrives, and she enjoys breathing in the pungent and moldy odor of the soil and fallen leaves, knowing they'll be soon be buried under snow and ice.

Suddenly, she hears someone in back of her clearing his throat. She rises quickly and wipes her hands on her apron. Turning around, she is surprised to see Mr. Chew.

When Margaret curtsies, he holds up his hand. "I wanted to talk to you alone, Margaret." He gnaws at his lip and starts, "I haven't had a chance to thank you for helping my wife during her ordeal."

Margaret feels awkward, unsure of what to say.

Before she can respond, he continues, "Sarah . . . Mistress Chew can be difficult . . . she doesn't easily . . . show . . . or say. . . ."

It embarrasses Margaret how uncomfortable and vulnerable he looks. "Anybody would have done the same," she says quickly.

He gives her a grateful glance and rubs his cheek. "Dr. Pott tells me that, without you, things could have gone much worse."

"I'm glad I could be of service."

"He says you would make a good midwife."

Margaret is astonished. Uncertain of what to make of it, she says, "Surely, he is too kind."

Mr. Chew's eyes search her face as if he were evaluating her, looking for any sign of disingenuousness. He walks closer to the garden and pretends to look it with interest. His mind made up, he faces Margaret again. "He would like you to assist him in similar situations from time to time—during deliveries. Would you like that?"

At first, Margaret is too surprised to answer. Then she considers and finally says, "I will be pleased to do what you think is best."

Chew again looks at her searchingly. "It is always best to stay on Dr. Pott's good side," he offers, smiling. "There won't be much occasion, but when it happens you will make yourself available."

Margaret nods to herself and says, "As you wish, sir."

More relaxed, Mr. Chew says, "Tomorrow morning, I want you to go and see him so that he can tell you what he has in mind for you. I'll let William know."

"Yes, master."

He looks significantly at her in a way Margaret doesn't fully understand and adds, "But I want you to continue to look after my wife when I am not here."

Without hesitation, Margaret answers, "I will."

Chew nods and heads back into the house. Margaret sits down on a wooden log in the garden and breathes deeply. She considers what new adventure fate has in store for her. The idea of helping and learning new things away from Mrs. Chew's overbearing presence appeals to her. When Lady Isabel's words, "You must conquer your fear," echo in her mind, she smiles, realizing that for the first time in her life, she does not feel afraid about what's ahead.

* * *

Captain Jope kneels in prayer in his cabin aboard the *White Lion*. He asks God for a successful journey home and forgiveness for any transgressions he has committed. Then he gets up and looks at the lurid colors of the sun setting among the windswept clouds that hover above the horizon. He shivers in the chilly sea breeze, a reminder that it is already November, unusually late to return to England from the New World.

He has just completed another successful raid of a Spanish galleon, using the same ruse as before. Interposing his ship broadside between his consort's vessel and their quarry, he robbed another of Warwick's captains of his share of booty. Although the man was a more experienced privateer than Jope's first victim, he was a garrulous sea dog who liked his liquor more than was good for him and never became suspicious. Happy and eager to talk, he dragged out their conversation even after the successful raid and Jope was ready to move on. By the time the *White Lion* finally surged ahead, the pinnace had already rounded the prow of the Spanish frigate, and picking it up proved an easy task.

With everything on the voyage having gone so smoothly, his crew is in high spirits. Jope can hear them on deck celebrating and singing bawdy songs. They're heading home to England and looking forward to spending their share of the plunder in dockside dives and brothels.

Jope settles in his chair. He breaks off a piece from a loaf of bread lying on the table and starts to chew slowly, savoring the salty taste of the coarse grain on his tongue. For the first time in decades, he feels content. He is returning with enough treasure to satisfy his brother and start building the fortune he has wanted to amass ever since he bought the *White Lion* and made it seaworthy for privateering.

He picks up a silver necklace studded with rubies resting on the table. The gemstones glint in the dying sunlight. He hopes that Mary will like it. He imagines it adorning her slender neck, set against the lace collar of her best blue dress. He has already put aside several bolts of fancy cloth for her—she deserves a new wardrobe. Now that he is heading home, with the stress and burden of being in the hunt for treasure behind him, he misses Mary and his two daughters and can't wait to see them.

There is a knock on the door, and John enters. He goes to the writing desk in the corner where a pile of books lies next to an inkwell and a lit candle.

As he reaches for one of the volumes, Jope says, "Leave it. No lessons tonight."

John comes over to the table, takes a chair across from the captain, and rests his chin on his arms. He puckers his lips and raises his eyebrows in a quizzical expression.

Jope can't help grinning at his inquiring look. He notes the sinewy forearms, well-muscled from frequent climbs up the ratlines to the crow's nests. He has a fleeting memory of the youngster using the books as a cushion in order to sit up high enough to clear the table and realizes that he hasn't needed to do that for some time.

"We've had a good haul this trip, and you've been doing a good job, more than what's expected of a cabin boy," Jope says. "Next spring when we ship out, you'll go as a mate's helper."

The youngster's eyes widen with surprise and pleasure. "No more swabbing decks and scrubbing the woodwork?" he asks.

Jope bursts out laughing and says, "I can't promise that, but you'll be working under our first mate and have many new responsibilities."

Beaming with pride, John says, "Oh, good. I like Gareth."

Jope breaks off another piece of bread and hands it to him. John starts to gnaw at the hard crust. Suddenly, he stops and asks, "When are we going to visit Margaret again?"

The question gives Jope pause. Since he ordered a homeward course, his own thoughts have turned to her as well. He wonders how she is coping in Chew's household in Jamestown. Realizing how much John has changed since he first met him, he imagines that she must be turning into a young woman by now.

"I miss her, too," he admits. "We will do our best to visit her next year, but privateering is an unpredictable undertaking."

"I know," says John. "It is in God's hands."

PART TWO

SETTLING IN

9

DAWN OF A NEW ERA

London, Plymouth—Spring 1625

The Earl of Warwick feels a small prick in his thigh and cries out more in surprise than in pain. Eyes blazing with fury, he rounds on the tailor kneeling at his side who has stabbed him with a pin while hemming his black satin wedding coat. Mortified, the thin, wizened man gets up slowly. His face is white as ashes, and his lower lip starts to quiver. His apprentice at a sideboard looks horror-struck as well.

"I am terribly, dreadfully sorry, m'Lord," the tailor manages to get out in a high-pitched, strangled voice. "It was an accident." He lowers his head with his arms pressed to his side and pleads, "I humbly beg your forgiveness, m'Lord. It is an unpardonable offense, I know. I . . . I . . . I am beside myself with shame and—"

Warwick, back under control, waves his rambling apology away like a bothersome fly. "Continue," he says dryly and tries to retrieve the thoughts the man interrupted.

"Oh thank you, Your Grace. Your generosity knows no bounds. I know I am but a fleck of dust in your exalted presence, and I am filled with eternal gratitude."

Irritated, Rich holds up a hand. "Enough!" he barks. "I said, 'Continue.' Do not wear out my patience!'"

"Of course, m'Lord, of course. It will take only another moment."

As the tailor hunkers down again on the carpet, Warwick catches the eye of his son, who has been watching the exchange with barely concealed amusement. Young Robert is dressed in a similar black outfit that makes him look like a smaller version of the earl. At least the youngster can see the humor in the situation. Perhaps there is hope for him yet. Let him learn how to deal with underlings—when to be generous and when to be strict.

Warwick is looking forward to finally sealing the union with Susan Rowe Halliday. At their first encounter, arranged and chaperoned by his clever stepmother at her London townhouse, they took each other's measure, and he quickly realized that Lady Frances had made an excellent choice for him. As a prominent leader of the Puritan cause, he needed a wife befitting his rank, power, and influence, who could hold her own in the pompous atmosphere of the Court, yet remain modest and gracious enough not to alienate his more austere religious associates. Lady Halliday was attractive, poised, and worldly and would suit his purposes very well.

By their second meeting they understood each other well enough to come to terms. Warwick would provide a safe, financially comfortable haven for her. In return, Lady Halliday would run his household and attend social events by his side. The earl was pleased that, while she expressed a willingness to oversee the education of his younger children, she did not demand extra support for her daughters, who were both of age and married.

A week later, they signed papers drawn up by his cousin Nathaniel, sealing the agreement, and made plans for an early spring wedding.

But then King James died on March 27, and they had to delay the ceremony. It would not have been seemly to celebrate their union while England was in mourning, not that the Puritans and other English Protestants were especially upset about the passing of their Catholic monarch, who had barely tolerated them and savagely persecuted some of their more radical leaders. Still, order and decorum had to be observed.

Fortunately, the new king, Charles I, was so eager to wed his 15-year-old French princess that he decided to marry her a mere two months after ascending to the throne, even though his actual crowning was still months away. Warwick muses that it takes a great deal longer to plan a coronation than a royal wedding after the requisite period of mourning. In any case, with the new king leading his young bride to church, the earl and Lady Halliday saw no reason to postpone their nuptials any longer.

Warwick eyes himself in the large looking glass. He will be wearing black, in acknowledgment of his being a widower. At the same time, his outfit will signal his wealth without flaunting it. Everyone at the ceremony will know that his satin black wedding garb cost a pretty penny. He smiles at his reflection and decides he looks ravishingly handsome. Perhaps it is time to have his portrait painted.

"Please be so kind and raise your arms, m'Lord," the tailor prods softly.

As Rich turns and complies, spreading his arms like a giant raven, the slender white-haired man at his side takes a step back and narrows his eyes to evaluate the fit.

"It looks a bit tight under the shoulders, m'Lord. We will have that taken care of in no time," he says.

As the tailor marks the garment under the arms with chalk, Warwick sighs. This is the third fitting he has had to endure, and it always takes longer than expected—more time than he wants to spare when he has so many more pressing things to do.

Many of the challenges facing the realm, not to mention Rich's concerns, predate King James's death. Nearly a year earlier, shortly after the monarch gutted the Virginia Company, he suffered a bout of dysentery from which he never recovered. While he lay ailing in Whitehall Palace, his 24-year-old son, Charles, and George Villiers, the Duke of Buckingham, took over the reins of government. In Warwick's view, shared by many other English nobles, they have exercised poor stewardship.

Buckingham had been James's favorite, too—there were persistent rumors that they were frequent bedfellows. He and Charles had grown close on a secret mission to Spain to negotiate the marriage between the English crown prince and the Infanta Maria Anna. Apparently, the devout young woman had detested Charles only slightly less than the boorish Buckingham. Outraged, the Spanish ambassador had addressed Parliament and demanded that Buckingham be executed for his rude behavior, but the duke countered by calling for military action against Spain. His demand proved more popular with the Protestant public.

King James acquiesced, declared war, and sent an army to Holland and the German Palatinate to battle the Spanish occupiers there. Warwick supported the decision. He didn't care that Charles wanted the fight for personal reasons, not on religious grounds. He was pleased that the conflict would lift the prohibition on privateering, allowing his fleet to raid Spanish ships with impunity. What appalled him was the lack of preparation—the youthful arrogance of the crown prince and Buckingham to think that it would be an easy military outing and that the Dutch people would hail them as liberators and rise up against the Spanish. The ill-conceived campaign stalled quickly and cost the lives of many English soldiers, including the Earl of Southampton and his son, who both caught a fever and died near Antwerp in November of 1624.

Warwick did not attend the funeral in Hampshire, after the bodies were brought back to England, but he regretted their deaths. Despite their falling out over the Virginia Company, Southampton had never treated him unkindly. Rich's quarrel had been with Edwin Sandys and his crony, Nathaniel Ferrar.

To Warwick's surprise, a few weeks after James died, the new king and his consort asked to meet with him to discuss military matters.

"It must be about money," Nathaniel Rich opined. "Parliament has just refused to provide the funds for another war against Spain on the European mainland."

Rich nodded. "I imagine Charles was apoplectic. He believes in royal infallibility and the divine right of kings even more than his father did."

"Yes, he'd like nothing better than to tear up the Magna Carta."

Looking out the window of his residence, Rich mused, "Now that he is on the throne, I wonder if he still stammers."

While they had a good laugh about that, they knew the King and Buckingham meant serious business, which might provide additional opportunities for Warwick's causes. Rich decided it would also be a good time to introduce his son to the new monarch.

On the appointed day, when they arrived at Whitehall Palace by coach, they were ushered into the throne room. Charles, wearing a fur overcoat trimmed with ermine, sat languidly in a golden chair on a red carpeted dais, surrounded by a number of advisers. His facial hair was still filling in. The Duke of Buckingham, with a full pointed beard and mustache flaring prominently, stood off to one side, hand on his sword.

The earl strode up to new monarch, knelt on the second step, and said, "My liege." Then he kissed the diamond-studded ring on Charles's extended hand.

Gesturing him to rise, the King said, "I am pleased that you are here, L-L-Lord Rich. I . . . I hear you are getting m-m-married again."

"Yes, my liege," Warwick said, repressing a smile. "For me it is my second time, though." He looked back and continued, "Allow me to present my eldest, Robert Rich Jr."

When the youngster hesitated, Charles's voluptuous lips broke into a beneficent smile. "Come closer, boy," he said. "I am not going to bite."

All the courtiers chuckled, as if enraptured by their monarch's wit.

Robert Jr. came forward, knelt, and kissed the ring just like his father. As he withdrew, Charles graciously said, "You have a handsome lad, Sir Robert."

"Thank you, my liege."

With a glance toward Buckingham, the King rose and said, "Let us repair to the study so we can talk at leisure." He signaled to a butler in livery. "Show the lad around the palace and give him something to eat."

Warwick bowed and followed Charles and Buckingham into a large room with several chairs and a large oak table covered with documents and maps. The King nodded to his adviser.

Buckingham cleared his throat and said, "Sir Robert, we are seeking your advice on how to obtain Spain's silver and gold from the New World mines, to cut off Phillip's lifeblood. You have considerable experience in this matter, I believe."

Warwick was both relieved and pleased and quickly warmed to one of his favorite subjects. "It is an excellent strategy, my liege," he said, looking at Charles. "Without a steady supply of bullion, Phillip won't be able to pay for his large armies and fleet. How were you contemplating accomplishing it?"

Buckingham, taking a map from the table, said, "We mean to attack the main Spanish ports in Mexico and the Caribbean to disrupt the empire's supply lines."

Warwick pursed his lips. "Those cities are well fortified. Why not let the Spaniards dig the ore out of the ground and take it from them when their ships carry it across the ocean?"

"Privateering?" Buckingham asked.

"Yes, it is more efficient and effective. Building up our fleet to dominate the seas will give us the flexibility to defend ourselves and attack Spain where it is weakest."

"Tell us more," said Charles, intrigued.

Rich quickly warmed to the subject. Naval preparedness was a topic he felt passionate about. But as the conversation continued, he could tell that neither Charles nor Buckingham were all that interested in what he had to say. They clearly had other ideas, although they did not share them with him. Warwick left the audience, impressed only by both men's self-importance and youthful arrogance and wondered why they had called on him at all if their minds were already made up.

His son, on the other hand, was awestruck by the visit and could not stop talking about everything he had seen. Warwick was happy that he had enjoyed himself, but didn't like seeing the lad with eyes aglow, almost as if he was in love.

A few days later, the earl found out what Charles and Buckingham were up to when Samuel Argall came to see him. Since James had knighted the old sea dog and put him in charge of developing the navy, he had not visited Rich as often as before. Warwick had missed his gruff presence and advice on how to establish more Puritan colonies in America. It turned out that the King and his consort were planning to attack the Spanish port of Cadiz with the help of France and the King of Orange. They were ready to commit a large portion of the English Navy to the undertaking. Now Warwick understood the reason they had called him. They had wanted his fleet to join the expedition but decided not to pursue it when they saw where his real interests lay.

Like Warwick, Argall was always ready for a good fight with Spain, and the idea of destroying its main port guarding the entrance to the Mediterranean struck him as sound. But then he heard how they planned to go about the assault.

"Buckingham is putting Sir Edwin Cecil in command of the expedition," Argall snarled in disgust.

Warwick immediately understood his concern. "We can only hope that his military experiences on land in the wars in Holland and Germany will translate to the seas."

Argall shook his head in disgust. "I've spoken to the man. He knows nothing about maritime strategy and naval battles."

Rich nodded in agreement. His quicksilver mind touched on the implications. Whatever the outcome, he would be able to conduct his own war with Spain on the high seas and reap financial benefit accordingly. But what would Phillip's response be to a direct attack on his country? Would he retaliate and send another armada to ravage the English coast? Would he attack the English colonies in North America? Warwick no longer cared about Virginia, although he still owned property there. But the Plymouth Colony would be vulnerable. He'd need to alert the board of the Council for New England and send letters of warning to Massachusetts.

"We are finished for today, m'Lord."

The tailor's voice brings Warwick back to the present. As he waits for him and his apprentice to peel the unfinished garments from his body, he wonders if his future wife is undergoing a similar ordeal with her dressmaker.

His thoughts turn to the new king's religious beliefs. His being a Catholic is more worrisome than his military inadequacies. His French bride, Maria Henrietta, the youngest daughter of King Henry IV, is rumored to be as devout as a nun. Although Charles has promised the members of Parliament who opposed the marriage that he would not loosen religious restrictions on recusants—Catholics who refused to attend the worship services of the Church of England—Warwick does not trust him. Charles's father prosecuted Puritans viciously, and his stammering son is not likely to be kinder. He hopes that Captain Elfrith and his young bulldog disciple fulfill the mandate he gave them soon. The Puritan cause needs new territories in the New World.

* * *

The Crown and Anchor, a dockside alehouse in Plymouth, is buzzing with excitement. Light from the early spring sun slants through the windows into the smoke-filled room, and the sour smell of beer permeates the atmosphere. Sitting on one side of a long table with their backs to the wall, Captain Jope, flanked by Teague and Gareth, now the *White Lion's* quartermaster, is mustering men for his new privateering venture. Off to the side, John looks serious and studious, as befits his first-time role as scribe. The captain, having assembled crews before, is more relaxed.

One at a time, seamen and gunners step up, doff their hats or caps, announce their names, and state their eagerness to serve with him. Jope greets his veterans from previous voyages with good-natured ribbing. But there are also a large number of newcomers who require a thorough vetting. Since word got out about the *White Lion's* success the previous summer, sailors eager to join him have come out of the woodwork. Although most of the regulars kept mum about Jope's special way of marauding, some couldn't help bragging about their successful haul while bandying about their trinkets and doubloons. Now there are many others who wish to share in the bounty.

Looking at some of the candidates, John recalls one of Captain Jope's favorite sayings: "The smell of money attracts all kinds of riff-raff."

With the sailors he knows, Jope just checks with Gareth and Teague. When he gets a nod, he says to the man standing before him, "Aye, I'd be glad to have you aboard again." Then he names the compensation, usually a quarter or half of a share. Upon consent, he signals John to dip his quill in the inkwell and enter the name in the logbook along with the agreed-upon stake.

With newcomers, a number of rough men who have seen better days—some have lost most of their teeth—he takes longer to find out with whom they have shipped before. In the end, after conferring with his quartermaster and navigator, he follows his intuition and accepts or rejects the candidates accordingly.

It is late afternoon by the time they're done. Leaning back against the wall, Jope calls for tankards of ale for himself and Gareth and Teague, and a smaller mug for John, who stifles a yawn. His hand is sore from scratching away with the quill for hours without a break.

"I think we have a fine crew, Captain," says Gareth. "More than three-quarters are men we know and can count on."

"Aye," says Jope. "It's a fine company of rough-and-tumble men."

He takes the logbook from John. "You did a fine job, lad. Your writing is better than mine!" As he looks down the list, he stops, surprised, and says, "I see you've put your name here, too."

John meets his eye and, with a small grin, replies, "Yes, but I didn't know what share to put down for myself."

For a moment, Jope is at a loss for words. Then he roars with laughter, slaps the table, and says, "Well, aren't you a saucy one!" He turns to his quartermaster. "What do you think of this brazen fellow? Should I give in to his demand or have him caned?"

Gareth's lips twitch in amusement. "Why not?" he says. "The lad pulls his weight."

Jope looks at John, whose raised eyebrows and compressed lips betray both uncertainty and determination. "I'm proud of you for speaking up for yourself," he says. "Put yourself down for an eighth of a share."

He cuffs the youngster's head with affection and is pleased to see his apprehension turn to relief and a huge smile blossoming on John's face. The corners of Jope's mouth twitch in merriment.

Later, alone in his cabin by flickering candlelight, he is more pensive. When he returned to Tavistock in early December, he was amazed to hear that England had declared war on Spain. He realized at once that it would make privateering more difficult because the Spanish silver transports would be heavily armed and their captains more likely to put up a fight. On the other hand, it would encourage English ships to conduct their raids in consort, giving him plenty of opportunities to make off with treasure. Greater danger, greater gain.

The trouble was that Mary, with her uncle in Parliament, understood the implications all too well. Jope loved seeing her eyes light up when he gave her the ruby necklace, and they had a good month together enjoying each other's company and spending time with their daughters. But as the time approached for him to depart, he began to notice her melancholy expression when she thought he wasn't looking. Mary knew enough not to argue with him again about his decision to become a privateer, knowing how much their livelihood depended on it, and Jope silently thanked her for it. But it pained him to see the worry lines on her forehead, and when he overheard her praying in their daughters' room at night, "Please keep big and little John safe," it nearly broke his heart.

He wishes he could stay with her, but he knows that his destiny lies elsewhere and prays that God will grant him success.

The day before shipping out, John and Jope go the harbormaster's office to obtain the documents for their departure. Unlike the previous year, it is a routine matter. With England and the Netherlands at war with Spain, there is no longer any need to disguise their military cargo and purpose of their voyage.

As they return to the docks, they see a middle-aged man in conversation with Gareth at the gangplank leading up to the *White Lion.* He is dressed in the cloak and doublet of a well-to-do merchant. When Gareth notices Jope and John, he points in their directions, and the man starts to walk toward them. As he approaches, his rolling gait characterizes him as someone who has spent considerable time at sea.

"Captain Jope, it has been a long time," he calls out.

The man, who has an unusually prominent wart on his cheek, looks somewhat familiar to John, but he can't recall where he has seen him before. Jope squints at him, too, but then his eyes widen in recognition.

"Captain William Ewen . . . Point Comfort . . . You were there with John Rolfe and William Pierce. . . . It has been, what—six years?" he says. "What brings you to Plymouth?"

Ewen shakes his hand heartily and replies, "I normally sail from London—I have a home in Greenwich—but on this trip I'm taking some men and women from here to my plantation in Virginia. I don't travel there as often as I used to." He scrutinizes John. "Is this the boy who was with you then? He certainly has grown!"

John's pulse quickens. The man remembers him. Does he know anything regarding Margaret's whereabouts? "Do you know what happened to the young girl?" he asks before Jope can silence him.

"Margaret? Of course," Ewen says with a smile. "I saw her at John Chew's house just last fall. She is becoming quite a comely young woman."

"Is she well then?" John blurts out.

"Oh, quite well, and well thought of by everyone."

Although John is eager to learn more, a look from Jope stops him from asking further questions.

"Why don't you come to my ship tonight? The *Charles* is docked yonder." Ewen points toward a merchant ship moored farther down the pier.

Jope hesitates. There is much to do before shipping out in the morning, but he knows from experience never to pass an opportunity to gather information.

"We're honored by your invitation, but we're leaving tomorrow," he says. "Why don't we have a quick pint in the Crown and Anchor?"

Ewen is pleased. "I understand. Next time we'll have more time, Captain."

As they make their way toward the alehouse, John can hardly contain his excitement. He is eager to know more about how Margaret is faring.

10

A WEDDING

Jamestown—Spring and Summer 1625

During the winter and early spring, Dr. Pott occasionally calls on Margaret for help when examining female servants and their mistresses who have fallen ill but are not comfortable with a man touching them. He tells her what to look for, which part of the body to palpitate or prod, and makes his diagnosis and prescriptions based on her observations. Margaret also attends two births with him and the local midwife. She learns about the use of birthing stools, how to help the mothers push during contractions, and how to cut the umbilical cord afterward. After her ordeal with Mrs. Chew's miscarriage, she is happy that both deliveries are routine and result in healthy baby girls.

Although performing medical tasks allows Margaret to get away from the strained, spiteful atmosphere of the Chew residence, it is not always a pleasant experience. People in pain are often at their worst—verbally abusive and mean—and the sweaty, noxious smells of sickbeds linger with her long after she finishes seeing a patient.

Nor is Dr. Pott the easiest person to get along with. He can be impatient, irritable, and prone to imagined slights to his reputation. One of his servants, Jane Dickson, tells Margaret behind his back that he turns every penny over twice before spending it. Margaret feels sorry for the emaciated, embittered woman. Jane was taken captive by the Powhatans during the 1622 massacre, and Dr. Pott rescued her and other women prisoners a year later by offering the Indians a pound of beads. But then he insisted that Jane owed him for the ransom he paid, as well as for the three years of service that her husband had left on his contract of indenture when he was killed in the carnage. When she petitioned the Council of Burgesses to be released, complaining bitterly that her new servitude was no different than being a slave with the Indians, her appeal fell on deaf ears.

Overall, Margaret's experience with Dr. Pott is positive. He always treats her with respect, even when he is annoyed. He proudly shows off his garden and the medicinal plants he grows there, and is eager to find out what she knows about herbs and flowers. Student and teacher exchange roles as Margaret learns about beneficial and poisonous plants unfamiliar to her while teaching Dr. Pott about the effects of certain flowers, mosses, and barks, knowledge she acquired from an Indian brave at Warrosquoake.

Mrs. Chew resents Margaret's absences and criticizes her more harshly than usual upon her return. When she finds out whom Dr. Pott has been treating, she always finds something negative to say about the patient. In the case of Mistress Harrison, ill with a fever, she comments, "I don't know why anyone would bother to help her get well. She looks like she's near death's door most of the time already!"

Margaret takes her insults in stride. By now she is used to the hot and cold winds of her mistress's moods and knows not to take them personally. They usually worsen when Mr. Chew goes on business to Hogg Island or Elizabeth City near the mouth of the James River. Then Mrs. Chew unleashes her wicked tongue and not only in the privacy of the residence.

One day, while picking sprigs of sage and thyme in the garden, Margaret observes Mr. Chew returning from a visit to his plantation and warehouse on Hogg Island. She is surprised to see him hurrying up the road from the harbor instead of walking with his usual measured gait. When he notices her by the side of the house, he stops, looks about, and discerning no one in the vicinity, marches over to her.

Margaret rises, surrounded by the smell of the herbs, and says, "We weren't expecting you so early, sir. Mistress Chew is resting yet."

"I'm not here to exchange pleasantries," he snaps vehemently.

Margaret, taken aback, wonders what has provoked his ire. Has she done something to offend him?

Mr. Chew takes off his hat and knocks the dust off the brim. Then he stares at her with burning eyes and says, "I have heard suggestions that Mistress Chew has been unable to hold her tongue. What do you know of it?"

Margaret's feeling of relief that he is not angry with her quickly yields to alarm. If she repeats Mistress Chew's venomous comments, she will most certainly earn more verbal punishment or worse when Mr. Chew is gone again.

Pacing back and forth, the merchant insists, "I must know! Have you heard your mistress speak ill of George Yeardley's wife?"

"Lady Temperance?" Margaret asks to gain time. She knows exactly what Mrs. Chew said from Embeline and Lucy. The Yeardleys' servants repeated it word for word, delighted to share with her how outraged their mistress was hearing about it.

"Yes. What did she say?" Mr. Chew barks impatiently. "Out with it!"

In a small voice Margaret admits, "She has spoken mockingly of the elaborate outfits she wears at social affairs."

Running his fingers through his hair, he asks, "What else?"

"On the way home from church, she said that the dress Lady Temperance was wearing would look better on a harlot."

Mr. Chew blanches. The emotions washing over his face turn from disbelief to worry to outrage. With great difficulty, he brings himself under control. His voice sounds hoarse when he says, "I will have to make my apologies to the lady, tell her that my wife misspoke, and hope she will be merciful."

Slapping his hat against his breeches, he stomps toward the house. Margaret looks after him, shaken, before returning to her task. Soon she hears loud arguing issue from an open window. Not knowing what the consequences will be, she takes as long as possible before going inside.

By the time she returns with her savory harvest, the shouting match between Mr. Chew and his wife is over. But the household staff is quietly abuzz. Walter takes her outside again and quickly recounts what has happened with much merriment. He especially enjoys mimicking his master saying, "Why did you have to pick on the most important women in town? If she complains to the council, you'll have an assignation with the dunking stool!"

Apparently, Mistress Chew retaliated with equal fervor until Mr. Chew threatened her with moving the household to Hogg Island. That knocked the wind out of her sails. In a panic-stricken voice, she begged for indulgence and promised to mend her ways.

Margaret does not believe it for a moment. Nor do any of the other servants. Even William, the head butler, chimes in, to everyone's surprise, with a quotation from the Bible, "Can the Ethiopian change his skin, or the leopard his spots?" he says ponderously while glancing pointedly at Margaret.

While the others laugh in approval, Margaret does not find it amusing. It hasn't once occurred to her that she would want to change the color of her skin, and William has never made a comment about it before. She chooses not to say anything, but wonders if it stemmed from mere snobbishness or a deeper resentment of her African origin.

For the next week Mrs. Chew is meeker than a lamb. She makes the effort to compliment every servant about something or another and seems more charming in public. Lucky for her, Lady Temperance decides to keep mum about the indiscretion, no doubt realizing that bringing it up will only lead to more ridicule.

And so, relative calm returns to the Chew residence. It helps that there are several large supper gatherings at the house, where Mrs. Chew receives plenty of attention from the male guests, including Dr. Pott, John Harvey, Richard Stephens, and other merchants and burgesses from town. Discussion covers the usual topics—how the Virginia Colony will fare now that Charles is on the throne, what Indian threats the summer will bring, and how large the tobacco crop will be.

The biggest news is the announcement of the upcoming marriage of Abraham Piercey and Lady Frances Grenville West. As the recent widow of Nathaniel West she is as close to royalty as one can get in Virginia. Her brother-in-law was Lord De La Warr, one the founders of the Virginia Company and its first governor. For Piercey, a man who worked his way from relative poverty to riches in Jamestown, the union is emblematic of his wealth, reputation, and standing in the colony. Lady Frances is more than a decade younger than him and brings with her a three-year-old son, named Nathaniel after his father.

But what has everyone in town tittle-tattling—servants, masters, and mistresses alike—is the rumor, soon confirmed, that the ceremony is to take place at Floridew, the plantation the wealthy merchant recently purchased. He has renamed it Piercey's Hundred and plans to settle there, leaving his townhouse with a caretaker for the use of his daughters, Elizabeth and Mary.

Everyone of rank in Virginia has been invited, but there are some who are unwilling to make the journey upriver for the event. It requires rising early to be able to return late the same day. No one wishes to spend the night on the plantation under primitive circumstances.

Sir George Yeardley, for one, and his family have decided not to attend. According to Driggers, when Yeardley received the invitation, he said, "I never set foot on Floridew when I owned it, and I'm not about to do so now that it belongs to Piercey."

A Wedding

At first Margaret doesn't pay much mind to the endless gossiping. She assumes that Mrs. Chew is one of the Jamestown society women who does not wish to subject herself to the hardship of the journey upriver, so Margaret is surprised when she overhears Mrs. Chew say to her husband, "We really must be there, John. I would not miss it for the world!"

Margaret's heart beats faster when she realizes that, if she could go along, she would be able to see Frances and Peter again. But since she is not Mrs. Chew's personal maid, there is no reason to get her hopes up.

To her surprise, three days before the event, Mr. Chew seeks her out and says, "Margaret, we'd like you to come with us to Floridew. Ann gets hopelessly seasick and won't be much use by the time we arrive. She will take care of the boys while we're gone. I've spoken to Master Piercey, and you will help out after the service as well."

Doing her best to contain her excitement, Margaret curtsies and says, "Yes, master. Of course. I am at your service."

She doesn't sleep well the night before the journey and is already wide awake long before dawn when the rest of the household gets up. It takes Ann only an hour to get Mrs. Chew ready, despite a few blistering words of reproach. Her husband paces impatiently at the foot of the stairs to their bedroom. When she is finally ready, she descends in a hazy aura of candlelight, like a vision of transcendent beauty, and Margaret watches Mr. Chew's face radiate with pleasure. He is ready to forgive her for anything. There is barely time for breakfast before they have to leave and make their way down to the harbor.

Shortly before sunup all the wedding attendees from Jamestown assemble at the dock. Some of them arrived the previous day from plantations farther east and spent the night in their townhomes or with friends. The women wear capes over their dresses to keep warm. Many stifle yawns with gloved hands. It takes awhile for everyone to board the three small ships before they cast off to make the 12-mile journey upriver to Piercey's Hundred.

Margaret has never seen the northern section of the James before. For a mile or two the river remains as wide as at Jamestown, then it narrows by half and meanders in ample curves. With the help of able navigators, a favorable breeze, and powerful oarsmen they make good time, and by mid-morning Margaret, sitting close to the prow in the leading ship, can make out a wooden building on the south bank. It is the windmill Yeardley had built—the distinctive structure everyone has heard about but few have seen. As they get closer, Margaret thinks it looks like a big wooden box standing on its side and mounted on a large post, with four large, canvas-covered blades up top that turn slowly in the morning breeze.

They soon reach a small dock and disembark one boat at a time. Margaret holds the bottom of Mrs. Chew's dress while her husband helps her climb awkwardly onto the narrow walkway to shore. From there, a wide path leads to a palisaded enclosure with the entrance gates standing wide open. Piercey's Hundred may be only a fraction the size of Jamestown, but it looks just as well fortified. No wonder the plantation withstood the assault during the Indian massacre well and suffered only six casualties.

As the guests slowly walk inside the enclosure, they stop in surprise. Up ahead is a large two-story house that would provoke gasps of amazement in Jamestown. Here in the countryside surrounded by low, thatch-roofed houses, it looks like a grand mansion with its solid stone foundations, redbrick walls, stone masonry, a large porch to one side, and a red tiled roof. Not since her time in England has Margaret seen such a substantial building. Abraham Piercey has spared no money in constructing his new home.

As other ships unload, the rest of the guests arrive and gather on the grassy area in front of the porch. Margaret looks for Frances, but there is no sign of her. She recognizes John Upton coming around the corner of the house. He seems preoccupied and doesn't acknowledge her. She is surprised when Captain Stephens comes out of the house and stands to the side on the porch. He is wearing a dress uniform with boots and a sword by his side.

Then a group of servants comes from the kitchen behind the house carrying wicker baskets filled to the brim with kernels of corn. Margaret almost leaps for joy when she sees Frances and Peter among them. Her friend looks just as she remembers her, but Peter has grown visibly taller. The servants walk around the crowd, urging each guest to take a handful of corn. When Frances comes up to the Chews, her eyes light on Margaret, and a radiant smile blossoms on her face.

Chew dips his hand in the basket and takes some of the red, brown, yellow, and white kernels. Then he whispers to Margaret, "You should go and help."

Margaret curtsies gratefully and follows Frances. But before she can get a basket herself, the crowd quiets as the door to the house opens and Governor Wyatt steps onto the porch, followed by Abraham Piercey and his two daughters. Mary and Elizabeth are dressed in identical lavender gowns, complementing their father's lavish, wine-colored doublet and matching breeches. Between them, holding their hands, stands a small boy with blond curls, wearing a darker outfit. Margaret figures it must be young Nathaniel, the son of the bride. Captain Stephens positions himself next to Piercey, acting as his best man. As Margaret joins Frances, standing with the other servants next to John Upton, her friend catches her hand and squeezes it as a warm gesture of welcome.

Meanwhile, the wedding guests have quieted down and look eagerly toward the porch. Abraham Piercey steps forward, exuding confidence, dignity, and satisfaction. He lets his eyes wander over the crowd and says, "Thank you, friends, for joining us for this happy occasion."

When he steps back, Governor Wyatt takes his place, raises his arms, and calls out, "Let us pray."

All bow their heads and listen in silence as Wyatt, in his role as minister of Jamestown, asks for the Lord's blessing. Margaret, glancing up at him from time to time, can't help but notice how serious he is and wonders if he will smile at all at some point during the celebration. When Wyatt finishes, the wedding guests all murmur, "Amen," and look around expectantly.

Wyatt gestures to the crowd to part in the middle and make a walkway. At his sign a bagpiper begins to play a stately melody. From the rear, Frances Grenville West slowly walks up the aisle. She is wearing a green silk taffeta dress with fancy embroidery and strands of pearls hanging from her shoulders. Cradled in her arms, she carries a bouquet of rosemary, symbolizing fidelity and luck. A number of women gasp in admiration. Margaret sees Mrs. Chew's eyes narrow and her lips pucker. The bride looks magnificent, and her gown is even fancier than Mrs. Chew's extravagant French dress. If she had hoped to upstage the bride, her efforts did not succeed.

Helped by Captain Stephens, Mistress West ascends the stairs of the porch and takes her place next to Piercey in front of Wyatt. The governor begins reading the formal vows from the *Book of Common Prayer*: "Dearly beloved friends, we are gathered together here in the sight of God, and in the face of his congregation, to join together this man and this woman in holy matrimony. . . ."

The ceremony goes on for quite some time, but no one except the bride's son gets fidgety. Elizabeth and Mary do their best to keep him standing still. When the bride and groom finally exchange vows, their faces glow with surprisingly tender expressions, and Margaret is moved.

After the governor pronounces them man and wife, they kiss. There are further prayers, and the ceremony finally concludes. Stephens draws his sword and solemnly points to an honor guard of militiamen lined up next to the house. They fire their muskets into the air to the cheers of the crowd. Then the newlyweds step down from the porch and walk down the aisle as the guests toss the kernels of corn at them to wish them prosperity and good fortune. They lead the company to an open meadow near the house, where there are wooden tables, stools, and benches off to the side, and a group of fiddlers and drummers have started to play lively music.

Frances signals to Margaret. They join the other servants at the back of the house where the cook and kitchen maids have readied trenchers and plates heaped with wedding buns, sweetmeats, and custards, and crystal decanters filled with dark red wine. The servants take up the food and libation, along with plates and glasses, and bring them to the guests milling about. Soon everyone is in a boisterous mood, toasting the happy couple, lining up for lively jigs and reels, and eating and drinking to their heart's content. Margaret and the other servers have to go back several times to refill their serving trays and bring more wine.

In time everyone is sated, and many of the women guests rest on the stools and benches. John Upton and other male servants go around offering pipes of tobacco to the men who congregate in small groups for conversation. A few couples enjoy the warm spring weather and stroll along the river. Others walk farther inland past the houses of tenants and freshly seeded tobacco fields.

The lull in activity gives Margaret and Frances time to rest on a bench by the kitchen and catch up. They enjoy the warm sun and watch Peter sitting on the ground nearby, whittling away at a small maple branch. Eager to hear about life in Jamestown, Frances listens with amazement and growing dismay to Margaret's account of her experiences with Mrs. Chew and Dr. Pott. She asks occasional questions to reassure herself that Margaret isn't being physically mistreated. Her kind, caring responses allow Margaret to unburden herself for the first time in years.

In comparison, life on the plantation seems ordinary, filled with daily routines determined by the season, although Frances imagines there will be changes, now that Piercey and his new wife will live there. When Margaret marvels at how much Peter has grown and sees Frances swell with pleasure and pride, Margaret realizes that it is Frances's son who gives joy and meaning to her life.

At some point Frances looks at Margaret and says, "You're growing into a pretty young woman. I bet you catch the eyes of all the eligible young men."

Margaret blushes and squirms on the bench. "You're not the first person who has told me that," she says. "What do you mean?"

Frances's eyes dance mischievously. "I'm sure you've met someone who caught your fancy," she teases.

When Margaret shakes Frances head, she reacts with puzzlement. Could it be that the girl is really so innocent? She decides to keep things light and says reassuringly, "Don't worry. You will."

"I don't meet many new people," Margaret says sullenly. "The *malungu* who came from this plantation are the only ones I get to talk to about anything other than work."

Suddenly, Frances becomes quiet. Then she asks softly, "Have you seen Emmanuel Driggers?" When Margaret nods, she continues, "Is he well? Has he found someone yet?"

Margaret looks at her friend with curiosity. "I don't think so."

"Oh," says Frances.

Then Margaret notices the wisp of a smile form on Frances's lips. "You're sweet on him!" she cries out triumphantly.

Frances replies, too quickly, "I am not. Whatever gives you that idea?"

Margaret looks at her, grinning.

"All right, I like him," Frances admits. Then her face drops. "But there is no chance for us. Our lives are headed in separate directions."

Margaret wishes she could say something to make her feel better. She barely gets the chance to put her arm around her shoulders and hug her when the cook calls to them to come help with cleanup.

By the time they are done, it is mid-afternoon, and the guests gather by the porch. It is time to go home. Piercey and his wife thank everyone for coming. Wyatt offers a prayer for a safe journey. Margaret embraces Frances and Peter, kisses them good-bye, and walks away quickly, not wanting them to see her tears.

She has almost reached the entrance of the palisades, looking for Mr. and Mrs. Chew, when a middle-aged man in merchant garb calls out to her, "Margaret?"

Although she didn't see him before among the guests, she recognizes him immediately as he walks toward her. She curtsies and says, "Master Ewen. How have you been, sir? I hope you got to see Master Chew here."

"Yes, I did, thank you," he replies courteously. "I'm glad I caught you. I have a message for you, from Captain Jope."

Margaret's heart skips a beat. "You've seen Captain Jope?" she asks incredulously.

"Yes, and John, too . . . in England. They were about to leave Plymouth Harbor on a privateering voyage."

"Are they all right?"

"Oh, yes," Ewen says, smiling. "John asked after you, and I told him you were becoming a fine young woman."

Margaret would like to hear more, but Mr. Chew calls out for her from the dock. She curtsies once more and says, "Thank you, kind sir. Please tell them I am well when you see them again."

On the way home, riding with the current and taking advantage of the breeze at their back, the boats move quickly. Still, it gets dark before they reach Jamestown, and the crews hang lanterns from the prows of the pinnaces to light the way. Many passengers have nodded off, but Margaret's mind is a cauldron of swirling thoughts: When will she see the captain and John again? Or Frances and Peter, for that matter? What will she say to Emmanuel Driggers? What does it mean that two very different people told her she was becoming a young woman?

She takes in the cool night air, watches the moonlight dance on the waves, and wonders what lies ahead for her.

11

AN UNEXPECTED MEETING

Caribbean—Summer 1625

John watches from the poop deck as Captain Jope and Samuel Teague expertly guide the *White Lion* into Havana's harbor. They are not flying any flag, indicating that they are sailing under the banner of neutrality. Since England and the Netherlands are at war with Spain, Jope hoists the English colors only during privateering raids in consort with another British vessel to show off their joint power and intimidate their prey. Although Havana remains an international port of trade of sorts, as captain of a warship he knows he has to be careful. The authorities are willing to look the other way so long as the ducats and doubloons flow freely into their coffers and their customers don't flaunt their nationality.

A number of ships are anchored in the bay and sitting at the docks. Some of the masts display the Spanish flag. Others have struck the banners identifying their countries and raised only colorful streamers that flutter in the occasional gusts of wind. John figures that they are probably English frigates. The weather is hot and humid, and many of the sailors on the other ships have stripped to the waist, sweat pouring off their half-naked bodies while they swab the decks and do repairs. They all look up from their chores to check out the new arrival. They raise their hands in greeting, and John waves back.

The decision to trawl in southern waters has turned out to be a good one. At Port Royal in Jamaica, the *White Lion* hooked up with another one of Warwick's warships. After a week out at sea they came upon a Spanish merchant vessel from Cartagena that had been thrown off course and badly battered during an unexpected storm. The captain and his crew, still bailing water from the hold and sewing up the many sails torn by the merciless blasts of wind, had no stomach for a battle and hoisted the white flag of surrender without a single shot being fired. Once again Jope's trickery worked smoothly, even with the new hires aboard, and the *White Lion* absconded with several chests of coins and jewels.

John hopes that the early success will be followed by another soon, so that they can end their pursuit of treasure and pay Margaret a visit in Jamestown before heading back to England. Since the chance encounter with John Ewen in Plymouth, he has thought of her often. Talking further with the merchant in the Crown and Anchor didn't yield much additional information about her, but John and Jope learned a great deal about Ewen's plantation—conveniently located across the river from Jamestown and housing a surprisingly large library. John wouldn't mind checking it out when they go to see Margaret.

In the meantime, John is working hard at his new job as Gareth's mate's helper. The quartermaster is in charge of every operational aspect of the *White Lion*, and John is getting quite an education of what it means to run a warship. He likes it, although it means more work and responsibility. Every morning the boatswain and cannon master update to Gareth about the state of the ship—the condition of the sails, ropes, spars, and masts; the readiness of muskets and cannons; and any problems above and below deck. John writes it all down in order to deliver a report to Captain Jope. While keeping a log is normally the job of the quartermaster, Gareth has been happy to delegate that task to John because of his facility with quill and ink.

To get a better grasp on the welter of details involved, John spends considerable time observing what's going on in all areas of the ship. He already knows a great deal about sails and rigging from previous voyages. But he has more to learn about the steering mechanism, what it takes to feed the entire crew, and above all, taking care of the weaponry on the *White Lion.*

The cannon master, Jake Harkness, is an experienced veteran of many battles and skirmishes at sea, and a good teacher. Lean and leather-skinned, he has only partial use of his left arm because a Spanish soldier speared him in the shoulder with a pike some years back. Because of his no-nonsense approach mixed with wry humor, his men venerate him.

Harkness has them check the barrels of gunpowder and canvas bags filled with powder for the individual cannons every day to make sure they are dry. Then he inspects all the cannons and muskets himself for any sign of rust. "The salt sea air eats away at the iron like a hungry wolf," he explains to John. "Wouldn't want any of them to misfire in the middle of a melee."

Even though the *White Lion* has managed to gather considerable bounty without firing a single shot, he continues to hold frequent practice drills. The men all know how important it is to be battle-ready. Harkness orders the crews to mimic loading powder, wadding, and shot into the cannon chambers and push them all the way in with a rammer. His booming voice is loud enough to wake an army of the dead. When the men have closed the breechblocks, they pull the cannons in place with ropes and tackle as fast as they can until their barrels poke out of the open gun ports.

The first time he stood near Harkness when the cannon master bellowed, "Aim!" John involuntarily covered his ears.

While the sailors adjusted the angle of the cannons, Harkness smiled grimly and yelled to him, "You should hear the din when these cannons roar. Most of the lads who've been in a sea battle are practically deaf."

Now John just winces in anticipation of his ears ringing and is glad that Harkness doesn't bellow, "Fire!" at an even louder pitch. But he is always happy to report to Gareth and the captain that if the *White Lion* does get into a pitched naval battle, they can be confident that it will more than hold its own.

Now that John is old enough to learn the rudiments of combat, Jope suggested that Harkness teach him how to use both muskets and pistols. The cannon master has him practice shooting at candlesticks, placed on the railing of the forecastle deck, when the spritsail above the bow has been rolled up to prevent errant bullets ripping holes in it. The first time John fired a musket, the recoil sent him backward, sprawling on the deck, to the general merriment of the sailors watching. Embarrassed but undeterred, John picked himself up and tried again, earning the respect of the gunners when he hit the target after only three additional attempts.

Watching the Havana dock approach as the *White Lion* reaches its mooring spot, John has a moment of regret, knowing that further practice will have to wait until after the next raid.

It is late afternoon by the time Gareth gives the order to drop anchor and Jope finishes his business with the harbor authorities. Then they and Teague go ashore to see if they can find another suitable candidate to sail in consort with them on their next privateering venture. They take John with them because his presence helps disarm even the most suspicious mariners.

But although they visit a number of taverns, filled with dense smoke and carousing sailors, they don't encounter any ship officers who would suit their purpose.

By the time they enter the fifth inn, it is almost midnight, and John stifles a yawn.

Noticing, Jope smiles and says, "I think it's time to turn in. Perhaps we'll have better luck tomorrow."

It is pitch black outside when they walk down a dark alley on their way back to the ship. At the corner up ahead, light spills onto the cobblestones from the entrance of another tavern. As they pass the doorway, a group of unruly sailors come tottering out, loudly joking, catcalling, and taunting one another.

The stocky, bearded fellow in the lead looks back over his shoulder to return an insult from another tar and collides with John. Staggering drunkenly, he peers at the youngster before him and blinks in surprise. Then he hollers, "Out of my way, clumsy fustilarian!" and raises his fist to throw a punch.

In an instant, Jope grabs him by the throat and shoves him up against the wall.

The man's cheeks flush red in anger. He coughs and rasps, "My fight is not with you."

Jope smells his sour, rum-saturated breath and fights off a wave of nausea. "Now it is!" he growls. But when he locks eyes with the man and sees the flickering madness, a shiver runs through him. Never before has he seen such a look of malicious spite and lust for violence.

Suddenly a loud voice roars, "Hold on! Hold on!" and two powerful arms pull the adversaries apart.

Jope is about to take a swing at the newcomer for interfering when he recognizes the rotund shape and plump face of Daniel Elfrith.

The corpulent captain holds up his beefy hands and thunders for everyone's benefit, "No need for violence. We're all friends here!" He throws his arm around Jope's shoulder and announces to his drinking mates, "By Charles's prickly cock, this is my old consort, Captain John Jope."

Ready to brawl, the sailors slowly relax their fists and take their hands off their swords and daggers. John, Gareth, and Teague breathe a quiet sigh of relief but remain on guard.

Elfrith gestures in the direction of Jope's foe, who is rubbing his throat, a sneer on his face. "That's Captain Ray Bullard, a fine sailor." He chuckles and adds, "He's usually harmless."

Jope has his doubts. He'd seen the glimmer of crazed malice in the brute's eyes.

But with Elfrith poking him, Bullard's scowl fades and he mutters, "My apologies, Captain. I meant no harm."

He bows awkwardly and walks away unsteadily in the direction of the harbor. His efforts to appear dignified are spoiled when he trips on one of the cobblestones. At a nod from their captain the other sailors follow him, resuming their unruly banter.

Looking after them for a moment, Elfrith turns to Jope and slaps him on the back. "Bugger all, John, it's good to see you. Quite a while since we've crossed paths." He points to young John and says, "I see you still have that Negro with you."

Jope stiffens. "Yes, he's a good mate's helper," he volunteers cautiously.

Sensing his uneasiness, Elfrith responds with exaggerated joviality. "Why don't you all come inside with me and have a drink? My treat."

"I'll take you up on that," Jope agrees quickly. He knows that his old friend is still in the employ of the Earl of Warwick and likely to report back to his master. Best to see what's on his mind. Looking reassuringly at John he says, "You and Gareth go back to the ship. I'll be all right."

Elfrith ushers him inside the tavern. The hazy, dimly lit room smells of sweat, vomit, and human waste. Pushing past drunken seamen, they find an empty table off to one side.

"I'm sorry about Bullard. He can be a real firebrand when he's in his cups," Elfrith offers, as he squeezes his sizeable body into the corner.

Before Jope can answer, a buxom barmaid appears. "Back so soon?" she asks, grinning.

Throwing his arm around her waist and cupping one of her ample breasts, Elfrith says, "Normally for only you, but I ran into an old friend."

She giggles, disentangles herself from his clutches, and says amiably, "Then what will it be?"

"Another tankard of rum for me," says Elfrith, clearing his throat and spitting on the floor.

Jope nods. "Me, too."

When the barmaid leaves, Elfrith looks after her swaying hips with a wolfish grin. Then he rounds on his friend. "By God's bones, you've finally taken to a worthy libation," he teases.

"Yes, in moderation," Jope admits.

"So, what brings you to Havana this day?

"Restocking our supplies before we set sail for England." He adds casually, "Been to Virginia's shores recently?"

"Not since I scuttled the *Treasurer* in Bermuda," Elfrith replies with a chuckle. "I now command the *Warwick* for Lord Rich." He lowers his voice. "You and I stumbled upon a good thing. Bullard and I have been privateering together. We now take Africans off Spanish slavers, not just treasure, and transport them to Bermuda. They're much sought after on the plantations there. It's a lucrative enterprise."

The barmaid returns and plops two pewter mugs on the table, dangling her ample breasts at Elfrith. She gives him a pert glance and asks, "Anything else you'd like?"

Scratching his belly luxuriously, he says, "Another time." Then he takes swig of rum, belches, and turns his attention back to Jope. "And what have you been doing? Still carrying trade goods across the Atlantic?"

Taking a tentative sip, Jope nods.

"You miss marauding and cracking Spanish heads?"

Jope smiles, wondering if there is any undercurrent of suspicion in the question. He leans forward and says deliberately, "Since we're at war with Spain, I've been considering it."

Elfrith slaps the table. "By God's nails, that's my boy!"

He looks around the room to see if anyone is paying attention to them. Then he bends close to Jope and mutters softly, "Why don't you join Bullard and me? The three of us sailing in consort can take on any Spanish warship and blast it to kingdom come!"

Jope takes a moment, as if considering the offer seriously. Then he shrugs and says, "I'm tempted, Daniel, I really am. But at the moment my hold is full."

Elfrith drains his mug and burps. "Pity," he allows.

He is about to order another round when Jope puts his hand over his cup, signaling he's done for the night. Elfrith looks at him with bloodshot eyes, nods, and fishes a silver coin from his purse. He drops it on the table and struggles to his feet. It takes several tries before they can head outside. On the way to the docks, the portly man keeps bumping into Jope. He is drunker than he's been letting on.

When they reach the water, Elfrith rests a fleshy paw heavily on Jope's shoulder and slurs, "That was a fine thing we did together in Campeche Bay and in Virginia. Zounds, I would have never gotten away unscathed without your help. I'm indebted to you."

"You would have done the same for me."

"No. You're a good man, John," Elfrith says, his voice a little maudlin. He throws both arms around Jope and gives him a bear hug. Then he disengages himself, executes a surprisingly elaborate bow, salutes, and declares, "May fair winds fill your sails."

Jope looks after him as he staggers down the pier. Then he looks for the rowboat waiting to take him back to the *White Lion*. On the way, passing the dark shadows of the other ships, he thinks back on the conversation. It seems that his old friend does not suspect that he's gone back to privateering, but with Elfrith, you never know.

When he climbs aboard, John is waiting for him on the quarterdeck, a searching expression on his face.

Jope smiles and says, "There is nothing to worry about."

12

ARRIVALS AND DEPARTURES

Jamestown—Fall/Winter 1625

The Piercey nuptials remain the talk of Jamestown for some time. In wealthy and poor households, at the dock, on the market square, at church, and at various social functions, everyone who didn't attend the wedding wants to know: What did the bride and groom wear? What does the famous windmill look like? What does the inside of the new house the merchant built for his wife look like?

When Margaret goes into town on her errands, other servants and workers shower her with requests to tell them what happened. Good-natured, she answers all their questions, although she soon grows tired of having to give the same responses over and over.

There is one thing she doesn't mention. In the pinnace on the way back from the event, sitting in front of the Chews, she overheard them argue.

"Yes, John, that house is very impressive, but I would never want to live there," Mrs. Chew whispered in a low and severe voice.

"Why not?"

"It is in the middle of nowhere!"

"But Hogg Island is just across the river from town."

"I would not set foot on it if my life depended on it!" Mrs. Chew hissed.

Exasperated, her husband put his finger to his lips and muttered, "You'll have to watch your tongue then, or we'll have no choice but to leave Jamestown."

From that point on, they traveled in silence. They arrived late that night, and Margaret, exhausted and grateful to be home, expected them to turn in without another word. But Mrs. Chew surprised everyone by smiling at Ann and saying, "Thank you for taking care of my boys while I was gone. I knew I could count on you."

The young woman, unused to kind words, burst into tears.

Bemused, Mrs. Chew exclaimed, "What? What did I say to make you cry?"

It was up to Margaret to smooth the ruffled feathers. Accustomed to scolding and indifference herself, she understood that the compliment acknowledging Ann's worth had overwhelmed her emotions. She put her arms around the servant girl's shoulders and murmured, "There, there. It's all right."

Nodding reassuringly to the flustered Mrs. Chew, she took Ann to their room and calmed her down by telling her all about the wedding. The wide-eyed girl responded exactly as Margaret had anticipated and soon nodded off, allowing Margaret to finally go to sleep herself.

More surprising to her account of what happened at Piercey's Hundred is the response of Emmanuel Driggers. When she tells him, "You know, Frances asked after you," a brief smile flits across his face, followed by a sigh.

Without thinking, she exclaims, "You're sweet on her, too!"

He struggles briefly as if wanting to deny it, then smiles wistfully and admits, "Yes, I am." Then his expression sags. "I'm afraid we're doomed to lead separate lives. We're indentured in different households, beholden to different masters, and I don't know if we'll gain our freedom to follow our own desires."

The sadness in his eyes touches Margaret's heart. She puts her hand on his arm and says, "You don't know that. Considering everything that has happened to us since Africa already, you can never tell what fate has in store for us."

"It is kind of you to say so, Margaret," he offers gratefully, then changes the subject. "Now tell me more about the house. It wasn't built yet when I left the plantation."

He tries to listen attentively, but from his wandering eyes and distant, forlorn look, Margaret can tell that his thoughts are elsewhere.

Once again, she wonders if she will ever feel that way about another person.

A few days later, a very different event takes place that affects Margaret personally. Early in the day a loud knocking at the front door resounds through Mr. Chew's house, startling everyone inside. When William opens the front door, two young uniformed soldiers, officers of the court, stand awkwardly on the stoop.

One of them thrusts a warrant at him and says, "I demand to see the master of the house."

A minute later Mr. Chew arrives in his dressing gown. "What's the matter?" he asks huffily.

"Are you John Chew?" the taller of the two soldiers asks.

"Of course I am. You know that, Jonathan. And you, Andrew, do too," the merchant says, exasperated. "You've both bought goods from me for your families."

The young men blush, but quickly regain their composure.

"Sir, we have been ordered to place you under arrest. Dr. Pott has sworn a warrant against you for failing to pay your bill."

They give him enough time to get fully dressed before marching him to the jail in town. As they pass the houses on Merchants' Row and beyond, curious gawkers, both owners and servants, come out to watch. Some look on solemnly, others point and grin. Mr. Chew avoids their eyes, although he is seething inside for being made the laughingstock of town.

When the general court convenes in the church the next day to hear the case, a nattering crowd gathers. Governor Wyatt, the presiding judge, bangs his gavel to quiet the noisy onlookers, and they hurriedly take their seats on the wooden benches. The court bailiff reads the accusation, and both sides present their claims. Dr. Pott explains that he treated Mrs. Chew when she miscarried more than a year ago and never received payment. Not only did he send a bill but he had a servant remind Mr. Chew of his outstanding debt. The merchant in turn insists that he "lent" one of his own servants, Margaret, to help the doctor in his medical practice, which was more than ample compensation.

Margaret's heart pounds when the bailiff calls on her to give testimony. As she stands up, the spectators murmur in surprise. Wyatt raps his gavel and scowls at her. For a moment their eyes meet, and his angry, penetrating stare strikes fear into her. But then she hears Aunt Isabel's voice in her mind, giving her courage. She steps into the witness box and attests in a clear voice that she aided Dr. Pott with delivery of babies on three occasions, and at other times, examining women who were sick with the flux. When she finishes, there is renewed buzzing from the crowd, and Wyatt knocks his gavel on the table again.

After a short deliberation, the court holds for Dr. Pott, and Wyatt orders Mr. Chew to pay up.

The merchant settles his bill and stomps off in a huff, looking neither right or left as he parts the people milling outside the courtroom. Margaret and the other members of the household who attended the trial have a hard time keeping up with him.

When they get back to the house, Mr. Chew turns on Margaret and shouts at the top of his voice, "I forbid you to help that man ever again, do you hear me?"

"Yes, master," Margaret says, meeting his apoplectic outburst calmly.

Later she overhears him railing to his wife that Dr. Pott had the members of the court in his pocket and that his preferential social standing made a mockery of justice. Margaret has another idea, wondering if Wyatt held against him because he hates her. More than anything, she regrets that she will no longer be able to work with Dr. Pott. Not only did he appreciate her help, it gave her a good feeling being able to participate in bringing a new life into the world.

For a while, there is plenty of chin-wagging regarding the "much ado about nothing" altercation between two prominent members of Jamestown's elite. But Mr. Chew's humiliation is short-lived, and before long, all of his friends and acquaintances are happy to return and enjoy his ample supper gatherings. Soon, animated banter mingles with the smells of rabbit stew, pork, and roasted venison in the candle-lit, smoke-filled dining room. Conversations cover the usual topics—local gossip, war with Spain, the tobacco harvest, and the need for vigilance in the face of potential Indian attacks, although some of the dinner guests with military backgrounds suggest that the "savages" have been quiet this season because they are still reeling from the disaster of having their crops burned the previous year. But the most frequent complaint, from local and visiting burgesses and plantation owners alike, is how difficult it is becoming to get good workers. Tobacco is a labor-intensive crop, and the Royal Virginia Council in London is not sending new immigrants quickly enough to keep up with the demand.

Margaret, serving dinner, listens to the hodgepodge of opinions, rumors, gossip, and revelations and shares them with her African friends whenever possible on her frequent trips into town.

One evening, John Harvey comes to say his good-byes. He announces, "My time has come to leave for England. I will embark on the next ship." Then he turns to Mrs. Chew and, gesturing to the assembled guests, says gallantly, "None of these knaves can keep me here, but I will miss the pleasure of your company, madam."

Blushing with pleasure, she rewards him with an appreciative nod and says, "We're sorry to see you go, Sir John, and hope you'll hurry back soon to grace us with your company."

Margaret is amazed to actually see Mrs. Chew respond so girl-ishly to his heavy-handed flattering, but what Harvey says next takes her breath away.

"When I went to meet with Governor Wyatt this afternoon, he declined to see me because he had just received a letter from England that his father died. I expressed my condolences, of course, and trou-bled him no further."

The news surprises everyone at the table.

"What will happen?" asks Richard Stephens.

Harvey, basking in his insider's knowledge and familiarity with colony matters at the highest levels, opines, "He will surely petition King Charles to allow him to return to England to settle his father's affairs."

Mr. Chew, still smarting from the court verdict, mumbles, "Good riddance."

Harvey pretends not to notice and continues, "Someone else will have to take over as governor in his absence. The likely candi-date is George Yeardley, I suppose. He lives in town and has previous experience leading the colony. But there is also Francis West, and of course—" He is about to say, "Dr. Pott," but thinks better of it.

Meanwhile, Margaret's heart is beating faster. She has to contain her joy at the thought of Wyatt departing from Jamestown, perhaps for good, and no longer having to fear him.

A week after Harvey ships out, Mr. Chew brings a newly arrived visitor to the house. Although dressed in travel clothes, his coat and doublet are made of noticeably finer material than what most men wear in the colony. Richard Bennett, a cousin of Edward Bennett and namesake of his uncle who died during the Indian massacre at Warrosquoake, has come from England to evaluate the state of the plantation there. Since Mr. Chew has kept Edward Bennett in-formed all along, this trip is really about providing the young man an opportunity to broaden his horizons in the New World. Not yet 20, with just the first sprouts of a brown beard and mustache, he nonetheless conveys intelligence and lively curiosity. When he meets Margaret, he looks at her with marked interest.

"Master Chew tells me that you were at Warrosquoake during the Indian massacre and after my uncle died," he says. "I would like to hear what happened from your own lips, if John can spare you for a while."

Mr. Chew nods his agreement and suggests, "Why don't you get settled first, and we'll find the time anon?"

The following afternoon Ann informs Margaret that the family and their guest are waiting for her. When she enters the sitting room, Mrs. Chew is ensconced on the sofa with her children, John and Nathaniel, perched on cushions at her feet. Mr. Chew occupies a chair next to them, and Richard Bennett stands by his side. He gestures at a stool near the empty fireplace facing the family. Margaret looks to Mr. Chew for guidance. When he nods, she moves it farther into the room and sits down while Bennett settles in a chair immediately across from her.

For the next two hours Margaret talks about the events at Warrosquoake during the Indian massacre and the plague. Her words flow freely and fail her for a moment only once or twice when a painful memory threatens to overwhelm her. Bennett rarely interrupts her narrative, but glances from her to Mr. Chew several times, surprised by her ability to recall details and relate what happened in such well-chosen words. When she describes Richard Bennett's gruesome death during the Indian attack, the young man actually gasps and puts his hand to his heart.

At the same time, Mrs. Chew rises, visibly upset, and calls out, "John, Nathaniel, come! These are not proper matters for children's ears!"

As she stalks to the door, the boys get up reluctantly to follow her. Young John casts a longing glance toward Margaret, obviously wanting to hear more.

When they have left the room, Margaret resumes and talks about the plague and Robert Bennett plunging to his death. When she describes his broken body by the river at the bottom of the cliff, a tear escapes young Bennett's eye. She realizes that he is not yet hardened to the rough, merciless ways of the world, especially in Virginia, and thinks well of him for it.

In a quiet voice he says, "All my uncles who came here died before their time."

Margaret nods, knowing that he is also referring to the late Reverend Bennett, who died just a year ago of a fever, shortly after his wife, Elizabeth, gave birth to their son. With no one to take care of her, she returned to England.

Bennett runs his hand through his hair, expels a sorrowful breath, and asks, "So what can I expect at Warrosquoake now?"

Margaret wrinkles her forehead and says, "Mr. Chew has visited the plantation more recently than I have and can surely give you a better account. But the people I knew there who remained are all hard-working men and women. Although fate hasn't treated them kindly, they are hardy survivors."

After a moment, Bennett nods and replies, "That is well said. Thank you, Margaret."

"Yes, thank you," echoes Mr. Chew.

Taking her cue, Margaret gets up and leaves for the kitchen. Gratified that recounting her experiences turned out to be easier than she anticipated, she feels as if a burden has lifted from her shoulders.

The next morning, Bennett and Chew depart for the harbor and hire a pinnace to take them to Warrosquoake. In their absence Mrs. Chew, still upset, gives Margaret a tongue lashing over the "careless" way she folds the freshly washed bed linens. She also refers to Richard Bennett as a "most ill-mannered young knave."

Two days later on a warm, humid morning Margaret is busy weeding the garden when she hears someone clearing his throat next to her. Startled, she leaps to her feet. The sunlight is in her eyes, and she squints to make out Richard Bennett looking at her.

"Oh, it's you!" she exclaims, quickly wiping the dirt from her hands and curtsying. "You are back so soon."

"Yes, I just gathered first impressions," he explains. "I'm going back tomorrow with more provisions to explore the plantation and environs further."

He looks at her searchingly for a moment, as if seeing her in a new light. Margaret, fingering her apron awkwardly under his scrutinizing gaze, doesn't know what to say.

Bennett notices her discomfort and smiles. "You have a surprising number of admirers at Warrosquoake," he tells her. "I bring greetings from Anthony and Mary, and from Lieutenant Shepherd. They all asked after you."

Immediately, Margaret's spirits lift. "How are they, and how is their little boy?" she says excitedly.

"Well, and Mary is with child again."

Clapping her hands in delight, she continues, "That's wonderful news! Please give them my very best when you see them again."

Surprised at seeing yet another side of Margaret—this one younger, freer, less deliberate—he responds quickly, "I will. And what message do you have for the lieutenant?"

Margaret furrows her brow. It confuses her that Shepherd would make a point of singling her out. She tells herself that it must be because he doesn't come to Jamestown that often and she is one of the few people here whom he has known for some time.

Richard, seeing her bafflement, clarifies, "He told me all you did for his men during the plague."

Margaret relaxes. She thinks for a moment and chooses her words carefully. "Please thank him for guarding the plantation against the Indians and the Spanish."

Bennett nods. "I will convey your words to them. Now I must take my leave and prepare for my trip."

He bows smartly, and Margaret curtsies in return. Looking after him, she realizes that he just treated her like a lady, not a servant, and it amazes her. As she returns to her garden, she glances toward the house and notices Mrs. Chew watching from her bedroom window, her lips puckered disapprovingly.

Over the next few weeks, Bennett ferries back and forth between Warrosquoake and Jamestown. He no longer wears his fancy clothes but has adopted the more practical garb of plantation owners. When he stays at the Chew residence, he treats Margaret respectfully, but he never bows to her again.

* * *

Late in August a letter arrives from King Charles granting Governor Wyatt's request to return to England. When Margaret hears the news, she is elated. True to John Harvey's prediction, George Yeardley becomes acting governor.

The next time Margaret meets Emmanuel Driggers in the market square, she teases him on coming up in the world—being a member of the governor's household now. Driggers grins in good humor and confirms the effect on everyone at the residence. "The master has been walking two feet taller ever since he received the news."

Margaret can't wait for Wyatt to depart, but before he ships out, he presides over one more court case. All the Africans in Jamestown follow it with special interest because it concerns one of their own, a black worker whose name is Brase. Although he is a recent arrival and not *malungu*, his legal fate has significant implications for their own status.

The case came about because Nathaniel Basse, owner of Basses Choice, a plantation close to the mouth of the James River, needed indentured servants. So when a merchant ship arrived with a laborer from Africa aboard, the planter bought Brase from its captain. But when Basse wanted him to work without a contract, like a slave, Brase brought a suit against him.

After hearing arguments for both sides, the court reaches its decision in late September. To everyone's surprise, it voids the original sale's contract, removes Brase from his current master, and awards temporary custody to Lady Temperance Floridew, the wife of George

Yeardley. It also orders her to pay "forty pounds of good tobacco per month for his labor, so long has he remain with her."

While discussing the case, Emmanuel Driggers says with bitterness in his voice, "Well, now we know what we are worth to them."

His caustic tone, so different from his usual, gentle speech, surprises Margaret. "What do you mean?" she asks.

"It's a pittance. The rich, white landowners and merchants don't care for us one whit and only value us for their benefit!" he says harshly.

Margaret doesn't understand why the judgment has made him so angry and decides to keep quiet.

But that is not the end of the matter. Two weeks later in early October, the court changes its ruling. This time it assigns Brase to the custody of Governor Wyatt to sail with him to England. Coincidentally, Richard Bennett takes the same ship.

Before he leaves, Bennett seeks Margaret out, away from the prying eyes of Mrs. Chew. He meets up with her as she returns from the docks carrying a basket filled with fish and oysters.

Looking seriously at her, he says, "I wanted to thank you again for all you did for my relatives, Margaret, before I leave."

Margaret is pleased. "I wish I could have done more," she answers.

"I don't know when I will return to Virginia, but I wish you well."

"Thank you, sir. Safe journey and Godspeed to you," she says, curtsying, reminding him of their relative stations.

He gazes at her for a long moment. Then he smiles and nods. "And to you, Margaret."

He turns without bowing and walks toward the town. Margaret looks after him, wondering if she will see him ever again and if, by then, he will have become just like all the others who see her only as a servant.

Arrivals and Departures

* * *

The fall comes and goes without any further memorable events. The leaves turn glorious colors, but their splendor hides the fact that the colony is in trouble. What becomes clear from conversation Margaret overhears at supper gatherings and in town is that Virginia is once again in dire needs of supplies—from farm implements to weapons and ammunition—so much so that Governor Yeardley writes a letter to King Charles humbly asking him to get personally involved with the Privy Council and the Royal Virginia Council in England and encourage them to hurry in making decisions on behalf of the colony to "ensure its present and future survival."

Unexpected relief comes in December when a frigate, the *Flying Hart*, arrives carrying a sizeable group of men and women who want to work and make Virginia their home. The welcoming committee at Point Comfort at the mouth of the James River quickly establishes that most of the passengers are penniless servants. More significantly, the ship has no authorization from the Royal Virginia Council in England. While the ship is under quarantine to make sure there is no sickness aboard—the memory of the pestilence brought by the *Abigail* is still fresh on everyone's mind—Governor Yeardley and his council in Jamestown debate how to treat the immigrants.

Margaret listens carefully to the arguments conducted at the Chew residence and in town, but keeps her own counsel. Many laborers and servants insist that the *Flying Hart's* passengers should not receive the same contracts of indenture that they did when they came to Virginia, abiding by the official immigration rules. When the council decides to admit the newcomers under the same terms—seven years of servitude and, upon completion, freedom dues of 50 acres of land, a quantity of corn, and new clothes—there is much grousing and resentment around town.

Margaret goes down to the harbor and watches with a host of other Jamestown citizens as the *Flying Hart* finally reaches the docks.

The immigrants who step ashore are a gaunt, sallow-faced collection of mostly men and a few women, looking worse from the journey than many of the inhabitants, and the carping quickly dissipates. The newcomers are taken to the governor's office, where they receive contracts of indenture and learn of their plantation assignments. Margaret sees John Upton with three new servants—two men and a woman—in tow, heading for a pinnace to continue their journey to Piercey's Hundred.

Before long, all the passengers have gone off to their respective households, and daily life in Jamestown continues apace.

13

HOMECOMING

England—Winter 1625

The bone-chilling December wind gusts from the east across the *White Lion's* deck, causing the sails to flap and strain against the creaking spars. Watching the gray whitecaps slap noisily against the hull, John shivers and pulls his wool overcoat more tightly under his folded arms. He has not yet grown accustomed to the winter weather, and his mood doesn't help. Another season without seeing Margaret leaves him feeling melancholy and alone.

He wishes he could share the excitement of the rest of the crew. Ever since they sighted the tip of Cornwall jutting out from the Bay of Penzance, everyone has worked with renewed energy. Their destination, Plymouth Harbor, is less than 40 leagues up the English Channel, and as the seamen haul ropes and trim sails to tack northeast, they brag about what they will do with their share of the booty. John figures many will just drink their earnings away and spend it on prostitutes. He has seen what sailors do with their money on land leave in various Caribbean ports and has no illusions about their behaving differently in England.

Things had looked promising for a visit to Jamestown in late fall, but the day before they were to set sail for Virginia, Captain Jope met another one of the Earl of Warwick's unsuspecting captains and decided to go on a privateering hunt together. They hoped to find and intercept some Spanish ship straggling in the wake of the West Indies treasure fleet, perhaps a merchant vessel that had stayed behind for repairs and had to leave port late in the season. After searching for a week, they were in luck and came upon a trading frigate from Brazil. Once again the *White Lion*'s crew picked the ship clean of treasure and left their consort with an empty hold. It was the third successful raid and swelled their coffers by more than another third.

Jope was so pleased that he had the ship's surgeon pierce his earlobe and, when it healed properly, emerged from his cabin one morning with a large pearl drop dangling from his ear. He strutted proudly across the quarterdeck and basked in the cheers and good-natured kidding from his crew that he was finally one of them.

Unfortunately, their final raid left them a considerable distance southeast of Puerto Rico, and they headed back to England directly to escape the winter storms of the Atlantic and make it home by Christmas.

Jope noticed John's lips tighten when he ordered the navigator to call out the change in course. Later that evening he invited John to join him for supper in his cabin. Although the steaming pork stew smelled tasty enough to make his mouth water, John poked listlessly at the dish with his spoon.

He was surprised when Jope said softly, "I know you're disappointed that we won't be able to see Margaret until next year."

John refused to meet his eyes and stared out the rear gallery window at the wake churning behind them.

It was not the first time that Jope had observed his young charge remain silent and sullen when he was sad or bothered. He decided to take it easy on the lad and said, "I don't owe you an explanation, John, but I *am* sorry. I had no choice."

In fact, he was unhappy, too, that he missed the opportunity to visit Margaret. God entrusted her to his care, and he really should have made sure she was doing well. But the possibility of capturing more riches had been too good to pass up, and he would have lost the respect of most of his crew if he had not pursued the opportunity. He also was feeling his age again and knew there was no guarantee that the easy privateering successes of the past two years would continue. He had to provide for Mary and the children, and the big haul, a Spanish gold transport that would allow him to retire, had escaped him thus far. Perhaps it would never come, but whenever that thought crossed his mind, he dismissed it. Jope wasn't ready to give up on that dream.

"I tell you what," he said, extending an olive branch. "I promise we will visit her next summer. We'll go early, on our way to the Caribbean."

John looked up at him for the first time. "Do you really mean that?"

"You know I am a man of my word. I want to see Margaret as much as you do."

At the time, John felt as if a heavy stone were lifted from his chest. But now, looking at the overcast, lead-colored skies, he is not happy about the long wait ahead. Watching a flock of seagulls dipping and diving in welcome around the *White Lion*, he realizes that he feels more at home aboard ship than where they are going. At Tavistock, he is only a welcome visitor with no sense of purpose. Here his new work and responsibilities at least make him feel important and needed.

Under the tutelage of Jope and at the side of Quartermaster Gareth he has matured and learned a great deal. He knows now what it takes to run a ship, including performing unpleasant tasks like keeping peace among a crew of unruly, headstrong privateers, and meting out punishment when needed.

When a deckhand named Cuthbert accused his bunkmate—Ambrose, a slow-witted gunner—of stealing a doubloon from him, Gareth and John searched the cabin and found it hidden away among Ambrose's belongings. The brawny lunkhead just stood there sullen-faced and did not deny it. Nor did he offer any excuses when they brought him before Jope on the quarterdeck.

The captain fixed his sternest gaze on him and asked, "Do you admit to stealing and hiding the money?"

Ambrose, unable to hold Jope's fierce stare, looked away and mumbled, "Aye."

Sighing exasperatedly, Jope said, "You have broken the Eighth Commandment! You know what that means, Ambrose?"

The thickset cannoneer nodded, resigned, and muttered, "Twenty lashes."

He didn't complain or resist when two sailors stripped him to the waist and tied his hands around the main mast. John saw that his back was already crisscrossed with welts from other whippings.

Gareth took a long cotton rope and put knots in five strands close to the end. "The next time, this will be your job," he said to John, grim-faced.

Then he administered the punishment before the assembled crew. He wielded the lash with considerable force. Having seen plenty of bloodied men in stocks and disemboweled corpses dangling from the hangman's rope in various ports they had visited, John was not unduly upset witnessing the punishment. It might have been different if he liked Ambrose, but the man had a short temper and no kind words for anyone. Still, John inadvertently held his breath with each stroke as bloody cuts appeared on Ambrose's back. The cannoneer had his eyes closed and his jaws clenched with each blow, but he did not cry out until it was over and a sailor tossed ocean brine from a bucket on his bleeding, lacerated back.

The men cut Ambrose down from the mast and dragged him, stumbling, to the ship's surgeon for treatment. The rest of the seamen went about their business as if nothing unusual had happened. John overheard a few muttering with admiration that "Ambrose took his punishment well."

The cannoneer stayed in his cabin and did not return to work for several days. When he did, what amazed John most was that he did not seem to carry a grudge for the beating, not against Gareth, nor Cuthbert, nor Captain Jope. John saw him working side by side with his mates and playing cards with them. No doubt he was still hurting, but he did not let on, except for keeping his elbows tight by his body to keep the skin and muscles of his back as still as possible.

As the white cliffs and rocky shores of the English coastline pass by on the port side of the *White Lion*, John muses that Captain Jope has managed to run a ship of rough, foul-mouthed men without adopting their coarse ways. True, he smiles more than in the past at some of the bawdy jokes of the crew and even curses once in a while, but he has not lost his essential kindness, good manners, and faith, even if he seems more concerned with money and treasure than ever before.

John recalls one unguarded moment in his cabin, when the captain pointed to the pearl drop in his ear and asked, "Do you think Mary will like it?"

Nodding earnestly John said, "I'm sure she will." Then he frowned and asked, "But why did you do it?"

Jope thought for a moment before answering, "So everyone at home—all the doubters and naysayers at home—can see that I was right to pursue this course."

Then he mentioned Sir Walter Raleigh, a fellow Cornishman and privateer, whom Jope had looked up to as a youngster. He had often worn a double pearl in his ear at the Court of Queen Elizabeth and even had a portrait painted with it prominently displayed. "His was wider, but mine is bigger," he confided with a smile.

Watching the coastline, John considers if he should have his ear pierced, too, and wear a pearl or diamond stud, but decides it is not for him.

A call from the crow's nest, "Plymouth ahead!" brings everyone on deck. John moves to Gareth's side to carry out his orders along with the rest of the crew for approaching the seawall and sailing into the harbor. He sees Jope on the quarterdeck looking ahead, his bright blue eyes blazing with excitement.

Homecoming

* * *

After they drop anchor, the entire crew—seamen, musketeers, and gunners—assembles on the main deck. They doff their hats and caps, and Jope offers a prayer of thanks to God for blessing them with success and bringing them safely back home. When he is finished, the men erupt in lively shouts of approbation. Jope acknowledges their accolades by shaking his fist high in the air, bringing on another wave of boisterous cheers. Swelling with pride at their accomplishments, the men slowly disperse.

It takes another two days for them to secure the *White Lion* for the winter, pack up their personal belongings, receive their share of treasure, and make their way ashore. By nightfall the decks are empty except for Jope, John, Gareth, and a handful of sailors, constituting the skeleton crew that will remain behind and maintain the ship until spring.

The next morning there is fog on the water when Gareth and two seamen row John, the captain, and their travel chests to the dock. Jope hires a coach for the 20-mile journey north to Tavistock. The coachman and his helper strain under the weight of the trunks as they load them onto the boot and secure them.

When they are ready to go Jope turns to his quartermaster and says, "Thank you, Gareth. Take good care of the *White Lion* for me."

Gareth straightens and replies, "I'll send you regular reports, Captain." Then he looks at John, grins, and says, "I'll see you in the spring, mate!"

John salutes smartly and climbs into the carriage. The coachman snaps his whip, and the horses start to pull away. Soon they reach the edge of the city, and hard-packed earth replaces the cobblestones on the road. A few miles later they travel along the outskirts of the Dartmoor, a vast, bleak expanse of brown heather relieved only by outcroppings of gray, mottled rocks and an occasional lonely tree. As they get closer to their destination, the terrain becomes hillier, but the weather is still overcast—long, low banks of somber clouds hovering above the horizon.

They ride in silence, entranced in their own thoughts. At some point while looking out the window, Jope absentmindedly fingers the pearl drop in his ear.

John startles him, saying, "Don't worry, Mary is sure to be pleased."

Caught, Jope grins sheepishly and mutters, "I hope so."

When the coach pulls through the gate into the courtyard of the mansion in Tavistock, Jope takes in the familiar gray stones, slate roof, and smoking chimney, promising a warm, cozy interior. His heart beats faster in anticipation, and he can barely contain his impulse to leap from the moving carriage and run to the house.

By the time the carriage stops and he and John climb down, the front door opens and Mary appears. She doesn't dash to him, as in the past, but approaches in a measured, ladylike manner. Suddenly she stops in midstride, her face lights up, and she claps her hands together in girlish delight. A mischievous twinkle appears in her eyes.

"Why, Husband, what a wonderful way to bring me a present," she says and rushes into her captain's arms.

As he kisses her passionately, she relaxes visibly, letting all the worries she's carried for the past months melt away. After a long embrace, she disengages herself and holds him at arm's length to admire the pearl drop in his ear.

"It becomes you," she says.

Relieved and gratified, he exclaims, "It is but a preview of what's to come. We've had a good voyage, a most excellent voyage!"

Mary turns to John, scrutinizes him from head to toe, and says, "My, how you've grown since I last laid eyes on you. You're becoming a handsome young man."

John flushes with pleasure as she embraces him.

By now the entire household—servants, cook, and kitchen maids—spills from the house to welcome their master. They fuss over him and John, but Jope keeps looking around until he sees Agnes carrying his youngest daughter with little Margaret at her side, holding her hand. He runs over to them and lifts his older daughter in the air. The expression of joy in his face brings tears to John's eyes. Only after Jope has kissed his rosy-cheeked children does he pay the coachman and order his servants to bring the travel trunks into the house.

As he steps inside, John breathes in the smells and relishes the musty, comfortable warmth he hasn't experienced while at sea, and realizes that he is glad to be back. Meanwhile, the house becomes a beehive of activity, with servants bustling about, unpacking clothes from the travel trunk to mend and store in chests in the bedrooms.

When things finally calm down, Jope and Mary settle in the living room on the sofa by the crackling fire. He opens the treasure chest and takes out a silver necklace and a matching pair of earrings. Presenting them to Mary, he says, "These are for you."

Once again, her eyes sparkle with delight. Holding them up and watching them glitter in the sunrays coming through the window, she says, "They are very beautiful, John." She indicates the chest filled with glittering coins and jewels. "Does that mean you can give up privateering and stay home?"

Jope's face clouds. "No. Not yet. But soon, my darling, soon."

Mary is pensive only for a moment. "Where are my manners? You must be starving," she says and calls for a servant to bring food and drink.

Soon everyone eats heartily. For John, used to the salty stews and rock-hard scones aboard ship, the odors and taste of fresh-baked bread, butter, and cheese are an overpowering pleasure. Once again, he is happy to be part of a real home.

* * *

Over the next weeks, there are special welcome church services, receptions at various houses, and feasts with Mary's family as Jope becomes a regular member of his community again. He doesn't wear his pearl drop for all occasions, but he makes sure to display it proudly on a visit to his brother Joseph. Everyone wants to hear about their exploits, and Jope obliges with stories of exotic Caribbean ports and daring captures of Spanish galleons, leaving out any mention of his devious approach to privateering. John takes his cue from him and responds in kind whenever anyone questions him about his adventures at sea.

In turn, Jope and John learn about what has been happening in England. With Charles on the throne for less than a year, there is much talk of the upcoming coronation, religious matters, and the ongoing war with Spain. Many people are not fond of the new monarch.

Mary's uncle, Sir Granville, is particularly acerbic in his comments. "Not only does the King demand that Parliament do his bidding without complaint, but he keeps asking for more money to fund his military expeditions," he fumes at one of the family gatherings.

At another dinner, he complains, "Charles is worse than his father. He thinks that God has put him on the Earth to do as he pleases. At least King James asked us for advice on foreign policy. Charles trusts only his favorite, Buckingham, who wants elected officials to kiss the hem of his cloak."

News and rumors about the English and Dutch sea venture to capture the Spanish treasure fleet and attack the Spanish port city of Cadiz are trickling in, and the news is not good. Apparently, things are not going well. Jope hates to hear that, but he also realizes that war with Spain will continue for some time. Considering that the Dutch are worthy allies, continuing to fly the flag of the Kingdom of Nassau will aid him on his marauding endeavors because English privateers will continue to welcome him as a consort with open arms.

John doesn't understand all the talk of politics and warfare. He enjoys the attention he receives at the various get-togethers, but after the initial novelty wears off, people become less interested in his life at sea. Many treat him as an appendage to Jope, a mere bystander to the more significant ventures of the captain.

John is happy that Jope has decided to further advance his training in combat. Every morning they go out into the woods behind the mansion and practice shooting muskets and pistols, using the nubs and gnarls of trees as their targets. Jope also instructs John on the use of the sword and dagger—how to feint and dodge and step inside an opponent's reach to slip the blade between his ribs.

"You're still small, so you need to be quick and swift. Once a bigger man can go on the offensive, he usually gets the upper hand," Jope advises. "Better to strike first than retreat from someone else's blows," he advises.

John enjoys these lessons and practices on his own. In the afternoons he withdraws to the small library in the house and passes the time reading. Surprisingly, he finds the account of legal cases especially interesting. There is something about the logic and certainty of reasoning based on a body of laws that appeals to his orderly mind. But in the evenings sitting by the fire and at night as he drifts off to sleep, his thoughts invariably turn to Margaret and the New World.

14

CORONATION
London—February–March 1626

The Earl of Warwick, resplendent in his ceremonial robes of red velvet and ermine, as befits his status as a peer of the realm, processes up the central aisle of Westminster Abbey. The accompanying anthem, sung by two choirs and accompanied by organ, viols, trumpets, and drums, rings loudly from the galleries. Rich takes his seat next to his wife, similarly arrayed, and nods to the other nobles and their spouses who are seated already.

It is good to be inside the cathedral after the bracing walk from Westminster Hall, but his coronet pinches his temples and reminds him that he would prefer to be elsewhere. Still, it is his duty to attend the ceremony, and a royal coronation does not occur every year. He will have to have Nathaniel rake the crown maker over the coals, though, for providing him with an ill-fitting diadem.

Watching the rest of the nobles arrive—the dukes and barons decked out in their lavish, official robes and gowns—he muses that while the Stuarts may have replaced the Tudor dynasty, they have certainly carried on their tradition of excessive opulence. To Warwick's Puritan mind, all the pomp and circumstance is unnecessary, too much of a waste, and it exemplifies the profligate quality of Charles's brief reign. As if to illustrate his thoughts, the Duke of Buckingham appears, strutting proudly up the aisle. The royal favorite, dressed more extravagantly than everyone else, looks around as if everyone owes him obeisance before he takes his seat.

Warwick marvels resentfully at the arrogance of the man who has nothing to be arrogant about. The Cadiz naval expedition has been a disaster, and the blame for it lies entirely at Buckingham's door. As far as the earl is concerned, the adventure was doomed to failure from the start, when neither Charles nor his favorite consulted with him. After their initial meeting, they never summoned him again, an astonishing slight and oversight considering that Rich owns the largest private navy in England and has shown extraordinary success as a privateer.

How foolish and ill-conceived the whole venture was from the start became crystal clear when Rich's old friend, Samuel Argall, visited him again shortly before his departure. It was as if the captain, now commander of the fleet, came to say his good-byes for good. If he had been unhappy about the chain of command before, he was now alternately furious and dejected.

"It is bad enough that Buckingham is in charge, but he made Sir Edward Cecil commander of all forces," he fumed. "I fear many lives will be lost unnecessarily."

None of Rich's efforts to reassure him had borne fruit, and now, in retrospect, he had been painfully prescient. The news came in trickles and told of one disaster after another. First, the early October storms scattered the ships, and by the time they regrouped, it was too late to capture the Spanish treasure fleet, which had received warning ahead of time and taken a safe, southerly route.

So Cecil decided to attack the port of Cadiz. The English fleet managed to take the fort near the entrance to the harbor, with much of the heavy fighting done by the Dutch allies. But no one grasped how well fortified the city was. When Cecil disembarked his troops for a land assault and realized that they had no food or drinking supplies, he stupidly allowed the men to raid the vats of wine in local homes. With much of his army drunk and Cadiz putting up a spirited defense, he had no choice but to withdraw. Unfortunately, the Spanish troops captured more than 1,000 inebriated English soldiers and put them all to the sword.

Many members of Parliament rightfully blame Buckingham for the debacle and are out for his blood. To keep his favorite safe from their sharpened talons, Charles dissolved Parliament and insisted that he would not reconvene it until after his coronation, but he can't stall forever.

Warwick is worried that he has heard nothing of Argall, although his flagship apparently escaped unscathed. He hopes his friend is alive and safe.

There is a stirring among the assembled nobles, churchmen, and spectators. The organist strikes up another anthem. Everyone's eyes turn to the entrance from the nave of the abbey and watch as the Lord High Steward of England carries in St. Edward's Crown, a purple cap trimmed with ermine surrounded by a golden frame studded with an array of precious jewels.

Then Charles makes his way up the central aisle in a crimson robe, carrying the staff of King Edward the Confessor. To Warwick, he looks younger than his 25 years, but his overbearing features remind the earl unpleasantly of King James. *Like father, like son,* he thinks.

When the new king halts before the large wooden throne of King Edward, which has been used to crown English monarchs for more than 600 years, the archbishop of Canterbury presents him to the assembly. Charles slowly turns in all four directions, his features placid and arrogant. The archbishop's feeble voice does not carry well, and there is some confusion about when everyone must call out the traditional accolade. Finally, one of the dukes starts, leading the audience in a rousing chorus of "God save the King."

Then Charles and the archbishop proceed to the altar for the administration of the coronation oath. It goes on for some time, and Warwick's mind wanders to the conspicuous absence of Charles's wife, Princess Henrietta Maria of France. A devout Catholic, she refused to attend the Anglican ceremony. It may have been her peevish nature, but Warwick knows that everyone in the government and administration breathed a deep sigh of relief. The marriage was already causing enough friction with the King's subjects, who, in Warwick's view, rightfully fear that Charles means to revoke the ban on Catholicism in England.

But it is not just Charles's choice of a Catholic queen. What really alarms Warwick is his support for the writings of the cleric Richard Montagu, signaling the monarch's disdain for the Puritans. When threats were uttered toward the priest after he published a pamphlet arguing against Calvinist predestination, Charles protected him by making him one of his royal chaplains. The prosecution of Puritans under King James was virulent enough. Warwick is afraid that it will not abate under his self-satisfied, ignorant, arrogant successor. The only good news is that, after four years of struggle, the Plymouth Colony in Massachusetts seems to be on firm footing as a haven for Puritans. Getting its charter renewed is as critical as ever. If only Captain Elfrith would find another refuge in the New World soon.

When the lengthy administration of the oath is finally finished, church officials remove Charles's crimson robe, revealing a silken white robe underneath—the anointing gown. The King then takes his place on the wooden throne while four Knights of the Garter come forward bearing a rich, golden canopy. They hold it over him, and the archbishop, attended by several bishops, proceeds to rub the consecrated oil on Charles's hands, breast, and head.

While the monarch is being invested in golden robes and the royal stole, all the nobles rise to their feet and remove their coronets. Rich is grateful for the temporary relief. He watches as various officials present the King with royal regalia and pile on more ornate robes. Then Charles receives a ring and the two sovereign scepters, one symbolizing kingly power and the other signifying justice and mercy, leading up to the climactic moment when the archbishop places St. Edward's Crown on his head.

Trumpets sound fanfares, and the assembled crowd repeatedly shouts out, "God save the King." As the nobles put their coronets back on, the boom of cannons fired at the Tower of London can be heard in the distance to inform the general populace that Charles has been officially crowned their king.

Now it is time for everyone to pay homage to the new monarch. First the archbishop and bishops swear their fealty. Then comes the nobility. When it is Rich's turn, he approaches the seated monarch and looks at Charles's youthful, bearded face. He bows, kneels, and says firmly, "I, Robert Rich, Earl of Warwick, do become your liege man of life and limb, and of earthly worship; and faith and truth will I bear unto you, to live and die, against all manner of folks, so help me God."

Returning to his seat, Rich sees his wife glowing with pride. Once again, he realizes that his stepmother did well to provide him with such a poised, accomplished spouse. As he sits down he takes Susan's hand affectionately, and she squeezes his in turn.

While the rest of the long line of nobles pay homage. Warwick takes stock of his affairs. Since the demise of the Virginia Company, his undertakings have been going very well. His merchant ships and privateering vessels have increased his wealth beyond measure. The only setback has been a renegade sea captain deceiving some of his marauding ships, depriving them of their rightful share of the bounty when raiding in consort with them.

The first time Warwick heard of it, he thought it was just a far-fetched explanation on the part of an incompetent captain, a meager excuse for his returning to England with empty coffers. But then another captain told a similar story, and this past summer there were more such occurrences. Somebody flying a Dutch flag was swindling his captains.

It made Warwick's blood boil and his temper got the better of him, resulting in a broken inkwell, several tobacco pipes, and a fine decanter of wine. When he calmed down enough, he discussed the matter with his cousin Nathaniel. The fact that the renegade flew both the Dutch and English flags suggested that it might be Captain Jope.

Warwick well remembers the captain with the piercing blue eyes who came to him for help to hide two African children in England. Those eyes, along with his rough Cornish brogue, were hard to forget. But the man had also impressed him as a pragmatist. When Rich told him that the agreement to keep the children in England needed to be changed, Jope's eyes had flashed with anger for only a moment before he had himself back under control. To his surprise, Rich had liked the man. Besides, Jope was a Calvinist minister who shared his own Puritan sympathies. It would not do to accuse him without definitive proof.

When Captain Elfrith came to see Warwick just a week ago, the earl asked him about Jope. The corpulent mariner exclaimed, "Zounds, I just saw him in Port Royal last summer. He told me he was still doing merchant runs. Had that African boy in tow."

It amazed Warwick that the captain had kept the boy with him. Perhaps Jope was more sentimental than he imagined. Considering how much he cared about those children, would he risk their lives by taking his ship into frequent battles?

"Could he be the Dutchman who has been pilfering my share of Spanish treasure?" he inquired, watching Elfrith closely.

The portly sea dog screwed up his face, scratched his bulbous nose, and intoned, "I'm of two minds about it. Can't say if he has or hasn't, by Charles's knobby cock. He's a sly one, though, is our John."

Frustrated, Rich ordered, "Well, find out for me. I need to know. And redouble your efforts to locate another suitable place for a Puritan colony in the New World. It's important!"

Since then, Warwick has been thinking hard on what to do. Although the loss of treasure is but a small bite in his vast fortune, he cannot let such slights go unanswered. His reputation is at stake. But how to determine with certainty if Jope is the culprit?

With the loyalty oaths of nobility concluded, Charles rises. The churchmen replace the crown of Edward the Confessor with a lighter, imperial state crown. Similarly, they exchange the royal robe and stole for a robe and overcoat of purple velvet.

The choirs sing a rousing *Te Deum*, and Charles, bearing his scepters, leaves the abbey. The churchmen and peers follow in a stately procession. Warwick offers his arm to his wife, and they walk slowly down the nave. Although pleased to be able to finally stretch his legs, he can't wait to get the coronet off his head.

The air outside is still chilly. Looking at the overcast sky, the earl suddenly has an idea on what to do about Jope. A crafty smile flashes across his face, and his heart beats faster. He can't wait to return to his house and confer with Nathaniel. Suddenly, he feels much better, even if he still has to endure the excesses of the royal banquet first.

* * *

Mary orders her driver to crack his whip and spur on the horses pulling the open cart. It is late morning, and she hopes to reach Sir Granville's house before her uncle departs for London and the opening of Parliament. It is icy cold, but she hardly feels the breeze, not because she is wearing a hat and bundled in a dark woolen blanket, but because she is so preoccupied.

Despite her sense of urgency, she is in a melancholy mood. Big and little John left just a week ago to ship out of Plymouth on the *White Lion*, and Mary misses her husband's nighttime caresses. Without his strong, comforting body next to her, she feels lonely, and if it weren't for her daughters, she would have no moments of joy at all.

But that is not why she is bouncing in a hurriedly arranged cart across the countryside. She wishes she could have hired a closed carriage, but the matter was too urgent. Earlier this morning a letter arrived from the Earl of Warwick for her husband. The messenger came directly on horseback from London, by-passing the normal postal service, and stayed only long enough to collect a tip and rest his mount. With Jope gone, Mary decided to open the missive herself. When she cracked the seal and read it, the content sent her head spinning.

Arriving at Sir Granville's estate, she is relieved to find that her uncle is still at home. She tosses all manners and formality to the wind, pushes past the shocked servant who opened the door, and barges into the tobacco smoke–stained study unannounced.

Sir Granville looks up from behind his desk and is barely out of his chair before Mary cries out, "Uncle, I need your help!"

Seeing her breathing hard, her brow furrowed under her travel hat, he immediately realizes that she is very upset. "Why, Mary, child, what's the matter?" he exclaims, alarmed. "Are the girls all right?"

"John's received a letter from the Earl of Warwick," she burst out. "He wants to see him in London, but John is at sea already and I don't know what to do."

Although he doesn't enjoy seeing his niece so beside herself, Sir Granville is relieved. Whatever news the letter from London may have brought, it is surely not a matter of life or death. He moves toward her and says soothingly, "Now, Mary, sit down and tell me all about it."

By now his distressed servant has caught up and stands at the door to the study, uncertain what to do. "I-I-I'm sorry, sir, but she just, just—" he stammers.

Granville waves him off. "It's all right, Wesley. Please go to the kitchen and fetch my niece a warm cup of milk."

The servant purses his lips but says, "Very good, sir."

As Wesley leaves the room, Granville looks sternly at Mary, who has started to shiver. "No arguments, you'll catch your death," he warns. When she bristles, then acquiesces, and the tension drains from her, he smiles and continues, "Come sit by the fire."

He offers her an armchair and Mary plops down, but her eyes continue to roam around the room like a frightened deer.

"So you have opened the letter already?"

"Yes."

"Let me see it."

She hands him the folded parchment with pieces of Warwick's broken seal still attached. Granville gets his spectacles, hold the missive up to the window, and reads out loud:

> To the honorable Reverend John Jope, greetings. My Lord, the
> Earl of Warwick, desires that you attend him at his London
> house at your convenience. He has matters to discuss that bear
> on your charges and your affairs. Sincerely, Nathaniel Rich.

If Granville is surprised, he hides it well. He scratches his beard and, after perusing the letter again, offers his opinion. "It is signed by the earl's cousin, who is an attorney. That makes it official, not merely personal."

"But what does it mean?" says Mary, anxiously.

"I don't know." Granville moves closer to her and puts his hand on her shoulder. "But there is nothing untoward here, Mary, nothing to worry about."

Relief crosses her face like the sun's rays emerging from a dark cloud.

Granville notes the change and smiles reassuringly. "I will draft a reply that John is away at sea for the unforeseeable future and that I will convey Lord Rich's message to him upon his return in the fall. In the meantime, I will make myself available to his Lordship. Perhaps I can find out what this is all about."

Mary rises, "Oh, will you, Uncle? I can't thank you enough," she exclaims. Impulsively, she rushes to him and covers his hand with kisses.

Embarrassed, but not entirely displeased, Granville pulls away. Handing the letter back to her, he says, "Now, now, Mary. It is the least I can do for my favorite niece. That's settled then. Why don't you stay for lunch? Your aunt will be happy to see you." Anticipating her protest, he adds, "I insist."

Mary sighs contentedly and says, "All right."

She takes off her travel hat and heads for the door.

"Go see your aunt. I'll be out in a short while," Granville says, reassuringly.

Alone in his study, he does not feel so confident. He remembers Jope staying twice at his London home several years earlier. Both times the captain visited Warwick regarding the two African children. With so much time having past, the invitation from the earl coming out of the blue is odd, to say the least. And Nathaniel Rich made a point of addressing Jope formally by his full name. Granville knows Warwick's capable cousin takes care of his day-to-day business affairs. Warwick himself does not concern himself with small matters, but a letter like this, written on his behalf, portends matters of consequence.

15

HOGG ISLAND

Virginia—April–May 1626

In April, Governor Yeardley finally receives a letter from the newly crowned king in answer to his urgent request for support. Initially, there is much excitement that the monarch has heard the Virginia Colony's plight and is ready to help. But when Yeardley reads the royal missive to a group of burgesses, elation yields to disappointment and dismay. Not only does Charles fail to address any of their needs—providing supplies and workers more quickly—he makes imperious demands. Foremost is the order to conduct "without delay" a census of the plantations and settlers, as well as an inventory of all the properties held by the Virginia Company before it was dissolved by King James. The latter is supposed to help His Majesty decide which lands to set aside for public use and which to appropriate for the crown's purposes.

"It's just like Sandys and the merchant investors of yore," fumes Captain Hamor, who has come from Hogg Island for the occasion. "He's only interested in enriching his treasury!"

Adding insult to injury, Charles's other exhortations range from the obvious to the ludicrous. He wishes that newcomers be welcomed and granted certain favorable privileges, a common practice already. Being at war with Spain, the colonists should be on the lookout for foreign agents, as if years of fighting with Indians have not made them alert to external danger. Drunkenness should be discouraged, which a number of Virginia governors have been doing already, with little success. Indeed, some of the recent arrivals from the *Flying Hart* who stayed on in Jamestown have caused more than their share of inebriated commotions and had to be reprimanded with a good scourging in front of the church.

But it is the final demand—that the settlers should be encouraged to plant corn rather than tobacco in order to become more self-sufficient—that provokes the most rolling of eyes and head-scratching. How can the monarch and his counselors be so out of touch with the conditions in Virginia that they would ask the colonists to limit the one crop that earns them any money?

At one of Mr. Chew's supper gatherings, Margaret witnesses spirited discussions of the royal letter among fellow merchants and visiting burgesses. The overwhelming conclusion, soon circulating among the general population, is that the King must be advised by imbeciles, and that the Virginia Colony is, once again, on its own.

The heated exchanges don't affect Margaret. With the coming of spring, she is happy to be outside again, away from Mrs. Chew's dark moods and viperous tongue. She prepares her garden and takes exploratory walks in the woods surrounding Jamestown. The pungent odors rising from the thawing earth and the chirruping of returning songbirds invigorate her, and she is happy to see the early blooming of bluebells, yellow trout lilies, blood root, and herbs she means to gather soon.

On one of the balmier days, her excursion takes her close to the James River, and she stumbles upon Elizabeth Piercey and Richard Stephens in a secluded thicket of willow oaks and birch trees. They are sitting next to each other on a fallen log, holding hands and gazing at one another with lambent eyes. The crack of a branch under Margaret's feet alerts them to her presence, and they jump up guiltily, like two thieves caught in the act. They know they should not steal time together without a chaperone. When they realize that it is

Margaret, they relax somewhat and try to hide their embarrassment under awkward smiles.

"You're not going to tell anyone about this, Margaret?" Elizabeth asks with concern and a note of warning in her voice.

Stephens intercedes quickly, "Of course she won't. Will you, Margaret?"

"It is not my place," Margaret says simply, holding Elizabeth's gaze for a moment before walking on.

From that point on, when Elizabeth meets Margaret in the street, she treats her with condescension, walking past her as if she didn't exist. Stephens, on the other hand, brings a sense of humor to their occasional encounters on the street and at the Chew residence, always catching Margaret's eye and giving her a conspiratorial wink. Margaret finds it all a bit silly. She has no intention of gossiping but wonders what Abraham Piercey would say if he knew what his oldest daughter and Richard Stephens are up to.

Soon, more important matters require her attention. One afternoon when she comes inside to get ready to serve the evening meal, Mr. Chew stops her in the hallway and says, "I'm going to Hogg Island tomorrow, and I want you to come with me. There are some things I have to take care of at my warehouse."

Surprised, Margaret says, "Yes, of course."

She can't imagine why Mr. Chew would need her there, but finds herself looking forward to the trip. She has been curious for some time to see what his plantation looks like.

The next morning before dawn, Margaret, along with Mr. Chew and two other servants, Walter and Ebenezer, board a pinnace at the harbor and sail across the river. It is still chilly, and the first streaks of sunlight illuminate a bank of clouds floating over the land to the east. Taking advantage of the river's current and early breeze, they make good time and before long sail past the reed-covered tidal marshes of Hogg Island. By the time they reach the dock of Mr. Chew's wooden pier, the sun has come out, bathing the shore and land in incandescent light and burning off the morning fog. It promises to be another fine spring day.

As Margaret disembarks, she notices a large barn nearby—Mr. Chew's warehouse—and a one-story house with a thatched roof and smoke issuing from a brick chimney on its side. It reminds her of the cottages at Bennett's Welcome, only larger. Farther inland, there are areas of dark, black soil, half-tilled fields waiting to be planted with root vegetables and corn. Unlike other merchants, Mr. Chew has made no efforts to become a tobacco grower.

Inside the house, Mr. Chew's servants—George Gooding, John Vaugh, and Thomas Winard—are waiting for them with breakfast: pancakes and bacon. Margaret has met all three at various times before from their occasional visits to Jamestown.

As she eats hungrily, Margaret takes a look around the dining room. It is warm and dark, with low ceilings and rough-planked wood floors. There are small piles of dust everywhere, and spider-webs festoon the windows. No doubt this is why Mr. Chew has brought her here—to help with spring cleaning. It amuses Margaret to think of how Mrs. Chew would react to the place. She'd take one look, tilt up her nose in disgust, stalk back to the boat, and set sails for Jamestown immediately.

After breakfast, they all head to the warehouse. The large wooden door creaks when George pulls it open. The barn is angled so that the sunlight spilling inside illuminates much of the interior. Margaret notes stacks of barrels, crates, chests, and hempen sacks sitting on the solid dirt floor. A makeshift table to one side displays iron pots, clay ewers, pewter plates, and kitchen utensils.

Mr. Chew lets his gaze sweep over the interior, points to one corner close to the entrance, and says, "We must make room over here. I'm expecting a new shipment later today."

As Margaret steps forward to join the others, he holds her back and says, "No, I want you and Thomas to clean the house."

For the next hour or so Margaret and Thomas, the youngest of the crew, sweep the floors, clear the spiderwebs, and wash the

windows, using water from a nearby spring. Thomas is a cheerful, talkative young man who uses the opportunity to make up for
months of self-imposed silence among his taciturn brethren. He has
ambitions to get a place of his own, and Margaret is happy to listen
to him babble on. It makes the work seem less bothersome.

When they are finished, Margaret takes the pail outside and starts
to clean the exterior of the windowpanes. As she makes her way to the
rear of the house, she hears distant shouts coming from the water. She
wipes her hands on her apron and goes to the front porch.

Another, larger pinnace is approaching. The sailors aboard have
struck the sail and are maneuvering with oars and poles to dock the
boat. George guides them with hand signals to the wooden pier as
Mr. Chew and the other servants watch impassively.

The first to climb up onto the wooden platform is a tall man.
The outline of his body and lumbering gait look familiar. Margaret
experiences a sudden jolt to her heart, and blood rushes to her face.
Could it be? She starts to walk, then run toward the beach, becoming more certain with each step. It is Captain Jope!

By the time she's halfway there, he has shaken hands with Mr.
Chew, who gestures toward the house. Jope sees the young girl flying
toward him, throws down his hat, and moves toward her as fast as his
boots allow. They meet on the path, close to the barn, and Margaret
throws herself into his waiting arms. Tears of joy spill down her face
as he lifts her off the ground and she buries her head against his
shoulder.

"You finally came," she whispers.

Jope pulls her close to him and strokes her hair. Then he sets
Margaret down and disengages himself from her arms.

"There is someone else who has come to see you," he says with a
smile and his piercing blue eyes dancing merrily.

He steps aside to reveal a young man, hands hanging by his side,
looking at her with uncertain anticipation. He is wearing a wool
shirt, breeches, and a dagger in his belt. For a moment Margaret
doesn't recognize John. He has grown at least a head taller since she

last saw him. His body has matured and become broad-shouldered and sinewy. His face is older, too, weathered by experience.

For his part, John is just as astonished. The young girl he remembers has become a young woman, soft-featured and fine-looking. Her body has developed womanly curves. With the sun behind her, she seems to have a special glow, leaving him speechless and if frozen to the ground.

Jope, amused by their amazement and awkwardness, burst out laughing. "Don't just stand there like two wooden statues," he roars. "Go on then."

He pushes Margaret forward, and she stumbles into John's enfolding embrace. John feels the soft swell of her breasts against his chest, and Margaret marvels at his muscular arms and body. As they hold each other it feels like the world has stopped.

When they draw apart, John says in a husky voice, "Margaret, you look beautiful."

Margaret answers, "And you are no longer a boy!"

Jope has returned to the dock to confer and negotiate with Mr. Chew. Then he orders his men to start unloading their cargo—muskets, pistols, hunting knives, and barrels filled with gunpowder. In the meantime, he examines the chests of corn and wheat and nods his approval.

By the time he returns to his charges, they are sitting on the steps of the porch, talking and holding each other's hands, as if to make sure by physical contact that they are real and not just figments of their imaginations.

"Let's go inside," Jope says. "The merchant has made his house available to us for the day."

As Margaret gets to her feet, she notices the pearl drop in the captain's ear. Her mouth drops open in astonishment. Then a smile blossoms on her face, and her eyes twinkle with admiration and merriment.

"You approve then?" Jope asks humorously.

"I do," she says and, turning to John, teases, "I'm surprised you don't have one, too, John. It would look good on you."

John grins. "I thought about getting one, but after I saw what pain the captain had to endure, I decided against it."

Jope slaps him playfully on the shoulder.

Inside, Margaret takes bread and cheese from a basket to the kitchen table, and they sit and eat and catch up on everything that has happened to them.

The first thing she wants to know is how they came to visit so early in the spring. It turns out that they met John Ewen again in Plymouth. Among other things, he talked about the sorry state of affairs in the colony—the need for more men, supplies, and arms. So Jope wrote to Mr. Chew and proposed a trade of guns for food supplies. He made seeing Margaret one of the conditions. Since Ewen would not be at his plantation but in England, they needed another meeting place. Knowing of the merchant's storehouse from Ewen, Jope suggested Hogg Island as a good spot away from the prying eyes and gossip mongers of Jamestown. He'd contact him when the *White Lion* arrived at Point Comfort and meet up two days later.

There wasn't enough time to wait for Mr. Chew's reply, so Jope took a chance that his offer would prove irresistible and departed Plymouth without prior agreement. Gambling that the weather would be favorable during their Atlantic crossing, he took on the extra cargo, although it weighted down the ship, stashing the arms and barrels of gunpowder on deck secured under canvas tarps.

When some of the sailors grumbled that they had signed up as privateers, not merchants, Jope pointed out that summer was a better time to hunt Spanish ships than spring. He appealed to their patriotism: they were providing their English brethren in the New World with the means to defend themselves against the Catholic Spaniards and heathen savages. Receiving extra food supplies in turn would provide the *White Lion*'s crew members a more varied diet and allow them to stay at sea longer to do their hunting.

His explanation didn't quiet all the dissenters, forcing Jope to pull the final ace from his sleeve. They would also take on a crate of tobacco, which would be worth its weight in gold. To lighten the mood, he added, "Unless we smoke it all before we get back home."

That brought cheers from everyone, and so the deal with his crew was struck. They left the *White Lion* in Gareth's capable hands, anchored on the other side of Hogg Island so as not to attract unwarranted attention from Jamestown.

"But there isn't any extra tobacco here this time of year," Margaret points out seriously. "Almost all of the crop gets shipped out in the fall."

"I just found that out from Chew," Jope admits, looking chagrined. Then he adds, "Good thing I didn't know that at the time," and burst out laughing.

As she and John join in, she realizes how much she has missed his infectious humor.

They talk for the better part of the afternoon, catching up on what has happened in their lives. John tells Margaret about their successful raids and brags about the barroom brawls he's witnessed at various Caribbean ports. Margaret recounts her time at the big wedding and her friendships with Frances and Peter at Piercey's Hundred and Emmanuel Driggers in Jamestown. Jope proudly shares news about Mary and his two daughters, including Margaret's namesake, who is now three years old.

At some point he asks, "Is Mr. Chew treating you well?"

Margaret nods. "Yes, well enough." Never one to complain, she decides not to mention Mrs. Chew's mean-spirited ways.

When the merchant comes into the house and lets Jope know that the exchange of goods is complete, the captain excuses himself and goes with him to take a look.

Margaret and John use the opportunity to walk and stretch their legs. As they amble past the fields toward the woods, John, acutely aware of Margaret's presence and scent, glances at her repeatedly.

Out of the blue, he asks a question that startles her. "Do you think our destiny is here in Virginia?"

Margaret stops and considers. "I haven't thought about that for some time," she ventures. "I like being out of doors, especially at this time of year and also in the fall." She looks at him seriously. "What about you? Do you like life aboard a pirate ship? I remember how sick I got on one of the Atlantic crossings."

John wrinkles his nose involuntarily. He looks at a flock of geese in flight and says, "I haven't thought about it much either. There is so much work, so many new things to learn, and the excitement of the raids, of course."

"I miss you and the captain," Margaret says softly, "and I am jealous that you can be with him all the time."

Looking at the ground, John remains silent for some time, as if struggling with himself. Then he blurts out, "You're the one person I miss all the time."

He looks up uncertainly and is pleased to see Margaret smiling. She leans toward him and gives him a kiss on the cheek. He feels it radiate through his entire body. For a moment, they look searchingly into each other's eyes and then, as if by mutual agreement, continue on their walk.

By the time they return to the house, the sun is starting to dip toward the land farther up the river. Their afternoon together is coming to an end.

Jope strides toward them from the water. "It is time, John, if we want to get back to the ship before dark."

"Do you have to go so soon?" Margaret asks plaintively.

Seeing her forlorn look, Jope feels an ache in his chest. Nodding kindly, he says, "I'm afraid so, Margaret. Is there anything you need?" As she shakes her head, he adds, "We'll come back sooner next time, I promise."

After a long embrace, he waits for John and Margaret to say their good-byes. They hug for a long time, as if trying to hold on to the feeling of their bodies close together and imprint it in their memories.

Margaret accompanies them down to the dock. When they get into the boat, Jope looks at her with his penetrating blue eyes one last time, waves to her once, and then acts busy, commanding his crew to cast off. But John, sitting in back of the pinnace, turns to her and watches as long as he can, his face bronzed by the afternoon sun.

Walking along the shore, Margaret follows the boat and waves until she comes to the edge of the tidal marsh and can go no farther. As the pinnace disappears around the tip of the island, a deep knot of pain gathers in her chest. She dries her tears on her apron and slowly heads back to the dock.

Chew has been watching discreetly while getting the barn secured. He quietly issues an order to the three servants staying behind. Then he gestures to Walter and Ebenezer to follow him to the dock.

"It is time for us to go home," he says gently.

Hardly hearing him, Margaret nods and climbs into the front of the boat. As they head toward Jamestown, she is glad that the others can't see her trembling lips.

* * *

Over the next few days Margaret feels a gray emptiness inside her. She keeps busy in the kitchen and digging in her garden, getting it ready for planting. Mrs. Chew mercifully leaves her alone, although she looks at her oddly from time to time. Perhaps Mr. Chew has said something to warn her off. Instead, she spends more time with her sons and torments the rest of the household staff.

A number of the servants are surprised and resentful that Mrs. Chew seems to be tiptoeing around Margaret, and at their expense. William, the head butler, looks at her darkly whenever she passes him and finds reasons to take her to task about her work. She does her best to ignore him.

Instead, she keeps thinking about the visit with Jope and John, especially at night before she goes to sleep. The captain looked older, although still energetic and handsome as ever, and the pearl drop in his ear was an unexpected surprise. But what unsettles her most, not in an unpleasant way, was the way John looked at her as if seeing her for the first time, and liking what he saw. The image of him smiling at her, his eyes glistening, stays with her for quite some time.

Over the next week the house becomes a busy place. After Mr. Chew quietly puts out the word to plantation owners and burgesses that he has a new stash of armaments for sale, visitors arrive from all over the colony. They confer with the merchant until they've struck a deal and then take a trip across the river to Hogg Island to pick up the weapons. Margaret recognizes John Hamor and a few others, but most of the men are not familiar to her. She hopes to see Lieutenant Shepherd, and perhaps even Anthony, but neither puts in an appearance.

One afternoon when Margaret returns from a trip into the woods, her basket filled with lily-leaved twayblade and spiderwort, she is surprised to see John Upton from Piercey's Hundred with Mr. Chew. They are deep in conversation standing on the other side of the house overlooking the riverbank. When Margaret passes them, they barely nod in acknowledgment.

By the time they finish, she is at work in the garden, and Upton finds her there. After saying hello, he says, "I'm sure you know what my talk with your master was about." Then he looks around to make sure they're alone and adds conspiratorially, "But I've come, among other things, to see how Mr. Piercey's daughters are doing. I imagine working next door you see a good deal of them."

Margaret decides to tease him and asks mischievously, "Why, Mr. Upton, are you asking me to spy on them?"

"Oh no, nothing of the sort," he replies, his face flushing red in embarrassment. That is exactly what he has in mind since Abraham Piercey told him to check up on the rumors surrounding Elizabeth and Stephens. To regain his composure, he continues, "Frances and Peter are well and send their greetings."

"I am glad to hear it. Please give them my best." Then she steps closer to him and whispers, "And you can tell Mr. Piercey that his daughters are fine, too."

Upton grins and executes a small mock bow. Margaret rewards him with a smile. As she heads for the Jamestown harbor, she looks after him for a moment before getting absorbed in her work again.

16
WARWICK'S OFFER
The Atlantic Ocean / London—Summer-Fall 1626

Jope and John don't talk much about their visit with Margaret except to note that she has grown and looks well. The captain is pleased that she seems to be happy with her situation and fails to discern the impact on John. If he notices the youngster frequently looking at the horizon with a melancholy gaze, he doesn't interpret it to mean anything more than what he feels himself about his wife and daughters when he is at sea—that he misses them. For his part, John doesn't know how to talk about the ripples of emotions his encounter with Margaret stirred in him. He has no words for his feelings, no way to articulate the strange, surprising longing in his heart.

Nor is there time or opportunity to explore them further. Two days after leaving Hogg Island and the Chesapeake Bay for the open seas, the *White Lion* runs into a late spring storm.

The signs of the impending tempest—the squawking seagulls that have accompanied them until now suddenly disappearing, the dark gray squall line in the distance, the smell of rain heavy in the air, and the increasingly powerful gusts of wind fluttering the sails— allow the crew to prepare for the encounter. After Jope, Gareth, and the navigator confer briefly and agree that they cannot outrun the storm, the quartermaster blows his whistle and shouts orders to everyone to get ready. The seamen fan out across the decks as if getting ready for battle. They trim a number of the sails, string ropes across the ship to grasp and latch onto when the seas get rough, and fasten everything above and below deck—sails, water barrels, cannons, supplies—as best they can.

Jope insists that John tie himself to one of the safety lines on the quarterdeck, and by the time he complies, the storm is upon them. The rain pours down with such force that John can't see farther than the bow. The navigator and helmsman struggle at the whipstaff to turn the ship against the wind so that it can ride the crests and troughs of the enormous waves without capsizing.

For two days and one night, the *White Lion* and its crew battle the unforgiving elements. The howling gale lashes the sails until some of them tear loose from the spars and flap about madly. The ships' beams and masts groan under the strain. Gargantuan waves batter the sides of the hull and sweep over the railings, hurling tall flumes of spray against the lower sails and sending water rushing into the holds.

Tied to the lifeline, John gets swept more than once against the railings and coughs up salt water he has swallowed. At some point Gareth orders him below to help bail water. As he stumbles down the stairs, a cannon tears loose and rolls across the deck. It barely misses him. A sailor named Robart is not so lucky. The cannon slams him against the wall and crushes his leg. Even the roaring wind can't drown his hysterical screams. As his mates pull the heavy gun off him, John sees the shin bone protruding from Robart's lower leg and blood pouring from the wound.

When Charles, the ship's surgeon, arrives and yanks at the leg until the bone goes back inside, Robart passes out. Then he wraps a rope tightly around Robart's thigh and inserts a wooden dowel into the knot to make a tourniquet.

"Loosen it every now and then and tighten it again, or he'll lose the leg," he shouts to John before stumbling away to deal with the next crisis.

John does as he is told and helps with bailing in between times. Mercifully, Robart remains unconscious for most of the time.

When the storm finally blows past and calm returns, Jope and Gareth assess the damage to the *White Lion*. They are happy to discover that the ship has taken some serious blow but is still seaworthy. It's a good thing they unloaded the cargo sitting on top of the decks in Jamestown. The barrels, caskets, and armaments would have turned into deadly missiles had they been blown around the ship. True, there is much to do and repair. The holds are still knee deep in water. Several spars have snapped like twigs, and a number of sails are torn to tatters. The cannons and muskets all need to be cleaned and oiled to prevent them from rusting, and the powder kegs need to be inspected to make sure the gunpowder remained dry.

All things considered, they've been lucky to escape with their lives, although when Gareth calls the roll, it becomes clear that a handful of men are gone, swept overboard and lost at sea. The rest have their share of broken bones, cracked ribs, dislocated fingers, and bruises, but only Robart sustained a life-threatening injury. The ship's doctor amputates his leg at the knee, after administering a shot of whiskey and placing a leather strap between his teeth to bite down on against the excruciating pain. John doesn't witness the surgery, but Robart's gurgling screams echo through the ship until Charles is done.

Afterward, in the welcome silence, Captain Jope assembles the crew. Then he offers a prayer of thanks for their safe delivery. Afterward, the spent sailors strip off their waterlogged clothes, hang them on the lifelines to dry, and crawl naked into their bunks to sleep while a skeleton crew keeps the ship on course.

When John wakes, he is still tired and sore. Every muscle in his body aches. He hobbles up on deck, retrieves his clothes, and looks for Gareth and the captain. He finds them in the cabin with the navigator looking at maps and deciding how best to get back on track for the remainder of their privateering voyage.

For the next month, the crew is busy from morning until night repairing the *White Lion*. At the end of each day, after grabbing a bite to eat, John falls exhausted into his bunk and drops off to sleep like an extinguished candle. He has no time to think of anything other than the tasks at hand. Margaret becomes a distant memory, an image that rarely flickers in his tired mind.

Jope is impatient and drives his men as hard as he can, but by the time the *White Lion* has returned to its former glory, he knows they have lost a good third of the privateering season. As a result, they manage to board only one merchant vessel, carrying spices and supplies to Mexico, and raid another in consort with one of Warwick's ships. That haul turns out to be better, and they head home in late October, satisfied that they have survived a trying season.

As they cross the Atlantic Ocean, John helps Jope inventory the spoils and figure out the value, writing it all down in the captain's log. It becomes clear that, after paying the crew and taking care of the ship, there will barely be enough left over to show a profit.

* * *

When they get back to Tavistock, further unpleasant news awaits them in the form of the Earl of Warwick's letter. Jope peruses it, his eyes squinting as he tries to make out the writing, Mary paces anxiously.

"My uncle has been trying to find out what Lord Rich has in mind, but he has had no luck," she says plaintively.

A knowing look passes between Jope and John. They both have a good idea what the summons is about.

"I will write the earl, informing him that I just returned to England, and if he still wishes to see me, I will be happy to make the journey to London at his convenience," Jope says brightly. "Come, John, you can be my scribe."

Two weeks later another special messenger arrives on horseback, not by conventional post, bringing the Earl of Warwick's reply. The tone is formal, courteous, and welcoming: Lord Rich desires Captain

Jope's attendance in two weeks' time. Jope sends the rider back with his acknowledgment. When he gets to London he will stay at Sir Granville's and arrange to call on the earl.

Mary continues to fret despite Jope's reassurances and air of confidence. He plays with his two young daughters and continues to tutor John on use of weapons and hand-to-hand combat. The captain's manner is not quite as self-possessed, however, when he and John take a walk in the woods on the estate.

"I have told Mary nothing of our special raids at sea," he says when they are out of earshot of the house. "You must act poised and confident during my absence. I don't want her to fret any more than she is bound to do on her own."

John nods seriously. He worries a wrinkled leaf on the ground with the toe of his boot and asks, "What if there is trouble?"

Jope's lips compress. He thinks for a moment and says, "Take her and the children to my brother's house and acquaint him with how matters stand. I may not always see eye to eye with Joseph, but I trust him to know what to do."

* * *

It is a raw December morning when Jope presents himself at the Earl of Warwick's home in London. He is dressed in his best doublet and overcoat. In defiance of convention, he is also wearing his pearl earring, hoping to convey a sense of self-assurance he doesn't entirely feel.

When Warwick's butler, Alfred, ushers him into the study, Jope is surprised to see the earl sitting at a table by the fire, playing a board game with a youngster not much older than John. Another, younger boy, positioned between them, looks on in fascination. Nathaniel Rich stands behind a table covered with documents and acknowledges Jope with a curt nod.

As Warwick glances up, the captain takes a step forward, doffs his wide-brimmed hat, and executes a deep bow.

The earl raises his black eyebrows and says, "Captain Jope, how good of you to come. These are my sons, Robert and Charles. You remember my cousin Nathaniel from our last meeting."

When Jope bows to each in turn, Rich continues, smiling, "Let me just finish this game. I'm trying to teach my sons chess. Do you play?"

"No, m'Lord, I have not had the pleasure."

"You would enjoy it, Captain. It is a game of war, and you must think several moves ahead if you wish to succeed." He shifts a black piece with a horse's head carved on top. "Check."

The youngster sitting opposite him wrinkles his brow. Jope observes that he has his father's thin lips and prominent nose, though his features are softer and his hair is curlier.

Rich leans back and continues to explain. "The pieces resemble kings, queens, knights, bishops, castles, and servants. Unfortunately, there are no privateering captains. I suppose when the game was invented, there was no need for naval warfare."

"I see," Jope says matter-of-factly. To him, Warwick does not look much older than the last time they met. The lines around his eyes are more pronounced, but he seems in excellent shape. He is wearing a fancy blue doublet made of satin and velvet that probably cost more than what Jope pays the crew of the *White Lion*.

The boy moves a white piece with a crown to an adjacent square. A small smile flits across Rich's face. He counters by pushing a piece, crowned with a bishop's miter, diagonally across the board and announces, "Checkmate! You must pay more attention to the clergy, Robert. They are a devious lot!"

The youngster, disappointed and embarrassed by his defeat, says, "Yes, Father." His younger brother suppresses a smirk.

Rich rises imperiously and says, "You boys can play a game with each other, while the captain and I conduct our business."

He picks up a half-empty wineglass, takes Jope by the elbow, and guides him over to the table, where nautical maps, charts, and a variety of documents are spread out.

Warwick sighs exaggeratedly and says, "The matter of educating my son to my ways is a challenging matter. Do you have any children, Captain Jope?"

"Two daughters, m'Lord, but they are still very young."

"And you have two African children as your charges as well. Have you seen them lately?"

Warwick's tone is smooth and conversational, and Jope decides to play along. "Yes, m'Lord, just this spring at Jamestown in Virginia. They are doing well."

"I'm glad to hear it," Rich says. He points to Jope's pearl earring. "It seems you are doing very well, too, Captain. It suits you."

"Thank you, m'Lord," Jope replies drily. He wonders how long Warwick intends to play this cat-and-mouse game.

"Sir Walter Raleigh liked to wear one, too, as I recall," Rich continues blandly. "Of course, it didn't prevent him from losing his head on the scaffold."

Jope represses a smile. Apparently, the earl wants to keep toying with him, but two can play that game. "I understand he was a good friend of your father's," he says drily.

Warwick eyelids flutter involuntarily, and he decides to change course. "I understand that you have gone back to privateering."

"Yes, m'Lord. I found the merchant life unfulfilling, and the war with Spain rekindled my desire to serve England more profitably. But I imagine you know all that from Daniel Elfrith."

Rich shares a glance with his cousin. "Yes," he drawls, "business and warfare have been a blessing. My fleet has prospered. The only fly in the ointment has been a Dutch privateer who has sailed in consort with some of my captains from time to time and makes off with the lion's share of the spoils." He looks at Jope casually and adds, "You wouldn't happen to know anything about this 'Flying Dutchman,' would you, Captain?"

Jope utters a small laugh. "A flying Dutchman. That would be a sight to behold!" Turning serious, as if he just realized that his joke might offend the earl, he adds quickly, "I don't mean to make light of your troubles, m'Lord, but no, I am not familiar with such a man."

Rich breaks out into a predatory smile. "You are quite certain, Captain?"

"Yes, but from now on I'll keep my eyes open and ears peeled."

Rich chuckles and goes to the mantle to refill his glass from a crystal carafe. "May I offer you a glass of wine, Captain?"

Jope shakes his head. "Very kind of you, m'Lord, but I don't indulge."

Warwick walks toward his cousin, "You see, Nathaniel. I told you, Captain Jope is a good Calvinist and a man of principle. I wish we had more like him rally to our Puritan cause."

As the lawyer nods, Jope notices that the two boys have suspended their game and started to watch the conversation with considerable attention. He wonders what they know of the earl's plans.

A look passes between Warwick and his cousin. The earl takes a sip of wine and looks at Jope searchingly. Then he smiles thinly and says, "I called you here, Captain, because I wish to make you a proposition."

Instantly on alert, Jope fingers his hat and says nothing.

After a moment, Rich continues, "I can use a man like you— smart, courageous, and loyal. I would like you and your ship to become part of my fleet, to sail under my banner. I am sure you would not let a renegade privateer get away with your rightful share of treasure, and in this time of war against the Spanish heathens, there is strength in numbers. I am assembling a special flotilla to take the Spanish gold transport." He pauses for emphasis before adding, "It would cripple our enemy and make you a fortune."

The offer takes Jope aback. This is not what he had expected. Recovering quickly, he says, "I am deeply honored by your faith in me, m'Lord. May I ask what terms you have in mind?"

Rich looks to Nathaniel, who clears his throat and says, "You would receive a guaranteed income and a percentage of the spoils. I am certain it would well exceed whatever treasure you garner now on your raids."

There is no pretense when Jope turns to Warwick and says, "I am overwhelmed by your generous offer, m'Lord. It is quite unexpected and begs serious consideration. With your permission, I would like to think on it."

"Take all the time you wish, Captain," Rich replies expansively. "We have three months before we all ship out on our next marauding season. In the meantime, I wish you a good Christmas feast and a pleasant time with your family."

Jope bows smartly.

Before he can withdraw, Rich fixes him with an imperious look. His dark eyes glitter dangerously, yet he smiles and his voice remains light. "Family and children are so important, Captain, wouldn't you agree?"

"Yes, m'Lord, they are," Jope acknowledges, holding Rich's gaze for a moment before turning and stalking from the room.

Rich looks after him, no longer smiling. When the door closes behind the captain, he turns to his oldest son and asks, "So, Robert, what do you think? Is he the Flying Dutchman?"

Young Robert furrows his brow again and says, uncertainly, "I don't know, Father. I could not tell."

The earl turns to Charles, who shrugs and shakes his head. "I have no idea."

Warwick sighs, disappointed. "You'll both have to learn to read men better. There is no doubt in my mind." He looks to Nathaniel, who nods as if it were a foregone conclusion, and continues, "I am curious what the Flying Dutchman will decide."

PART THREE

REUNION

17

SHEPHERD'S OFFER

Jamestown—Spring 1627

After hunkering down for the winter, the early spring is a welcome and busy time for everyone in Jamestown. With the warming weather, oaks, elms, chestnut, and beech trees sprout delicate green leaves. All kinds of migratory birds return, and courting and married couples go for walks along the river. Richard Stephens and Elizabeth Piercey no longer hide their affection for one another but parade it openly for everyone to see. Rumors that they are to be married within the year float about town, and neither does anything to dispel them. Margaret hopes the wedding will take place at Piercey's plantation and that she can attend it and see Frances and Peter again.

When Mrs. Chew starts to complain of being nauseous in the mornings, everyone realizes that she is pregnant again. Margaret wonders who will take care of her delivery when the time approaches since Dr. Pott is no longer welcome in the house. She does not feel confident that she can act as midwife on her own and knows she needs to talk to Mr. Chew about it soon.

In the meantime, she is busy with her many chores. Besides preparing her garden, helping in the kitchen, and serving meals, Margaret oversees the springtime increase of the poultry population, which has been kept small over the winter months to save on feed. After letting the cock loose among the hens in the backyard, she gathers a bounty of fertile eggs in no time.

Three weeks later, the baby chicks start to hatch, emerging from their eggs covered in wet, sticky yolk and fluid. Nathaniel, Mrs. Chew's younger son, watches enraptured as Margaret wraps the weaker chicks in wool, brings them into the house, and puts them in a crate near the fire to keep them warm. The others stay with their mother hens. During the next fortnight, Margaret feeds her hatchlings with corn-meal, breadcrumbs, and plenty of water. Those that survive join their fellow chicks in the henhouse and the backyard. Although she has to keep Nathaniel from chasing them, the sight of the fluffy little yellow creatures scurrying this way and that brings a smile to her lips.

With everyone involved in spring cleaning, Margaret is hopeful that Mr. Chew will take her to Hogg Island again for another visit with Captain Jope and John. In the evenings after she is done with her work, she sneaks out of the house to the river's edge and, looking at the stars shining brightly overhead, prays for them to come soon. But although she sees a number of ships each week sailing toward the Jamestown docks, the *White Lion* is not among them, and Mr. Chew never asks her to go to Hogg Island.

As the weeks pass, she becomes increasingly disappointed and worried. Where could they be? Did something bad happen to them? She tries to comfort herself with the notion that they will surely come in the fall and continues to send her nightly prayers to heaven. Once in a while, she hears someone on the road—a drunkard tottering past and cursing when he trips over a stone, or a merchant walking home late from a supper meeting—and she waits in silence, hidden in the shadow of a large water willow, until he has passed by.

At some point, scouts arrive with dire warnings of an impending Indian attack. As a result, Governor Yeardley issues a number of proclamations to help protect the colony. He orders male settlers to carry weapons with them at all times. Gunpowder is no longer to be wasted by firing muskets into the air during weddings and other celebrations. Finally, every household must meet for prayer at least once a day, and plantations that are not near a church have to provide a special place for worship.

There are lively debates in town and around Mr. Chew's supper table over the merits of such laws. Many feel that Yeardley's directives don't go far enough and that there needs to be more military action. The great Indian massacre affected many people directly, and memories of the horrific slaughter are still vivid in their minds. As far as the exhortation to daily divine appeals go, it doesn't escape Margaret that the daily morning prayers, led by Mr. Chew, occur with less frequency whenever the merchant goes away on business. His wife is not interested in getting up early, and by the time she is ready, everybody is busy with their tasks. Margaret wonders if the same happens in other households.

When news arrives from London that Spain threatens to retaliate for the attack on Cadiz and the maritime raids by English privateers, Yeardley convenes the advisory council at his house to discuss what countermeasures to take. After much debate, the attendees decide to send a military expedition to conquer the territory of the Kisiak tribe along the York River about 15 miles north of Jamestown. Although the Kisiaks participated in the great massacre four years earlier, they were greatly weakened and have been quiet ever since then. Securing the area would provide the colony with a refuge in case a Spanish attack meets with success.

Margaret is one of the first servants in Jamestown to hear about the deliberations when Emmanuel Driggers informs her of the decision reached at the governor's house. She doesn't know what to make of it and decides not to worry too much since there is nothing she can do about it.

But the decision soon affects her indirectly. A few days later, when she goes to market with her shopping basket, she runs into Lieutenant Shepherd, dressed in his uniform. He seems older, more mature. His light brown mustache is longer, and his beard, trimmed to a point below his chin, has filled out on the sides.

His eyes light up, and he exclaims, "Margaret, I am so glad I ran into you! I was planning to come and see you later!" In a lower voice he adds, "I'm in town to meet with the governor and other military personnel."

"The campaign against the Kisiaks?"

He looks at her in surprise and says, "I didn't realize it was common knowledge already."

To protect Driggers, Margaret decides to tell a small lie and replies, "It isn't. I happened to walk past the governor's house and overheard a servant in the yard mention it."

The explanation seems to satisfy him. He draws closer and asks, "Can you spare a moment?" When Margaret nods, Shepherd continues, "I've been stationed at the Treasury Plantation, where all the military supplies are kept. With my time there and at Warrosquoake, I have saved enough money to buy a farm. I'm going to get a place of my own near Hogg Island, but I need someone I can trust to take care of the house both when I am there and when I'm gone on military campaigns."

He waits for Margaret to respond, and when she doesn't, he says, "I can't think of a better person than you."

Margaret is both astonished and pleased. The thought of running a household hasn't occurred to her before. Although she has experience with many aspects of the job, she isn't sure she'd be ready to be in charge.

"You'll be taking a wife then?" she asks.

"No, not yet. I plan to get settled first with a handful of servants and workers, but then . . . well, yes, of course, I want to start a family."

Margaret doesn't know how to react. "I am under a contract of indenture with Master Chew," she says uncertainly. "Have you spoken with him yet?"

"No, I wanted to check with you first," Shepherd says brightly. "But I'm sure he and I can come to a suitable arrangement."

Looking at the ground, she fingers the handle of her basket absentmindedly.

Sensing her ambivalence, Shepherd says, "There is no need to make a decision right away. I'm not planning to occupy my homestead until this Indian business is taken care of and my house is built—certainly not until next year." He looks at her earnestly. "Will you think about it?"

Relieved, Margaret answers, "I will, I promise. I am honored that you would consider me. Thank you."

Shepherd gives her a boyish smile. "Think nothing of it," he says. "We'll talk of this anon."

Margaret watches him leave and stride purposefully toward Yeardley's house. She takes a deep breath.

But before she can give his proposal further thought, she hears someone clear his throat behind her. Then a deep voice says, "You know, it would be a good fit. The lieutenant is a good man."

Startled, she whirls about. It takes only an instant for her to recognize the dark-skinned, muscular man who is grinning at her. It is an old friend from Warrosquoake.

"Anthony!" she exclaims.

His eyes sparkle with delight. Margaret would like nothing more than to hurl herself into his arms and give him a big hug, but there are too many other people about, and it would not be proper. Instead she says, barely able to contain the excitement in her voice, "It is so good to see you. What brings you to town?"

Anthony chuckles and says, "The lieutenant and I came on the boat together. I'm here to buy provisions." He looks her over with appreciation. "I heard you were growing into a fine young woman, Margaret, and it was no exaggeration."

Once again Margaret flushes with pleasure.

They find a bench away from the main square and spend the next quarter hour catching up. Margaret talks about Captain Jope and John's visit, helping Dr. Pott, and life at the Chew residence.

When she mentions Mrs. Chew's miscarriage, Anthony's face grows sad. "Mary lost a baby, too," he says softly.

Margaret puts her hand on his arm. "I am sorry about that. But she is all right?"

Anthony nods, and they sit quietly for a moment. Then he says, "My daughter is doing well, too." As he continues to talk about life at the plantation, herding cattle and planting corn and vegetables, he grows more animated.

"Are you still planning to have a place of your own?" Margaret asks.

Anthony nods seriously. "When young Richard Bennett returns from England, I will know more. He made promises before he left."

When they part, Margaret throws propriety to the wind, embraces Anthony unabashedly, and says, "I'm so glad I got a chance to spend time with you, Anthony. Give Mary my best."

"I will," he replies. "And think about the lieutenant's offer, Margaret. The merchant you work for is a calculating man. I've seen it in his eyes when he visits the plantation. I wouldn't trust him to have your best interest at heart."

Margaret is taken aback. That has not been her experience of Mr. Chew. If it weren't for his shrewish wife, she couldn't think of a better place to be. But she decides not to pursue it any further, parting from Anthony and saying her good-byes.

On her way back from shopping, she thinks about Lieutenant Shepherd's surprising offer and feels at a loss about how to respond. She wishes more than ever that Captain Jope was here so that she could ask his advice. He would know what to do.

18

DECISIONS

The Caribbean—Summer–Fall 1627

Hot in pursuit of a Spanish frigate, the *White Lion* cuts through the churning ocean waves, sending plumes of salt water over the bowsprit. Next to it, as if pulling hard in harness, another privateering ship noses ahead. The *Penelope*, flying the English flag and the Earl of Warwick's banner, is a larger vessel more equipped for warfare than a swift chase on the open sea, but it manages to hold its own.

Although the *White Lion* is the faster ship, Captain Jope is content to let his consort take the lead. Standing on the quarterdeck, hand resting on the hilt of the sword at his side, he cuts a statuesque figure, and his blue eyes blaze with intensity. He looks over to the other ship, where his counterpart, a younger man wearing a naval uniform, paces back and forth excitedly, shouting orders at his men. He is on his first marauding venture, and Jope imagines that his heart is beating fiercely with the thrill of the hunt. He himself is eager, too, but as a veteran privateer he knows his crew is ready, poised to execute his orders when the time comes to take the treasure.

The meeting he had with Warwick in the spring gave him a great deal to think about. As he strode along the cobblestone street toward John Ewen's home in the Limehouse District close to the wharfs on the Thames River, he mulled over what had just transpired.

Rich had obviously staged the chess game with his sons to send him a not-so-subtle, yet complex message regarding his family. Jope admired not only the tactic to deliver a veiled threat, but that the earl had used it to double as a training session for his heirs. Jope always sought out such opportunities to further John's education. Looking at the youngster about to climb up into the crow's nest, he is pleased that John is much more mature for his years than Rich's eldest son.

But what to make of the compliments, the fishing for information Warwick already knew, and the generous and seductive offer to join his fleet? Certainly the possibility of hunting the Spanish gold fleet as part of a well-armed flotilla would set his heart on fire. But there was also the veiled threat to his family, not to mention the new name Rich had coined for him, fraught with ambivalent meaning: "the Flying Dutchman."

The offer put him in a quandary. He could not fully discuss it with anyone, not Mary, nor her uncle, nor even his own brother—and certainly not with Ewen, whom he was about to visit to discuss another mercantile voyage to Jamestown. If word leaked out about his singular way of privateering, everyone close to him would be at risk. He had to keep his own counsel.

Watching John nimbly scale the ratlines to take his place as the main lookout during the raid, Jope wonders if he has made the right decision. Fate bequeathed Margaret and John to him, and he has accepted it as his destiny to be their guardian and protector. But how to know what steps to take to secure their futures, to make the right decisions?

Up ahead, the captain of the Spanish galleon has realized that escape is impossible and given orders to strike her sails and heaved to, floating broadside in the water. But he is not yet ready to give her up. When the *White Lion* and *Penelope* get close enough to see the metal breastplates of the conquistador uniforms, a series of white puffs issue from the ship's gun ports, followed immediately by the roar of cannon fire.

The *Penelope*, being closer to the frigate, takes the brunt of the attack. Fortunately, most of the shots miss their target, but two missiles score a direct hit. Part of the railing on the poop deck disintegrates in an explosion of timbers, and a sail low on the main mast suddenly springs a gaping hole.

The captain of Warwick's vessel may be young, but he commands an experienced crew of cannoneers, who retaliate with full force and better aim. In the course of two exchanges, his ship takes another blow, but the Spanish frigate is much the worse for it. One of her masts comes crashing down on the deck like a felled tree, entangling the soldiers there in splintered spars, rigging ropes, and torn sails. Hopelessly crippled, the Spaniard gives up and hoists the white flag of surrender.

Now is the moment to execute the *White Lion*'s well-rehearsed ploy. With the *Penelope*'s crew preoccupied in assessing the damages from the battle, it will be easy pickings. Jope's men are on alert, ready to spring into action at their captain's command to unfurl extra sails, move ahead, interpose themselves between the two other ships, lower the pinnace, and abscond with all of the treasure.

But the command never comes. Instead Jope orders, "Heave to and prepare to board in consort with the *Penelope*."

There is a stunned silence. The men cannot believe their ears and, for a moment, seem as if frozen in their spots. Gareth, standing at the rail, ready to lower and commandeer the pinnace, is the first to move. He takes a step forward and looks up uncertainly at the quarterdeck, where the captain looms like a colossus, arms akimbo.

"Those are my orders," Jope shouts.

The moment of gliding between the *White Lion*'s consort and the Spanish ship passes. Gareth says, "Aye, aye, Captain," and gestures to the boatswain to blow his whistle and signal to the crew to proceed in normal fashion. The men lower and board the pinnace at a more leisurely pace and wait until the *Penelope* launches a skiff of its own.

Decisions

Up in the crow's nest, John watches the two boats approaching the Spanish ship together. He is as not as surprised by what just happened as the rest of the crew.

When Jope returned from his meeting with the Earl of Warwick, he was jovial and seemingly at ease. Mary had been much reassured. The earl's offer surprised her, but Jope's lighthearted account of the meeting made it sound like Rich only wanted to enlarge his fleet and that his old friend, Daniel Elfrith, had recommended him as a good prospect.

If Mary was at all suspicious of Jope's good cheer, she didn't let on. But for John there was no confusion about how the meeting had gone. He had been around Jope long enough to know that there was considerable turmoil beneath his cheerful exterior. He also noticed that the captain was more pensive than usual when he thought no one was looking.

Soon after, during their daily walk together in the woods, they stopped at the pond and idly sent stones skittering across the frozen surface. John, noticing the captain tightening and unclenching his jaw, as if he was locked in a difficult struggle, asked softly, "It was about how we conduct our privateering raids, wasn't it?"

Jope looked at him in surprise, as if John had read his mind, and chose not to turn the question aside. "Yes, that is the main issue," he admitted, "although Lord Rich raised it only obliquely."

"Well, you mustn't give in on my account or Margaret's, not when your freedom and independence are at stake."

After another searching glance, Jope said, "I appreciate your words, John, but I have my whole family to think about."

His tone made it clear to John that the subject was closed.

But two days later, the captain had reached his decision. He dictated a letter to John for the Earl of Warwick, thanking his Lordship for his generous offer, but respectfully declining. He gave no reason, knowing that there was nothing he could say to mitigate the implied challenge to Rich's authority.

John doesn't know what conversation Jope had with Mary or how much the captain really told her, but he became more solicitous toward her and spent more time with his daughters. She, in turn, became subdued again, as if resigned to her fate. John caught her looking at Jope with an intense longing on several occasion. When she noticed, she seemed angry for a brief moment, then blushed and smiled at him kindly.

Jope remained restless and, unexpectedly, decided to ship out at the earliest possible time, risking late winter storms on the Atlantic crossing. John had hoped that meant they would see Margaret again and was disappointed when Jope had Samuel Teague chart a southern course for the Spanish Main. Upon arrival in the Caribbean ports, Jope had trawled several ports, looking for consorts and news of treasure ships with almost feverish determination.

Yet now, when an easy opportunity presents itself to make off with the entire booty, he has backed away. Jope is not a coward and must have his reasons. Suddenly, it occurs to John that it could be that the captain is trying to protect him and Margaret. Although he would like to know for sure, that is not something he can comfortably ask about.

He watches the pinnaces returning from the Spanish vessel to the *White Lion* and the *Penelope*. They are both filled with caskets and chests—a substantial haul. The Spaniard must have been laden with a treasure hoard. The men cheer as the chests are heaved on tack and taken to the captain's cabin.

Jope assembles the crew and offers a prayer of thanks for their bounty. Then he has himself rowed to the *Penelope* to confer with her captain. After determining that the damage is not critical—the ship needs repairs that will take some time but is seaworthy enough to make it to harbor on her own—he says his good-byes. He promises to hook up for future raids when she is shipshape again. Until then, he will go ahead alone.

When he returns to the *White Lion*, he orders the navigator to set course for Havana.

Decisions

* * *

To everyone's surprise, the even-handed pilfering of the Spanish vessel is not a onetime event. For the rest of the voyage, Jope avoids depriving his consorts of their share of the prize and shares the spoils with them equally. He offers no explanation for his change of heart. The men start to grumble quietly, wondering why their captain has gotten cold feet.

But fortune smiles on Jope. By the time the *White Lion* sails back to England, its holds are filled with treasure from four successful raids, worth more than any of the previous hauls and laying to rest any rumblings about the captain's abilities.

John has taken to spending his free time in the crow's nest. The sound of the spars creaking and sails flapping in the wind soothes his disappointment that, once again, there hasn't been time to visit Margaret.

One afternoon, as he watches the men below hauling ropes to raise sails and cleaning the deck, he realizes that he has been aboard long enough to know most aspects of what is required to run a ship. Jope and Gareth have been good teachers, both by example and by their hands-on approach. But when it comes to his future, he knows he is not a privateer at heart. He will never own or captain a ship. He enjoys the excitement and adventures and is proud that the men respect him now. But going ashore with Gareth and other crew members, he has seen enough waterside taverns and brothels to understand that it is not a life he wants for himself. And even the roughest sailors on the *White Lion*, usually after several cups of rum, talk with longing about wanting to go home to their families and friends.

That is not an option for him. Although Mary and the servants do their best to make him feel at home at Tavistock, John knows he will never be truly accepted there. Too many of the neighbors look on him with tolerant condescension at best, and the occasional strangers he encounters always react with astonishment and bafflement. Jope and Mary are his only family, and he will always be an outsider in England.

He recalls that Margaret talked about the other Africans in Jamestown and on plantations—the *malungu* community. He remembers her mentioning someone named Anthony, who has dreams of having a farm of his own. Perhaps there is more opportunity there to make a life for himself. Like Margaret, he wonders what fate has in store for him and if it is time to take his future into his own hands.

A few days later John joins Captain Jope for supper in his cabin. He has been thinking all day about how best to broach the subject, even rehearsed what he wants to say. But as he screws up his courage and feels his heart pounding in his chest, all his well-prepared words fail him and he blurts out, "I want to go to Jamestown for good."

Jope, chewing on a gristly piece of salt pork, listens with only half an ear. "I know you're disappointed that we didn't visit Margaret this year as planned," he says. "Now that I proved that we can make plenty of money without irritating the Earl of Warwick, I feel more at ease. We will visit her next spring, I promise."

"No, you misunderstand me. I want to go and settle there," John asserts with passion. "I don't think there is a future for me as a privateer."

Jope leans back in his chair and takes in John's vehement, yet vulnerable demeanor. He looks along the timbered ceiling and to the windows at the stern of the ship to buy some time. He has known this day would come. He just didn't expect it to be so soon. His gaze settles on John, and his blue eyes shine in the flickering candlelight.

"You have thought about this a great deal," he says.

"Yes, I have," says John.

Suddenly he feels a stab of anguish in his chest. The thought of leaving Jope is almost unbearable. Tearing up, he would like nothing better than to take his words back, but he has said them and they lie irrevocably between them now.

Decisions

Jope sees John struggle, gnawing at his lips, and his heart goes out to him, but he holds himself back and says deliberately, "You are old enough to know your own mind, and perhaps it is time." Then he forces himself to smile and adds, "We will have much to talk about and plan for in the months ahead."

John nods with gratitude, manfully holding back his tears.

19

EARLY DEATH
Virginia—Fall–Winter 1627

When an early November snowstorm blankets Jamestown, Margaret realizes that Jope and John will not come to visit her this year. The almost unbearable anguish she feels in her chest quickly yields to a gnawing anxiety. It is most unusual for the captain not to honor his promise, and she fears that disaster has befallen him and John.

When she shares her worry with Emmanuel Driggers, he does his best to reassure her. Scrutinizing her from head to toe, he asks, "Do you feel it in your bones that they are gone?"

Margaret takes a moment to examine where her disquiet lodges inside her and then shakes her head no.

"Then there you are," he says, exuding confidence. "Nothing to worry about, not yet."

Looking at him doubtfully, Margaret checks herself again and realizes that she actually feels better.

The deep sense of calm lingers while other, more immediate concerns capture Margaret's attention. She continues to worry about Mrs. Chew's advanced pregnancy. The lady of the house is showing a large belly and, by Margaret's count, is due within the next two months. Margaret does not want to bear the responsibility for her delivery by herself. If something were to go wrong, she would not know what to do. When she finally mentioned this to Mr. Chew, he reassured her that he will take care of it, but so far she has seen no signs of him doing so.

Then, a momentous event occurs whose ripples impact Margaret's life significantly both in her immediate and distant future. In the middle of November, after taking to his bed for two weeks, Governor George Yeardley dies. His demise was not unexpected since he had complained of being "weak and sick in body, but in perfect mind and memory" a month earlier when he made his will.

As news of Yeardley's rapid decline reached the far outposts of Virginia, plantation owners, merchants, and other business partners traveled to Jamestown to pay honor and respect to a man who guided and championed the colony for nearly 20 years. Since his arrival in 1610, he had served twice as governor with unswerving loyalty, both under King James and King Charles, while amassing the largest fortune of any settler in the New World.

At the funeral service, Virginia's elite crowds into the pews and stands in back of the church in Jamestown to say their good-byes. Servants, laborers, and craftsmen assemble outside. The speakers laud Yeardley for his many accomplishments, while his wife, Temperance, and their three children, Argoll, Elizabeth, and Francis, sit erect in the front row, stoic expressions on their faces. But when the minister sermonizes about the fragility of life on Earth, they cannot hold back their tears.

While Mr. and Mrs. Chew attend the service inside, Margaret shivers with the others at the church steps as the chilly breezes, laden with moisture, penetrate their woolen wraps and overcoats. She draws her shawl more closely around her shoulders and considers that the governor was only 39, younger than her captain, and she prays that he and John are well.

When the service is finished, Margaret catches only a glimpse of the coffin being carried to the cemetery for interment. Far back in its wake, she meets up with Emmanuel Driggers, who looks serious. At first she imagines his deeply furrowed forehead and rigid lips are about holding back his emotions regarding his departed master, but then he shares what is really on his mind.

When they near the pillory and whipping post by the church, he takes her under the thatched eaves of one of the buildings and whispers, "I don't know what will happen to any of us."

Puzzled, Margaret asks, "What do you mean?"

Driggers quickly shares the rumor that the governor bequeathed his house in Jamestown to his wife and specified that the rest of his property be sold and divided among her and the children.

"Lady Temperance is likely to sell all of us African servants, and without a contract we will have no say in where we'll end up!" he finishes up in desperation.

His raised voice draws the attention of others, and Margaret puts a hand on his arm to calm him. "It won't be so bad," she assures him. "She will need servants to keep her household and take care of her youngest boy."

Driggers nods to let her know he has himself under control. Together they walk in silence to the cemetery and catch up to the crowd gathered around the grave and witness the burial. Then they join the long line of mourners filing past the new mound of black earth and pay their respects.

The following day, a group of burgesses meet and quickly elect Francis West as deputy governor to lead the colony until King Charles and the Royal Council appoint a new governor. West is the younger brother of Lord De La Warr, one of the wealthy founders of the original Virginia Company, and has been in the colony even longer than the man he is replacing. As a representative in the first House of Burgesses, a former commander of Jamestown, and a member of the general court, he has a pedigree almost as impressive as Yeardley's was, and everyone greets his succession with relief, confident that he will provide continuity and further success.

The new governor immediately moves to Jamestown from his plantation downriver in Elizabeth City. A widower himself, he openly starts to court Lady Temperance, and soon the town is rife with gossip about their impending marriage.

Meanwhile, Margaret, returning from a downtown shopping trip, sees her master and Dr. Pott in amiable conversation on the steps of the Chew residence. She waits until they shake hands, and Mr. Chew goes back inside while Dr. Pott walks toward his house down the road.

As he passes her, he tips his hat and says, "Mrs. Chew is doing just fine, Margaret. I expect you to be ready to assist me again when the time comes."

Margaret curtsies in reply and heads to the kitchen, happy that the burden of Mrs. Chew's delivery is no longer on her shoulders.

* * *

Knowing the course that his future will take imbues John with a sense of serenity and newfound maturity. It is the first time in his life that he has made a decision for himself, not just reacted to what fate sent his way, and it feels good. What he doesn't anticipate is how difficult and painful it is to say good-bye to all the people he has sailed with so closely for the past four years.

Captain Jope convinced him to let only a few crew members know about his ensuing departure. It is important to keep the news about his leaving England quiet and not give the wagging tongues of seaman drunk in their cups the opportunity to spread the word on shore. Let the privateers returning for next year's voyage of the *White Lion* discover for themselves that their captain's young mate is no longer aboard.

So John tells only Gareth and Samuel Teague when he finds them alone with Jope on the quarterdeck. Both are surprised and look to the captain for confirmation.

When he says nothing, Gareth asks John, "Why would you do that?"

For a moment John is at a loss for words as a wave of anguish sweeps over him with the realization that he may never see these men again.

Teague, seeing John struggling, scratches his beard deliberately and, with a wicked twinkle in his eyes, says, "It's that girl, that Margaret, isn't it?"

Before John can deny it, Gareth cuffs his shoulder and says, grinning, "You dog, you!"

Jope bursts out laughing, which gives John time to hide his embarrassment and bring his emotions under control. Nodding as if admitting Teague's humorous accusation, he grins sheepishly.

"Well, that's all right then," the navigator says gruffly. Returning to his charts, he adds, "We'll miss you, lad."

Gareth mouths to John, "We'll talk later," and he leaves, too.

For the next week, John does his chores with the awareness that it will be for the last times and tries to etch them in his mind. He runs his hands over the cold, rough barrels of the cast-iron cannons. He doesn't mind pricking his finger with the needle as he stitches up the tear in a sail before rolling it up for winter storage. He practices all the special knots for ropes he knows, notes the places where the wooden railing is gashed, and finds the planks that creak under on the various decks.

Above all, he finds time to say to the tars and musketeers he cares about, especially Jack Harkness, the cannon master, "I appreciate how much you have taught me."

When they sight land, he climbs up the ratlines into the crow's nest of the main mast for the last time and sits there alone for a while, looking at the approaching shore. The late autumn sun bathes the white cliffs in pale yellow, and the offshore breeze cools his face. He watches the seagulls riding the gusts of wind and knows he will miss this most of all—sitting in his own private perch high above the deck, alone with his thoughts. Then he turns toward the open sea, the Atlantic Ocean, and looks at the distant horizon, knowing that his future and destiny lie beyond.

The next day the *White Lion* reaches Plymouth Harbor, and the crew strikes the sails and closes the hatches for the winter. That night, Jope invites Gareth and Teague to join him and John for dinner in the captain's cabin. Over a savory, salty pork stew and scones made from the last of the flour, they tell their favorite stories of the voyages involving John.

Jope brings out two bottles of Spanish wine, part of the loot from the vessels they raided.

After the first taste, the navigator smacks his lips and says, "Those Catholic bastards may be the Devil's spawn, but they do know how to make a good wine."

John keeps up with the boisterous toasts, although he barely sips his glass. He has learned to tolerate beer in taverns while his compatriots swilled rum, but this red liquid tastes too sour and vile. It leaves more for the others to share, and Teague takes the opportunity to refill his cup frequently. The wine lubricates their tales, which become increasingly outrageous as the evening wears on. John's tumble from the spars to distract the harbormaster turns into a swan dive, and his embarrassment the first time he accompanied the crew to a brothel has him running away all the way to the other end of Havana.

It is quite late when the navigator turns his cup over, rises unsteadily from the table, mumbles a good-bye, and staggers out the door.

Gareth takes his last sip and totters to his feet, declaring, "You've been a good mate, John. Godspeed to you."

John gets up and stands uncertainly by the table. Then, impulsively, he rushes to the quartermaster and hugs him.

Gareth, a bit flustered, untangles himself and says, grinning, "Well now, lad, this isn't good-bye, you know. We will come and visit you in your new home in Jamestown, Don't you worry."

He exchanges a knowing glance with Jope, gives John a casual salute, and leaves, too.

Jope notices John's forlorn expression and says kindly, "You may sleep here tonight, if you wish."

John gratefully accepts the offer.

The next morning for final muster, everyone acts as if nothing had happened. Captain Jope sits down at a table on the quarterdeck and, with John next to him keeping the ledger, gives each man on the crew his rightful share of the spoils. He squints at the figures and asks John to decipher them for him, claiming he can't make out the writing. He has a good word for each runner and sailor and says he hopes to see him on the next voyage. After hearty good-byes, the tars remaining on the ship row their shipmates ashore so that they can head for the taverns and their homes.

Jope and John are the last to leave. They climb down the rope ladder and settle into the waiting boat, where their travel chests are already stashed. As they cast off, John sees Gareth watch and wave from the quarterdeck. Waving back, he feels a lump in his throat. He keeps looking at the *White Lion* bobbing gently at anchor, her sails struck and the masts and spars bare.

At the pier, a small carriage waits to take them to Tavistock. While the sailors load the travel chests and make them fast in the boot, John steps inside and sits down, eyes cast toward the wooden floor. When he hears the coachman's whip snap and feels the horses lurch forward, he takes one last look out the window. The ship looks like a toy boat in the distance. Jope, watching John's lower lip quiver, feels his eyes tear up, too.

The weather is overcast, but not too cold. Neither traveler says much along the way, both wrapped in their respective thoughts. But when they reach the edge of Tavistock and turn off toward Jope's estate, the captain breaks the silence and says, "Let me tell Mary in good time. We don't want to spoil her joy at our homecoming."

John nods his agreement.

Early Death

When they drive through the gate with mounting anticipation and pull to a stop in front of the house, something feels wrong. Mary isn't at the door, ready to rush into her captain's arms. Only when Jope is finished paying the coachman and the travel chests are safely on the ground does the entrance to the house open and Mary slowly emerge. Agnes with baby Joane in her arms comes out behind her. As Mary approaches, John notices that her eyes are red-rimmed. At some point she trips, and when Jope catches her, she throws herself into his arms and bursts into tears.

Alarmed, the captain cradles her head in his large hands, strokes her blond tresses, and asks, "Why, Mary, what's the matter?"

Trying to regain her control, his wife stammers between sobs, "It's our eldest, John. She's gone—dead," and bursts into tears again.

Jope sways as if his legs are about to give way, but he catches himself and exclaims, "Margaret? Our daughter?"

Mary nods her head against his chest.

"What happened?"

Weeping, Mary explains, "She caught the ague a fortnight ago. I sent for the doctor, but there was nothing he could do."

A cry like a wounded animal escapes the captain's throat and he sways again. John is about to jump forward to steady him when Jope straightens, clenches his jaw, pulls Mary closer into his embrace, and continues to stroke her hair.

Finally, her weeping subsides. Jope gestures to the nurse to bring his daughter to him. He gently touches Joane's cheek and kisses her on the forehead. Then he asks Mary softly, "Where did you bury her?"

In a low voice Mary says, "Out back near the lilac tree."

"Show me."

His arm firmly around her waist, they start to walk around the side of the house. As they pass John, Jope gives him a sharp glance. John nods, signaling his understanding. Until they've dealt with the grief of the loss to their family, not a word about his own news. Feeling a deep sadness, John slowly follows behind them.

20

COMINGS AND GOINGS

Jamestown—Late Winter–
Early Spring 1628

George Yeardley's death isn't the only departure of a ranking member of Virginia's elite. Just after New Year's, Abraham Piercey dies quite suddenly. The cape merchant, as everyone still calls him, apparently complained of pains in his chest and left arm at breakfast one morning and fell dead to the ground a few hours later. Because of the unexpected nature of his passing, there is not time for elaborate funeral preparations, and only members of his family and a few servants travel to the plantation to attend his burial.

When Mary and Elizabeth return to Jamestown, they have no peace. The next day the line of visitors coming to offer their condolences reaches almost to the harbor. Afterward, everyone in town talks about how shaken Piercey's daughters looked, although Mary seemed more affected than her older sister. Soon, expressions of mourning yield to conjectures about how the cape merchant's death will affect the wedding plans of Elizabeth and Richard Stephens.

Apparently the couple had plans, as soon as Elizabeth turned 18, to travel upriver to Piercey's Hundred and ask for her father's blessing. Expecting Piercey to be delighted, they were hoping to get married in June. But now everything is on hold until the reading of the will. Since their stepmother brought a considerable fortune with her into the marriage, Elizabeth and Mary expect to inherit most of their father's wealth, including the plantation upriver.

Margaret feels especially sorry for Mary, who looks drawn and wan whenever she sees her. But she has other things to worry about.

One morning in late January when it is unseasonably warm outside, Margaret is cleaning and washing the kitchen pots at the river when she notices Emmanuel Driggers hurrying up the street. She rises, wiping her cold, wet hands on her apron, and waves to him. He arrives winded, puts his hands on his sides, and takes a moment to catch his breath. Seeing his somber expression, Margaret feels a pang in her chest. He does not bear good news.

When he has recovered, Driggers looks at her sadly and says, "I have come to say good-bye, Margaret. I'm to go with Lady Temperance's son Argoll south to Point Comfort. She is sending the boy to his godfather, Francis Pott, and keeping her two younger children with her."

His words feel like a knitting needle stabbing her in the stomach. She cries out, "Oh, Emmanuel, so soon?"

He nods dejectedly. "Yes, me and three other African servants—Bshaw Fernando, Andola, and Maria. Francis Pott is commander of the fort at Point Comfort and has a big plantation there."

"That's Dr. Pott's brother?" she asks.

"Yes."

Margaret looks at the James River flowing steadily toward the Chesapeake Bay and feels tears welling up. "When are you leaving?" she asks in a small, choking voice.

"We're casting off at dawn tomorrow morning."

Heaving a deep sigh, Margaret closes her eyes for a moment. Then she opens her arms, goes to Driggers, and embraces him. Pressing herself to him, she says, "God keep you well, Emmanuel. I hope this is not the last time we see each other."

Surprised, he holds her for a moment. Then he untangles himself, takes her hands, and says more formally, "I am certain we will set eyes on each other again, Margaret. Perhaps I will be a free man by then." He adds with bitterness in his voice, "I don't aim to be like a leaf in the wind for the rest of my life, subject to the whims of the wealthy owners."

Then he straightens, lets go of her hands, gives her a parting smile, and walks away. Margaret looks after him until he disappears into Yeardley's house down the road. Then she returns to her kitchen duties with a heavy heart.

Getting rid of her servants is not the only change that Temperance Yeardley effectuates. She takes up the reins of executrix of her late husband's estate with determination. She sues a number of merchants and tradesmen in the colony to collect the money they owed to her husband. At the same time, she surrenders to Francis West the cattle under her care that are part of the governor's allowance.

Since she and the new governor are engaged in a whirlwind courtship, with plans to marry in the spring, the wags in town can't help noting that she is "killing two birds—or rather, two cows—with one stone, giving him what is his rightful due as her dowry."

Margaret doesn't pay much attention to the gossip. She and the rest of the servants at the Chew home are busy preparing for the arrival of a new addition to the household. Even so, Mrs. Chew goes into labor earlier than expected. Margaret sits up with her all night, doing her best to keep her mistress comfortable, wiping her forehead with a wet cloth and enduring her screams and curses as the contractions come at ever shorter intervals. Late the next morning, Dr. Pott signals that it is time. He and Margaret help Mrs. Chew climb onto the delivery stool, and before long, she gives birth to a baby girl.

Mr. Chew, who has been pacing outside the bedroom for most of the night, is beside himself with joy that both his wife and newborn daughter are healthy and safe. To Margaret's surprise, an exhausted and relieved Mrs. Chew takes a moment to thank her for her help.

It doesn't take long for her to recover from her ordeal, however, and castigate the servants again with her acid tongue, although she seems to spare Margaret her worst venom.

When the baby survives for two weeks, the parents decide to name her Sarah after her mother and have her baptized at the church in Jamestown. Many friends of the Chews and all their servants attend. Even the workers from the plantation on Hogg Island row across the river for the event. Everyone coos and congratulates the Chews when the child's hearty cries echo among the wooden pews during the ceremony.

But at the celebratory meal afterward, all conversation is about the reading of Abraham Piercey's will. Notable is the provision that, although his daughters are to inherit most of his estate after his death, they must have the permission of their stepmother to marry, or the disbursement will change, with much of the estate going to Frances Grenville Piercey. Everyone wonders about Elizabeth and Richard Stephens, Margaret most of all. She has seen them grow close over the past two years and knows that they are very much in love. She can't imagine what they will do if Lady Frances does not approve.

Meanwhile, the New Year brings a significant change in the legal status of the colony. In early March, at the behest of King Charles, Governor West convenes the first General Assembly in Jamestown since the demise of the Virginia Company four years earlier. From all over the colony, the burgesses and their wives arrive to take part in the historic meeting. They and their servants occupy all the extra rooms in town. Many stay with friends and acquaintances. Mr. Chew hosts two couples, John Uty, a fellow merchant and plantation owner from Hogg Island, and his wife, Ann; and Francis Eppes and his wife, Marie, who hail from the eastern shores of the Chesapeake Bay. The guests keep the servants busy making up the beds and preparing extra food for the meals.

The main item on the agenda, which the governor has revealed ahead of time, is the tobacco contract. On the eve of the assembly, the discussion at supper of the pros and cons is lively. Margaret listens with rapt attention. With Driggers gone, she no longer gets advance notice of the important matters that transpire in the governor's mansion.

"Why would the King want a contract requiring us to sell tobacco exclusively to England?" asks Mr. Chew. He knows the answer well enough, but it gets the conversation going.

Eppes, a gaunt man with penetrating brown eyes, clears his throat and opines, "Charles needs the tax money to pay for his extravagant tastes and foolish wars," he says. "When we were in London last summer, everyone talked about his clothes being worth more than the Crown jewels."

He looks to his wife for confirmation. Marie, a plain, plump-faced woman, nods eagerly.

Margaret notices Mrs. Chew looking longingly at Marie's fancy, brand-new dress, which puts even her own extravagant garment to shame. Imagining how jealous her mistress must be, she can't help smiling to herself.

"I will vote for the contract only with the proviso that we can continue to trade our crops for the goods we need brought directly to our shores," says Uty, pulling at the whiskers adorning his chubby cheeks. "Tobacco is our currency, better than silver or gold!"

"But is it in our interest?" asks Mr. Chew. "Would we not get better terms if the Netherlands and France were part of the competition?"

"Having one sure customer would make things easier," says Eppes.

"And what if the King won't give us a good price?" Uty challenges.

Mrs. Chew, bored with politics and financial matters, interjects from the other end of the table, "Did anybody find out when the governor means to wed Lady Temperance? I want to have plenty of time to get ready for that affair."

"Yes, I'd like to know, too," says Ann Uty eagerly.

Her husband, gnawing on a turkey bone, shares a look of understanding with Mr. Chew. The ladies must have their concerns. He digs with his finger in his teeth, dislodging a stuck sliver of meat, and offers, "I warrant it will be toward the end of the month. They've been quiet about it because they don't want a large ceremony."

"Temperance is minding her pieces of eight," says Mrs. Chew. "She's always been something of a skinflint."

Mr. Chew nearly chokes on his wine. He shoots an angry glance to his wife at the other end of the table and mutters loud enough for everyone to hear, "Watch your tongue, woman!"

Acting surprised, as if she doesn't understand what upset him so, Mrs. Chew coos sweetly, "What is it, John? I'm not speaking out of turn. Everyone knows that Temperance is nothing if not true to her name."

Margaret and the other servants in the dining room repress a grin. They enjoy seeing someone other than themselves at the receiving end of their mistress's acerbic tongue.

The next morning, the more than 30 attendees, dressed in their very best clothes, go the church in Jamestown where the House of Burgesses will hold its meeting. Mr. Chew wears a dark green doublet and pantaloons with golden trim and a cloak to match. The Jamestown ladies take the opportunity to show off, too. Decked out in their finest garments, they sit in the rear pews to bear witness to the historic occasion.

After leading the assembly in prayer, Governor West calls the meeting to order. There are some fine speeches rehashing various points made at supper the night before, but the contract for an exclusive tobacco contract with England passes unanimously. The burgesses also take up local matters and vote to prohibit any corn being traded with the "savages." Although the Indian tribes have been relatively quiet for the past two years, colonists heed calls for all households to strengthen their dwellings against attack. Finally they pass an ordinance against public drunkenness, and another requiring everyone to attend church on Sundays.

"We can't let things get lax in times of war," says William Tucker, who was one of the early settlers to arrive in Jamestown, coming on the ship that carried Governor West's brother, Lord De La Warr. Having led a number of successful military excursions against the Indians, his word carries weight and receives general approbation.

With a closing prayer, the governor ends the meeting, and the burgesses return to their domiciles. Some leave for home immediately, while others spend another night in Jamestown. Everyone ventures that the year is off to a splendid start and expects normal events to take their course. Everyone in Jamestown looks forward to the marriage of Temperance Yeardley and the governor, however small and intimate it may be.

Margaret starts to prepare her garden for planting and hopes that Captain Jope and John will visit soon. She resumes her nocturnal visits to the river to pray for their imminent return. On occasion she senses that someone or something is watching her and she feels apprehensive until, one moonlit night, she hears a branch crack nearby and sees a deer darting into the woods. From that point on, she feels comfortable, cheered by the silly thought that the forest animals are looking out for her and praying with her.

But one night as she walks up the bank to get back to the house, she has a strange, prickling sensation in the back of her neck, and it frightens her. Suddenly, a dark, heavyset figure looms before her, blocking her way. He grabs her roughly and throws her to the ground. Stunned, she tries to scramble away, but her attacker tosses her on her back, climbs on top, and starts to caress her body. His breath is heavy and foul and drenched with liquor. When the brute squeezes her breast painfully, Margaret cries out, and he clamps his hand over her mouth. As she desperately struggles beneath him, she feels his other hand clutching at her dress, yanking it up her thighs. She rakes her fingernails across his face, but he just grunts and slaps her so hard that her ears ring. Continuing his assault, he tries to pry her legs apart. Margaret fights him with every ounce of her strength, but he is more powerful.

Suddenly, she hears a voice yelling, "Get away from her!" followed by a loud thud.

Her assailant howls in pain and rolls off her. Holding his head, he totters to his feet and runs into the thicket by the river.

"Margaret. Are you all right?"

Looking up, she sees another dark figure standing over her. In contrast to her attacker, he is tall and thin. Relief washes over her when she recognizes William, the head butler. He is carrying a thick branch in his hand. Never has Margaret been so glad to see his pinched, disapproving face.

"Are you all right?" he asks again, this time with a note of concern in his voice.

"Yes," she says, catching her breath. "How did you—?"

"I've been watching you sneak out of the house at night for some time now, and I've been worried," he explains. "Good thing I came outside for a moment tonight and heard you cry out."

"Yes," Margaret says gratefully. "I can't thank you enough."

"It was nothing," he says. "I am responsible for everyone in the household."

He helps her up and steadies her when she sags against him. Margaret brushes off her dress as best she can.

As they walk slowly toward the house, he asks, "Did you recognize the man?"

Margaret shakes her head no. "It all happened so fast."

William sniffs contemptuously and says, "Probably one of the riffraff that came off the ship last year."

By the time they get back inside, Margaret has recovered enough from her ordeal to go to bed, although it takes her a long time to fall asleep.

The next morning, the house is abuzz with what happened to her. The other servants are shocked, angry, and solicitous. Even Mrs. Chew expresses her concern. Mr. Chew is especially outraged and vows to do whatever he can in his official capacity as a member of the Governor's Council, but Margaret asks him not to pursue the matter.

"I don't want to draw any more attention to myself about this," she says.

But over the next week, whenever she goes into town, she surreptitiously examines the faces of the men she meets, looking for any signs of scratches. While she doesn't see anyone, she continues to have nightmares from time to time and feels vulnerable. More than ever, she misses Captain Jope, with whom she always felt safe, and wishes there were someone like him in Jamestown who would take care of her. The one positive outcome is that William is now openly on her side and treats her with kindness and respect.

21

CHANGES OF FORTUNE

Jamestown—March 1628

In late March a pinnace arrives at Jamestown carrying a militiaman from Point Comfort. He brings news that an English man-of-war, the *Fortune*, has arrived with a large number of Africans aboard. They were taken in a raid on a Spanish slave ship off the coast of Angola on its way to Mexico. The British captain and privateer Arthur Guy wishes to trade them for tobacco and food.

Although the messenger reports directly to the governor, the news travels like wildfire around town. Francis West does not hesitate. The opportunity for getting workers to add to the colony's thin labor force is not to be missed. Within an hour, he sends the soldier back to Point Comfort with a letter to Francis Pott, informing him to clear the *Fortune* for travel upriver to dock at Jamestown.

Meanwhile, he calls a meeting of Jamestown's mercantile elite, Mr. Chew and Richard Stephens among them, to form an alliance to buy the Africans and profit by selling them to plantation owners throughout the colony. The men quickly agree and hammer out a plan. They send word to all the burgesses and their plantation managers in Virginia, informing them of the rare opportunity. They also commandeer all the soldiers protecting Jamestown and relay messages to other forts up and downriver, asking for reinforcements. Finally, they hire workmen to start constructing a simple holding pen on an empty meadow to the west of town.

That evening Mr. Chew takes Margaret aside and tells her to prepare herself for the arrival of the Angolans. "You will join the crew that will provide them with food and drink. Try to keep them calm and reassure them that they have nothing to worry about."

It is a rough night for her, filled with nightmares—frightening, helter-skelter images she hasn't experienced for years—of her burning village in Ndongo, the Imbangala attacking, she and John naked and chained on the way to Luanda and in the dark, fetid hold of the *San Juan Bautista*. Tossing in her bed, she awakens several times in a cold sweat.

The next day, everyone in town gathers excitedly in the square in anticipation of the *Fortune*'s arrival. Merchants and artisans have closed their shops as if it were a holiday, and the fishing tables on the pier have been cleared away early. Scouts head downriver on the lookout for the *Fortune*. By the time the ship rounds the last riverbend before approaching Jamestown, word has spread already, and the crowd surges toward the docks. Soldiers in uniforms and militiamen in leather doublets and breeches hold everyone back to allow the ship to anchor unimpeded.

Margaret is excited and troubled. Her "crew" consists of a few white servants and all of the Africans in Jamestown.

One of Temperance's remaining older maids, Ramona, stands next to her and whispers, "They want us to talk to them and keep them docile and happy."

Margaret considers that that is something Emmanuel Driggers would have said. She wishes that he were still here so that she could rely on his experience and leadership. She is surprised to see Lieutenant Shepherd commanding the soldiers lining the pier, muskets in their hands. When he notices her, he smiles and waves to her. Margaret wonders how far along he is in building his new homestead.

As the *Fortune* slowly approaches the dock, sailors from the main deck toss down thick ropes to the harbor hands below to tie them to the wooden mooring posts. An anchor drops into the water with a big splash. As soon as the gangplanks are laid across the gap, the Jamestown delegation—consisting of the harbormaster, Mr. Chew, Richard Stephens, and Dr. Pott—ascend to negotiate the terms of sale. Margaret catches a glimpse of Captain Guy, sword dangling at his side, welcoming them aboard. Like Captain Jope he has a commanding presence, although he looks younger, despite his full beard.

Guy invites the delegation to his cabin, and together they head to the interior of the ship. Meanwhile, seamen high above start to strike the sails. Some of them wave down from the ratlines, shrouds, and spars. Many of the children watching from below wave back. But since none of the Africans are visible aboard, the crowd soon grows restless.

Still, everyone waits until, two hours later, the delegation and the captain emerge on the quarterdeck, all smiling. While Dr. Pott and Stephens go below to inspect the cargo, Chew and the harbormaster return to the dock. They apprise Lieutenant Shepherd of what's about to happen. Dr. Pott and Stephens emerge on the main deck, nod down to their peers below with satisfaction, and confer once more with Captain Guy. He shouts orders to his men, and before long, the first Africans appear at the railing.

There are gasps from the crowd below. Several of the children point stubby fingers excitedly. But when the command, "Remove their shackles," echoes from above, everyone quiets and watches the first Africans walk down the gangplank. Some of them are so weak that their fellow passengers have to help them across the swaying timbers. It takes some time until the more than 100 Africans are gathered on the pier in a tight group. There are considerably more men than women. Most are naked and emaciated and shiver in the cool March breeze. Their eyes flit fearfully back and forth across the rows of gawking Jamestown denizens.

Dr. Pott, Stephens, Captain Guy, and his quartermaster, an older man with a scar across his forehead, bring up the rear. Up close, Guy's face looks just as leathery and weathered as Captain Jope's, but his dark, hooded eyes are more calculating.

He and the others head to the courthouse to meet with Governor West and to draw up the contract of sale, including a letter to the English secretary of state that Jamestown will send the agreed-upon number of hogsheads of tobacco to the English port of Yarmouth after the crop is harvested and cured in the fall. This gives Guy and his crew the opportunity to spend the summer roaming the Caribbean as privateers while knowing that a tidy profit in tobacco awaits them when the *Fortune* returns to England.

Meanwhile, the captain of the militia and his men start to herd the Angolans to the pen. They stagger slowly and awkwardly forward, having been imprisoned so long that their muscles have become weak and unreliable.

Margaret and the other servants walk ahead to a wagon loaded with food, water, and blankets. By the time soldiers have herded the Africans into the pen, Margaret and the others are ready with baskets of corn bread and buckets of water. As they start to walk among the arrivals, many of the spectators crowd around the wooden fencing and stare at the exhausted men and women with undisguised fascination.

Finally, Lieutenant Shepherd has enough and shouts, "These people need to rest and eat. Go home now. You can do your gawking later." Margaret thanks him under her breath as the grumbling crowd slowly disperses.

Steeling herself against the fetid smells emanating from the arrivals, who have had no opportunity to wash themselves for weeks, Margaret dispenses blankets for warmth and cover. She does her best to push away her own memories. It is even harder to still her anguish at witnessing such misery—men and women shivering on the cold grass, looking dull and lethargic, their eyes bereft of hope.

Ndongo words and phrases she hasn't spoken for a long time come back to her, and she says, over and over, "I am Margaret. You are safe now. Don't be afraid."

Some of the men and women perk up when they hear a familiar language. A few say their names—Caesar, Secundo, Francesca—and ask questions. Margaret tells them, "Later. Eat and drink first. We'll be back."

By the time all of the arrivals have been fed, a number have drifted off to sleep.

Margaret returns to the Chew residence exhausted and unsettled. Not since the Indian massacre and plague has she seen so many unhappy, frightened people. She wishes she could assure them that things will get better.

The next day, the *Fortune* is gone early, and the Jamestown residents spring into action. By the time planters and burgesses arrive from other parts of Virginia, the Angolans have had a chance to wash and put on the simple garments made for them.

Margaret converses with as many as she can, listening to their stories of being captured and answering their questions. As she tries to share some of her own history and telling them about life on the plantations, she often is at a loss for words. She stopped speaking Ndongo more than eight years ago, and her skills with the language are still those of a 10-year-old. She can understand the arrivals better than communicating to them what she has to say.

Some aspects of the New World are impossible to convey. When she tries to describe Indians and explain that they have reddish skin, she is met by bewilderment. She quickly apprehends by the incredulous, fearful looks she gets from the Africans that they either don't understand or don't believe her.

Discovering that many are from villages along the Kwanza River, she asks about Pongo and is disappointed that no one knows anything about her hometown, not even if it still exists.

At night she falls into a dog-tired sleep, and her rest is not as haunted as at first. When she wakes, she thinks about how far she has come in her journey from Angola and is grateful how different her life is by now from that of the new arrivals.

Margaret and the other black servants help the colony secretary, Colonel Claiborne, identify each of the arrivals by their Christian names—Francisco, Hannibal, Angela, Isabella—and in the cases where they don't seem to have one, provide it for them. By then, she knows which are husband and wife, although none of the women are pregnant. If there were any children, none have survived the voyage.

To prepare for the upcoming auction, carpenters build a wooden platform in Jamestown's central square. The day before, the plantation owners or their managers visited the holding pen to look at the men and women and decide who they want to buy.

Margaret sees John Upton among them, but when he recognizes her and says hello, she discovers to her surprise that he is not there on behalf of the Piercey plantation, but for himself.

"I bought out my contract of indenture and am renting land on the south side of the James River near Warrosquoake," he says proudly. "In time, I mean to buy it and have my own plantation. Richard Bennett has returned, you know. He intends to stay in Virginia."

Impressed by how quickly he attained his freedom, she says, "I wish you all the best. Please say hello to Anthony and Mary when you see them."

He smiles and replies, "Perhaps you will want to join me in my venture. I could use a good worker like you." He adds more softly, "There's no future for you here, Margaret. I'd make sure you're taken care of."

Margaret gives him a long look before answering, "I am honored and will give it due consideration."

"Do, Margaret." He sweeps his hand in the direction of the penned-up Africans and says, "None of them will get a contract of indenture."

Startled, Margaret asks, "Why not?"

"Governor West and the other burgesses decided not to give them any. What these Africans don't know, they won't ask for, and by the time they hear of it, if they do at all, it will be too late."

"So they'll be like slaves?"

"We will treat them better than that. But . . . yes."

Margaret is appalled but decides to say nothing. After Upton leaves, she remains lost in thought for some time. The presence of all these new Africans about to be sold makes her wonder about her own future.

On the day of the auction, a big crowd assembles around the platform on the central square in Jamestown, almost as large as for the arrival of the *Fortune*. The plantation owners and other bidders stand in front. They have all agreed to the terms laid out ahead of time. All proceeds are to be paid in tobacco later in the year.

One by one, the Angolan men and women are paraded up on the platform. Most stand there looking terrified, but a few glower at the assembled onlookers. Colonel Claiborne, sitting off to one side at a small table, calls out their names along with the price set by the Jamestown buyers' consortium. Many of the Africans go for the asking price or a bit more. But a bidding war develops over some of the stronger-looking men. Domingo, a tall, muscular black, and another who goes by the name of Bernardo bring more than twice the original asking price.

Margaret watches the event with anguish and growing alarm. When some of the married couples realize they are going to be separated, there are angry shouts, wails, and shrieks of distress. One husband and wife cling to one another so fiercely that it takes several attending soldiers to forcibly separate them.

It brings tears to Margaret's eyes. Thinking about Upton's words, she knows that the African couples are likely never to see each other again. If they had contracts, they could reunite after finishing out the terms of their indenture, but without they are bound to the whims of their masters.

By the time the last African is sold, the afternoon sun is low in the western sky, and Margaret is beset with weariness.

That evening at supper, Mr. Chew is in as celebratory a mood as she has ever seen him. For him and his partners, the auction was an unqualified success. "The profits exceed all of our expectations," he crows happily to his wife and guests and has his wineglass topped off several times.

Mrs. Chew is all aglow, too, no doubt thinking about what bauble or gown he will buy for her on his next trip to England.

Margaret does not share her master and mistress's joy and goes about serving him, Richard Stephens, and another town merchant quietly. She finds their easy laughter and self-congratulatory revels maddening in light of the pain they inflicted on the Africans.

Later that night as she goes to sleep, her thoughts are all in a tumble. Unbidden, an image of Lady Isabel at Aldwarke enters her head. "Keep your mind clear and rely on your faith," she says firmly. "You have been chosen."

The next morning, after breakfast, Margaret finds Mr. Chew in his study. She knocks on the door frame and says, "I wonder if you would spare me a moment of time."

Mr. Chew, although a bit hungover from the night before, is still in an expansive mood. Smiling broadly, he says, "Of course, Margaret. What is on your mind?"

Margaret says, "Thank you," and steps inside the room with determination. She takes a deep breath and continues, "I was wondering when my contract with you is up."

A look of puzzlement sweeps over Mr. Chew's face. "I don't understand," he says.

Calmly, Margaret reiterates, "I want to know when my contract of indenture with you is finished."

His shoulders tensing visibly, Mr. Chew glowers at her for a moment before his face takes on a cunning expression. "What has brought this on?" he asks.

When Margaret doesn't reply, an idea comes to his mind. "Of course, the auction yesterday! You heard about that."

"Yes," says Margaret.

Mr. Chew's eyes dart around the room. Then he looks at her with guile and says, "Well, there are several years to go. By my count at least five more years."

Margaret furrows her brows. She thinks for a moment, calculates using her fingers, and says, "I came to Virginia in the summer of 1621, and my contract was for seven years. By my count, that time is almost up."

Looking surprised—he figured the young woman would not be able to count at all—he drawls, "Well, Margaret, there is a problem. As you know, all papers burned during the Indian massacre, so there is no record of it."

Margaret is taken aback. "Do you doubt my word, sir? You told me at Warrosquoake that you would take care of it."

Mr. Chew clears his throat and says, "Oh no, nothing of the kind. But it bears looking into. Let me do that and get back to you."

Astonished, Margaret feels bile rise in her throat. She swallows and says slowly, "I would appreciate that, sir. When Captain Jope gets back, I'd like to be able to tell him that the matter is settled."

Chew's cheek twitches involuntarily. In a mawkish voice, he complains, "Don't you like it here? I know my wife can be difficult at times, but haven't I been more than fair to you?"

"You have, sir, that is true, and I thank you for it," Margaret replies. "But this is another matter entirely."

Chew scowls. "I thought you would be more loyal."

Margaret holds his indignant stare and says calmly, "I will await your answer," and leaves.

She does not hear back from him over the next two weeks, and Mr. Chew is dour-faced in her presence. His wife starts to pick on her again. Suddenly, Margaret can do nothing right. Mrs. Chew becomes so spiteful and vicious in her attacks that the other servants take notice and ask Margaret if anything has happened to provoke her rancor. Margaret shrugs and keeps her own counsel. To escape the vindictive atmosphere in the house, she spends as much time as possible in her garden.

* * *

One afternoon, Lieutenant Shepherd finds her there, digging and putting seeds in the ground. He is not dressed in uniform but wears travel clothes—leather boots, dark pants, a brown coat, and matching overcoat open at the front.

When she rises in greeting, he wastes no time and says, "My house is finished, and everything is ready for me to relocate to my plantation. I have come to see if you have changed your mind about going with me and running the household."

Margaret looks at him searchingly. She still feels vulnerable from the assault of the drunken lout who tried to rape her and is leery about moving to a more secluded place. But then she remembers Anthony saying, "The lieutenant is a good man," and makes up her mind.

"If you can settle the matter with Mr. Chew, I will gladly join you," she says. "But I have one condition: I must have a firm contract of indenture with you."

For a moment, Shepherd is speechless. He did not expect her to say yes, certainly not so quickly. Once again, he breaks out in his boyish grin and exclaims, "That is wonderful news! I will speak to Mr. Chew right away."

By the time he leaves, Margaret is working in the kitchen. When she hears nothing more from the lieutenant, she thinks that he did not succeed. But later that evening, Mr. Chew finds her and says, "This will be the last night you stay under my roof. Tomorrow you will go with Lieutenant Shepherd."

A surge of joy rises from her heart and fills her whole body, threatening to overwhelm her, but she composes herself and says, "Thank you, sir."

As she packs the few belongings in her room, she wonders what transpired between Mr. Chew and the lieutenant. Perhaps the merchant gave in meekly because he did not want to have to face Captain Jope's wrath. Then she says good-bye to the cook, the other servants, and the head butler. Most everyone expresses shock and astonishment. A few ask why.

Margaret has thought ahead of time about how she would answer. "I will be in charge of the whole household," she says.

The explanation seems to satisfy everyone and forestall further inquiries.

When she finds William and tells him, he screws up his face and looks at her disdainfully. Then he grins conspiratorially and says, "It's about time. All the best to you, Margaret."

The most surprising response comes from Ann. The young woman bursts into tears when she hears the news, but gathers herself enough to say, "I am happy for you, Margaret. At least you're getting away."

That evening, Mrs. Chew ignores her deliberately, tossing her head haughtily as she passes Margaret on the way to the stairs, but she cannot diminish Margaret's delight.

The next day, she joins Lieutenant Shepherd at his lodgings. He has a seven-year contract for her, and she signs "Margaret" slowly next to his, the first time she has written her name in many years, and she is pleased that she can still do it.

Later that morning, she steps into the pinnace that will take her across the river to her new life.

22

JOHN

The Atlantic Ocean—May–June 1628

John gazes from the main deck of the *Saker* at the receding coast of Brittany. He feels a dull knot of pain in his chest and wonders once again if he has made the right decision. The cawing of a seagull accompanying the merchant vessel distracts him from his thoughts. He follows the white bird's flight as it catches an upward draft and soars to join others hovering in the breezes that propel the ship forward.

From there, his eyes land on a sailor perched precariously on the spars as he lashes an additional sail in place to capture as much of the wind as possible on the open sea. Observing him, John remembers balancing high above the deck of the *White Lion* and muses that the crew he sailed with was more seaworthy. He realizes that he misses them. Deprived of activity, John wanders the deck aimlessly, unable to escape the memories of the past few months that are intruding on his solitude.

For a week after they arrived in Tavistock, the Jope mansion remained in mourning over the loss of little Margaret. The dreary December skies did nothing to dispel the somber mood inside, and John's occasional efforts to cheer Mary and the captain were met with sorrowful eyes and tightly pressed lips. They chose to spend much of the day praying together and attending to their remaining daughter. John often wondered if their bereavement would ever end.

Then one day after breakfast, Mary and the servants took down the black drapes and curtains, and the atmosphere inside the home brightened. John was pleased to hear bustling sounds return to the kitchen. The captain's gentle teasing brought a smile to his wife's face. He acted more solicitous toward her than John remembered from previous sojourns.

Two days later, while Jope went to see his brother to bring him his share of the *White Lion*'s bounty, Mary surprised John. After they finished lunch, she beckoned him to join her in the living room and sat down next to him on the sofa. John smelled the sweet odor from the pomander at her side. Her face still looked drawn, but her blue eyes were no longer red-rimmed and tired.

She contemplated him searchingly and said, "John told me last night that you want to leave us and go to Virginia." There was no reproach in her voice, but when John didn't say anything, she insisted, "I want to hear it from your own lips. Is your mind definitely made up?"

In a low voice he replied, "Yes, I want to make my own way in the world." Seeing a look of anguish cross her face, he quickly added, "I do not mean to cause you any pain."

Mary smiled wanly. "I know that, John. I'm being selfish. I have always enjoyed your company, and now I'm going to lose you, too."

John's eyes teared up, and before he knew it, words he had held back for too long spilled from his mouth. "I have to go. I don't belong here . . . never will . . . and the *White Lion* . . . it isn't really a home. I want to have a family at some point, like you and the captain, and I can't imagine that ever happening here."

Surprised at his passion, Mary said, "You have thought about this a great deal."

"I've struggled with it for some time. I know how valuable I am to the captain, how he has to rely on me for—"

Mary gasped. "So you know?"

John nodded. "Yes, his eyesight is getting worse. That's why he has me reading and doing the writing for him. It's not just to teach me."

She sighed. John watched her fingers fuss with her skirt.

Then she asked, "Is it about Margaret in Virginia?"

John's mind was a jumble of thoughts and emotions. Unsure how to respond, he remained silent. Mary closed her eyes for a moment and seemed to reach a decision. When she opened them again, John was surprised by the acceptance and kindness radiating from her face.

She took his hand in hers, squeezed it lightly, and said, "I understand."

For a while they sat together in silence, lost in thought. Then Mary leaned forward and kissed John on the forehead. Straightening her dress, she rose and said again, "I understand," adding, "It is your destiny."

The conversation changed something in their relationship, as if their shared knowledge settled things between them and allowed them to enjoy each other's company. Still, John observed Mary looking at him from time to time as if she wished to etch him in her memory. Caught, she would flush red and quickly look away.

John was glad that Jope didn't bring up the topic of his leaving for some time. It gave him a few weeks to relax and enjoy the time with the people he loves.

But the Sunday after the Feast of the Epiphany, the captain found him and said, "Let's go for a walk."

It was a gray day. There were patches of snow on the ground, and the air was heavy with moisture. Bundled into their coats with shawls covering their necks, they trudged in silence to the pond in the woods behind the mansion, their favorite spot. The edges were rimmed with a thin layer of ice, but the interior was open. Jope picked up a flat stone and skipped it across the exposed surface, counting the splashes before it disappeared into the dark water.

Then he said, "I have thought long and hard about what you wish to do, John, and discussed it with Mary, too. I have come to the conclusion that we should ask William Ewen for help."

John remembered the merchant well from their encounters at Plymouth Harbor and had a favorable impression of him. As he and Jope explored various options, John grew excited about his future. Back at the house, the captain dictated a letter to John and sent it to Ewen at his London address.

While waiting for a reply, Jope advanced John's training in the use of weapons. He drilled the youngster hard, often to the point of exhaustion, as if he wanted to instill in him everything he knows in the short time left to them. John didn't mind. He welcomed the feeling of emptiness after a hard workout.

In the meantime, he continued to participate in all aspects of the Jope household—going to see relatives, attending church on Sundays, and helping around the house—but although everyone treated him as a member of the family, he began to feel like a visitor, a stranger. He looked for the postman each day and was disappointed when there was no reply from London.

As the time approached to ship out for the season, John became increasingly worried that his future would remain unsettled for another year. Jope kept postponing his departure for the Caribbean to the point that Gareth started getting worried and sent letters warning that many of the veterans who have sailed on the *White Lion* in the past were getting restless and that some were hiring on to other privateering ships leaving Plymouth.

Finally, in early April a letter from Ewen arrived, apologizing for the delay and inviting Jope and John to come to London. Immediately, the captain hired a carriage to take them there. They said perfunctory good-byes to Mary and promised to return within a fortnight.

The four-day trip gave them plenty of time to discuss what to expect. Jope persuaded John that it was best for him to go to Virginia under a contract of indenture. If he arrived as a free man with substantial means—his share of the privateering booty—it would raise eyebrows and lead to awkward questions about his history. For the same reason, John needed to travel there on a ship other than the *White Lion.* Upon arrival he should claim that he spent time as a servant in the Netherlands. The less association with Jope and England, the better.

At night, when they stopped at roadside inns, Jope paid for a room and snuck John inside, away from prying eyes and wagging tongues. They took meals together in private and shared the lumpy straw beds.

By the time they reached London, they were tired from the journey. But as they entered the city, John perked up. None of his stopovers in Caribbean ports or Plymouth had prepared him for London's enormous size. As the carriage clattered along the streets, past alleys and public squares, he was awed by the throng of people everywhere. The sights of walking tradesmen, and sounds of hawkers selling all kinds of goods and wares and calling for passersby to visit alehouses and brothels, amazed him. Less pleasant was the pervasive stench of trash, rotten meat and vegetables, offal, and horse manure that assaulted his nose. He was shocked when he saw a young woman empty a chamber pot from the second story of a house onto the street below.

It was late afternoon when they arrived at an inn in Greenwich, on the south side of the Thames River close to the wharfs and docks. After settling into a room, Jope sent a note informing William Ewen of their arrival. By the time they received a reply inviting them to meet at him his house the next morning, it was already dark outside.

Since Ewen's home was within walking distance, they set off after breakfast. It was a blustery spring morning with frosty breezes coming off the river. Once again, John marveled at the bustling street traffic—carriages and wagons being pulled by horses and oxen, dockworkers carrying heavy sacks on their broad shoulders to load onto ships. No one paid any attention to them.

By the time they reached the townhouse—an impressive, three-story sandstone edifice—John felt overwhelmed. He couldn't imagine ever living in a place this busy, noisy, and malodorous. He was grateful to leave the raucous environment behind when they walked through the large wrought-iron gate into well-kept, quieter surroundings. As they strode toward the covered entrance, a butler opened the large oak door as if he had been waiting for their arrival and ushered them into a large sitting room. John marveled at the high ceiling lined with dark-stained beams and the large paintings hanging on the wall. He imagined that they were portraits of the merchant and his family. Only at Aldwarke had he seen such a lavish display of wealth.

Soon a door opened, and William Ewen walked into the room. He was as voluble as ever, greeting Jope like an old friend. "Hello, John, it is good to see you," he bellowed. "I'm sorry I was detained on business in the Netherlands and did not receive your letter until I got back." Then he turned to John, smiled, and with a crafty look said, "I am certain I can be of help accommodating your wishes, John."

Then Ewen offered Jope a pipe of tobacco. When the captain declined, Even asked humorously, "Not even my own crop from Virginia?"

Jope grinned and shook his head. "You know that I don't indulge."

"I hope that doesn't mean you'll drive a hard Calvinist bargain, Captain," Ewen teased as he prepared a pipe for himself and lit it from the fire crackling in the large stone hearth. He gestured to a nearby sofa and settled in a comfortable chair across from the captain and his young charge.

For the next hour, surrounded by the sweet, pungent aroma of tobacco smoke, they discussed how best to settle John on College

Land, the plantation Ewen owns across the river from Jamestown. They agreed on a seven-year contract of indenture. It seemed a long time to John, but Jope had prepared him. He understood that Ewen is, above all, a businessman who expects to reap a benefit even when he is being helpful.

At some point the merchant said, "You will like it at College Land, John. All the books from another plantation, called Henrico, were stored there after the Indians destroyed it during the great massacre of 1622. You'll have plenty to read when you're not otherwise too busy."

When the discussion reached the point of John traveling to the New World, Ewen agreed with Jope that embarking from the Netherlands would be best. That would leave no record of the captain's involvement and allow John's origins to remain suitably obscure.

"I'd be happy to convey you there on my ship," said Ewen, "but the *Charles* is under way with goods for New England." He took a puff on his pipe, thought for a moment, and continued, "I do know a ship that is due to depart from Vlissingen to Virginia—the *Saker*. And I know the captain who owns it. In fact, he named it after himself."

"When will it sail?" John asked eagerly.

"In a week."

John's heart sank. "That won't do," he said ruefully. "It isn't enough time for us to go back to Tavistock, pack up my things, and get there."

"Unless . . . ," Jope mused. He turned to Ewen and asked, "How soon can you have the documents for us?"

"I will take care of them this afternoon. Come back tomorrow."

Jope rose. "Then we must be on our way and get ready."

When John started to protest, Jope gave him a fierce warning glance. Cowed, John told Ewen, "I can't thank you enough for your troubles, sir. We will see you in the morrow."

Ewen bowed in return and rang for the butler to show them out.

When they were outside, Jope stopped on the paved path. He gripped John's shoulder and said with a serious expression, "We will go to Vlissingen directly from here. I will purchase what you need this afternoon."

Dismayed, John stammered, "But, but . . . I w-won't be able to say good-bye to Mary!"

Jope squeezed his shoulder kindly, but said firmly, "You will write to her. She will understand."

The impact of leaving right away didn't hit John until they got back to the inn. After Jope left their room, John suddenly felt a searing pain in his stomach and doubled over. Tears streamed down his cheeks, and he sat on the wooden floor for a long time. By the time he recovered, the pain had become a dull knot in his chest.

He wiped his eyes, stood up, and walked to the writing desk in the corner. He found a sheet of parchment in one of the drawers, poured ink into a small metal bowl, and sharpened the feather quill. Then, slowly and carefully, he started writing.

Later, when Jope returned carrying a small travel chest, a shirt, an extra pair of trousers, a leather purse, and a woolen blanket, he found John staring out the window. After looking over the purchases, John read the letter out loud to him. He saw tears well up in the captain's eyes.

"Mary will appreciate this," he said. To change the mood, he added, "I have another gift for you."

From behind his back, Jope brought out a brand-new flintlock pistol, made of brass and polished walnut, and held it out to John. "Here, for you."

John was dumbfounded. He took it, weighed it in his hand, ran his fingers over the smooth, curved handle, and aimed it at the wall.

"It is beautiful," he said. "I don't know how to thank you."

"I figured you'll need something to protect yourself against the bears and savages," Jope responded offhandedly.

That brought a smile to John's face, a moment of joy in a melancholy patch of time.

The next few days were a blur for John: meeting with Ewen, signing the two identical contracts—one for the merchant to keep, the other for John to take to Virginia along with a letter of introduction to Thomas Goodman, the plantation manager at College Land. Traveling down the Thames River in a pinnace. An uneventful passage to Vlissingen. Sailing up the Scheldt River and passing the gabled façades of the homes of wealthy Dutch burghers, with the twin spires of the church rising behind them.

They found Captain Saker, a sullen-faced man with small, beady eyes, aboard his merchant ship, a three-masted frigate. Jope introduced himself as an agent for William Ewen given the task of making travel arrangements to take the Dutch servant boy to Virginia. While Saker slowly deciphered the letter from the merchant to him, Jope and John cast their eyes about the frigate. A look passed between them acknowledging that the vessel was shipshape enough for the transatlantic voyage.

If Saker harbored any suspicion at taking on another passenger so close to casting off, the letter satisfied him. He actually smiled when Jope didn't haggle over the price he asked, even though it was considerably more than the going rate.

Before they left to get John's few belongings at the inn, Jope said, loud enough for the captain and some of the crew to hear, "I'll be sending your money after you, lad."

Later in their room, he handed John several pieces of silver and advised, "Put two in your purse and hide the others on you. I'll bring the rest when I come to Virginia. No need to test how greedy these knaves are."

During their last meal together, they agreed to say their good-byes in the morning and keep up the act of being strangers at the dock. John had no appetite and stabbed listlessly at the pieces of roast duck on his plate.

Looking at him with his keen blue eyes, Jope said, "I know it's hard to part, John, but we will see each other again—if not this fall, then next year, for sure. I am confident we will. I know it!"

John nodded gratefully, wanting to believe him to stem the tide of desperation threatening to inundate him. Having agreed with Mary not to raise the question of Jope's eyesight, he thought of other things to say. There was another matter. He had not planned to mention it, but now he decided he couldn't keep quiet about it. He took a deep breath and said, "I am glad Mary is with child again."

The captain's jaw dropped in surprise, and John realized that he really didn't know.

An array of conflicting feelings crossed Jope's face before he exclaimed, "How can you be sure? How do you know?"

"She told me before we left and swore me to secrecy."

As the news sank in, a beatific smile broke out on the captain's face. He laughed giddily and said, "This is wonderful news! Thank you for telling me. I will do my best to act surprised when she decides to let me in on the secret."

"I doubt you'll be able to sneak anything past Mary," said John, grinning.

He watched Jope's face darken for a moment, considering a reply and then deciding to remain silent and smiling instead.

The next morning, they embraced each other in the room for a long time. When they finally let go, John clenched his hands, determined not to betray any of his feelings.

They walked to the dock in silence, John carrying his belongings in a small strongbox under his arm. The knot in his chest ached fiercely as he made his way up the gangplank. When he stepped onboard the *Saker*, he glanced back. Jope gave him a casual hand wave, turned, and walked away.

Thinking about their paltry good-byes brings tears to John's eyes. He looks up and sees that the seagulls no longer accompany the ship. The brisk ocean winds fill the sails, and the *Saker* speeds along, cutting through the undulating waves. Looking back toward shore, John can no longer see land. He turns to watch the deckhands going about their tasks. It feels odd to be an idle traveler after his many years as a cabin boy and mate's helper. He would love to join the sailors and occupy his thoughts with work. But when he tells Captain Saker that he would be happy to help and pitch in, the dour mariner refuses, worried for the safety of his passenger.

23

JOPE

Plymouth—May 1628

The carriage taking Captain Jope from his home in Tavistock to Plymouth rattles along the rutted road, bounding over occasional rocks and tree roots. Mists rise from the meadows and fields, glowing in the early morning sunlight. Open patches reveal delicate spring green grass and budding leaves, but Jope pays no attention. He is eager to get back to the *White Lion* and set sail for the Caribbean. Although he is nearly two months behind most other privateers stalking Spanish ships, he is determined to succeed with a vengeance and become the Flying Dutchman again.

After watching the *Saker* disappear around the seawall of the Vlissingen harbor, he had walked to the inn to gather his belongings. Exhausted from a sleepless night and the rush to see John off, he'd felt spent and empty inside. Returning to the docks, he hired a pinnace to take him directly to Plymouth. With a brisk breeze blowing from the east, the ship made good time.

As they entered the English Channel, Jope suddenly experienced a wave of relief wash over him, as if a heavy burden had been lifted from his shoulders. The feeling of freedom surprised him until he realized that he did not have to worry about John's education, safety, and well-being anymore. Although he cared about him, the youngster's fate was no longer in his hands. Still, he wondered if he had fulfilled his duty regarding him and Margaret. Not until he saw them well established and thriving in the New World would he feel completely at peace.

But first he had to settle financial matters, provide security for his growing family, and fulfill his obligations toward his brother. He was not getting any younger, and the prize of raiding a Spanish silver galleon that would make him rich and take care of Mary and his children for good still eluded him.

Upon arrival in Plymouth, Jope had the pinnace take him directly to the *White Lion*. He was pleased to see that the ship was in good order and that Gareth and his men had stocked ammunition and dry goods in anticipation of a quick departure.

"Get a crew together and finish loading provisions. You have my authority. I want to sail in three days' time," he said.

"We can accomplish that," his quartermaster said confidently. He hesitated for moment before asking, "How is John?"

"On his way," Jope answered tersely. "I'll be back in three days. Be ready for departure."

He had himself rowed ashore, hired a horse, and gone straight to Tavistock. He hardly noticed the green forests and meadows on the way and thought only about how best to tell Mary what had happened.

When he arrived at his home, he leaped off his mount, handed the reins to his groom, and hurried inside, brushing past the startled maid, who was expecting the postman. He found Mary sitting on the sofa in the living room, knitting a shawl.

Her startled expression turned to pleasure. "You're back!" she exclaimed, her eyes shining with joy.

Jope rushed to her side and kissed her hands. The words tumbled from his lips in a torrent of affection. "I am so pleased, my darling. Why didn't you tell me? I do hope it is a boy," he said.

Mary looked at him with humorous exasperation and said, "So John told you. That young man needs to learn to keep a secret! I'll have to scold him. Where is he?"

This was the moment Jope had dreaded, but he plunged ahead, his face impassive. "He is on his way to Virginia. There was a ship leaving from Vlissingen. We had to hurry and go there directly. It was the only way to catch it in time."

Digging in the pocket of his overcoat, he retrieved John's letter and handed it to her. Mary unfolded the piece of parchment and read it out loud:

Dear Mary, I am writing to say good-bye. Events have overtaken us and I am leaving tomorrow for good. Captain Jope will explain. I can't thank you enough for all the good will you have shown me. If destiny so wills it, we will see each other again. Until then, may good fortune shine on you and your children. I will never forget you. John.

By the time she finished, her eyes glistened with tears. She leaned back and sighed. "I had an inkling that he would not come back, but I didn't want to heed it," she said softly. "So much leave taking, so much sorrow. I just hope he'll be safe and make a good life for himself and Margaret."

"John will do well at Ewen's plantation. He is nothing if not industrious," Jope said eagerly.

Mary gazed at him, resigned. "I suppose that means you'll be going, too?"

He nodded. "The day after tomorrow."

She took his hand, keeping the knitting in her lap. Then she set the needles aside, gave him a weary smile, and moved close to him. "Then let's make the most of it," she said and kissed him.

They spent the days in each other's company, taking walks in the balmy spring air, talking about their plans for the future. At night they stayed up late, wrapped in each other's arms, Jope taking comfort in her soft embrace.

At some point Mary raised the question that had been on her mind for some time: "Who will do your reading and writing for you now?"

243

Jope realized once again that she knew more about him than she let on, and that keeping things from her was foolish. But he did not worry her more than necessary and said, "Don't worry, I can write well enough, and Gareth will be my eyes when I need help with documents and charts."

The answer seemed to satisfy Mary. But the following morning when he left at dawn and saw her framed in the front door, waving after him, a dejected expression on her face, Jope wasn't so sure. Raising his hand in reply, he tightened his jaws and turned his thoughts to the challenges ahead.

The memory is hard to bear. Fortunately, despite the occasional bumps in the road, Jope nods off at some point and wakens only when the carriage reaches the outskirts of Plymouth and slows down.

By the time they reach the dock, he is eager to get going. He pays off the coachman and paces impatiently until the rowboat arrives to take him to the *White Lion*. He is pleased to see the unfurled sails ready to be lashed to the spars and hopes that Gareth has everything else organized as well.

When he gets to the hull, he clambers up the rope ladder and leaps aboard the main deck like a man a decade younger, his sword clanging against the railing. His vigorous appearance surprises tars who have sailed with him before. He reaches the quarterdeck in quick, easy strides. Gareth and Samuel Teague salute, beaming with pride and excitement at their captain's unexpected vigor.

Jope greets them and looks over the assembled crew. His bright blue eyes sparkle with delight as he tells his quartermaster, "I am pleased there are so many veterans from before."

"Your reputation is worth its weight in gold," says Gareth, smiling.

"Is everything ready?"

"Aye, aye, Captain, shipshape and ready!" Gareth shouts loud enough for everyone to hear.

"Then let us pray and head for the open sea!"

A roar of approbation rises from the main deck. Jope turns to sailors and quiets them. He removes his wide-brimmed hat and gets to his knees. The men below follow suit. His prayer is as eloquent as any he has ever preached. He speaks passionately of the men's God-given purpose to defeat the heathen Spanish wherever they find them. He inspires them with visions of serving England and Christendom while not forgetting to rouse them with promises of riches and treasure. When he finishes with a stirring, "It is our destiny," the men erupt into cheers as one.

Jope rises, turns to Gareth and Teague, and shouts, "It is time!"

The navigator heads below to join the helmsman at the whipstaff. Gareth blows his whistle, and the men scatter about the ship, each keen to do his part. Jope watches them head to the capstan to hoist the anchor, and climb the ratlines to the spars to make fast the fluttering sails until they swell and billow in the wind.

Bestriding the deck, his arms akimbo, he squints at the harbor entrance where the flickering light dances on the waves. He grins and says to Gareth, "Perhaps we'll beat John to the New World. He has a layover in Bermuda, after all."

As the *White Lion* clears the seawall and heads toward the channel, a deep sense of pride and satisfaction comes over him. He realizes that, as much as he loves Mary, his daughter, and soon-to-be-born son—he is certain that the child will be a boy—this is what thrills him more than anything. This is what he is made for.

24

MARGARET

Virginia—Summer 1628

For Margaret, going to Lieutenant Shepherd's land feels like starting over. Accommodations are modest and rudimentary, reminding her of the early days at Warrosquoake when everything was still under construction. The carpenters and roof thatchers Shepherd hired to put up the main house did a good job, finishing walls and wooden floors before they left. But except for a few furnishings—Shepherd's bed, a dining room table, a few storage chests, sitting benches and stools—the interior is spartan and bare.

Margaret takes the servant's room off to one side and sleeps on a makeshift wooden pallet covered with a straw mattress. It is not as comfortable as her bed at the Chew residence, but she doesn't mind. Nor does the smell of pine sap from the freshly cut timbers bother her. She actually gets a better night's sleep than she has for months.

She is less happy when she first sees the kitchen out back, which is little more than a shed with a brick hearth, dirt floor, and walls that still have the wattle showing on the inside. Outfitted like a soldier's camp, it has only a large cast-iron pot that can be hung over a fire, a frying pan, a ladle, a few knives and spoons, and some pewter plates and cups. She immediately demands that Shepherd purchase other essential items for her the next time he is in Jamestown.

He does not argue and says, "That is why I brought you here—to tell me what we need to make this a real home."

When she first arrived and Shepherd introduced her to his other three workers, Margaret was surprised to recognize one of them—a soldier from the fort near Warrosquoake. In fact, she had successfully nursed him back to health during the pestilence when so many others didn't survive.

Jason was no longer the scrawny youth she remembered. He had filled out and looked robust, although his reddish hair still refused to behave and stood out in tufts at all angles. His eyes lit up when he saw her, and he greeted her with genuine delight.

"I am pleased to see you again, Margaret, and very happy that you're going to be here with us," he said.

He walked with a slight limp, and later, when they had a chance to catch up, he told her that he was now a civilian. He had suffered a wound in a skirmish with the Indians and could no longer endure the long marches required when going on campaigns. Lieutenant Shepherd had hired him as overseer in anticipation of when the plantation was ready to grow tobacco, at which time the ranks of the field laborers would swell considerably.

The other two, Paul and Thomas, were indentured workers, young men recently arrived from London. Although inexperienced at farm work, their hands were covered with calluses already from wielding axes, shovels, and saws to clear the land around the house. They looked at Margaret with uncertainty and undisguised fascination, and she realized that they had never seen an African up close before.

Their awkwardness amused Margaret at first. But later, when Thomas's furtive glances suggest more than just passing interest, she becomes wary. She has seen plenty such looks before, and by now she understands what they mean. After what happened to her at Mr. Chew's residence, she knows she has to remain on guard.

Her worries are laid to rest one afternoon when she comes back from the river and overhears Jason say, "What about Margaret?"

She puts down her pail, carefully sneaks closer, and hides behind a button bush. The men, taking a break from felling trees, are sitting on the horizontal trunks, their faces covered in sweat and grime.

"So the lieutenant brought his doxy to live with him," Paul says. "Can't blame him."

Jason's answer startles her with its intensity. "Margaret is not his mistress, and we'll have no talk like that!"

Thomas laughs and asks, "So she is available then? Wouldn't mind playing at hot cockles with her."

In an instant Jason leaps to his feet, grabs him by the front of his shirt with both fists, and hoists him from the tree trunk he's been sitting on. "If you ever show disdain for Margaret again, in word or in person, you won't be able to walk straight for a long time," he snarls.

"We were just funning," Thomas squeezes out weakly.

"No need to get upset," Paul adds quickly.

"Do I make myself clear?"

Only when Thomas nods fearfully does Jason put him down.

Margaret tiptoes away, smiling to herself.

That evening at supper, Paul and Thomas eye Margaret cautiously. She acts like she knows nothing about what happened, but gives Jason an extra piece of meat.

In the ensuing days, the young men treat her with deference. Thomas even offers to fetch water for her in the mornings, and Margaret accepts gratefully. Not having to carry the heavy bucket down the ravine to the river and back again before daybreak is a big help and gives her more time to get breakfast ready.

From that point on, Margaret feels comfortable even during Lieutenant Shepherd's frequent absences, when militia business takes him to Jamestown and beyond. For his part, he is happy to see her upon his return and compliments her for the work she has done, yet he always treats her with a sense of formality and respect.

When she creates a garden near the house on some of the cleared land and starts to put in herbs, medicinal plants, and flowers, he says, pleased, "I was hoping you would do that."

Shepherd is not an aloof plantation owner, however. When at home he continues to make improvements on the house and does his share of the backbreaking work of clearing away the forest. Soon there is enough arable land to start growing corn and other vegetables, and Margaret helps with the planting and weeding. Meanwhile, the men continue to fell trees and remove shrubs. Shepherd has ambitious plans. He wants to have enough fields to grow his first tobacco crop the following year.

Margaret's days are filled with work and activities. Besides cooking, baking, and serving meals, she has her hands full—washing, cleaning, taking care of the chickens and goats, darning clothes, and tending her garden. There are so many things to do that she never feels like she can get on top of them all. She looks forward to the time Lieutenant Shepherd takes a wife who will relieve her of some of the burden of running the household.

Still, she finds time to explore the surrounding forest and realizes how much she has missed being in nature. Margaret loves walking on the supple ground of composting leaves and pine needles and smelling the musty air under the shady canopy of oaks, maples, and hickory trees. Collecting mushrooms, herbs, and wild berries, she often sees deer, rabbits, foxes, and opossums and delights in the sounds of woodpeckers, sparrows, and other songbirds.

The men come to appreciate her cooking after such excursions. Although Paul and Thomas wrinkled their noses the first time they smelled a stew flavored with thyme and hyssop and nibbled at it gingerly, they quickly discovered they liked the taste and found the raspberries for dessert an unexpected treat. Now, after a day of hard physical labor, they wolf down whatever Margaret puts in front of them.

On Sunday mornings, they all walk to Lawne's Creek Church together. It takes nearly an hour to get there because they have to use a rowboat to cross Chippokes Creek. From the surrounding lands on Hogg Island and its environs, settlers, plantation owners, and their servants gather at the wood-frame building sitting on a high, wooded promontory between two ravines leading down to the James River. The planters take turns reading from the Bible, giving sermons, and leading the congregation in hymns and prayer.

The first time Margaret attends, she recognizes several owners and burgesses, including John Uty and his wife, Ann, the overseer from Captain Samuel Matthew's plantation, as well as the three servants from Mr. Chew's plantation, who are surprised to see her. She is especially pleased when the workers from College Land arrive in a small pinnace, and there are three Africans among them—Michael and Katherine, who are a married couple, and Matthew, whose quiet sense of humor and twinkle in his eyes remind her of Emmanuel Driggers. They are excited to see her, too, having been among the Africans Captain Jope brought to Virginia on the *White Lion*. It feels good to have a small *malungu* community whose shared memories go all the way back to Ndongo.

The church is located on a pretty spot with Jamestown visible upriver on the opposite shore. After the service, people take the opportunity to walk, socialize, and share news from other parts of Virginia and beyond.

The latest gossip concerns the Piercey family. When the cape merchant's widow, Frances West Piercey, informed the court in Jamestown in late March that she had inventoried all of her departed husband's belongings, no one imagined that she would remarry so soon. Like Temperance Yeardley, who waited only four months after her husband died to wed Governor West, Frances found Captain Samuel Matthews, a well-connected planter, who owned a number of plantations along the James River and had close ties to the governor. Their nuptials were held in a small ceremony at Matthews's Manor near Blunt Point. Both of Piercey's daughters refused to attend, claiming they were still in mourning. In turn—or as some suggested, in retaliation—Frances refused to give her stepdaughter

Elizabeth permission to marry Richard Stephens, insisting that she was too young. That did not please the young couple at all, and they promptly eloped on a ship to England. Apparently, Stephens's mother still resides there and is likely to be more favorably disposed to their union. Everyone is waiting to find out how this will affect Abraham Piercey's will. There is a great deal of money at stake, and it seems Elizabeth is risking it all for love.

Margaret is happy for her and Stephens, delighted that they have the courage to take their future into their own hands. She is also glad that she didn't miss an opportunity to see Frances and Peter again. She was beginning to regret not being able to attend the wedding.

During the week, Margaret looks forward to these Sunday gatherings, which provide a welcome respite from the busy work and the isolation at Shepherd's plantation. In time, she finds that she doesn't miss Jamestown at all, certainly not the poisonous atmosphere of the Chew household.

One night after a long, exhausting day, Margaret falls into bed dead-tired. Before she drifts off to sleep, she takes stock of her situation. Although she would prefer that her indenture contract with Shepherd did not run to another seven years, it is a small price to pay for leaving the Chews without any strings attached. At least this contract is safely filed away in the court records in Jamestown. Overall, she is happy where she has landed, even if it is a bit lonely. If only John and Captain Jope would come to visit soon. Little does she know how soon part of her wish will come true.

25

ARRIVAL

*The Atlantic Ocean and Virginia—
Summer 1628*

The other passengers on the *Saker* are a collection of servants and laborers, haggard white men and women with pockmarked faces and sallow complexions. Not sure what to make of John, they eye him with suspicion and keep to themselves. More muscular and better dressed than them, yet unable to join in their Dutch conversations, he imagines he must seem like a strange creature to them, a blackamoor from another world. When they all disembark at Bermuda, John is happy to see them go.

He stays aboard while the crew takes on drinking water and other provisions. When they cast off the next day, he is the only passenger left aboard, along with the cargo of tools, hardware, and household goods bound for Virginia. He likes not having to share his cabin with others and endure their snoring. For the first time in weeks, he gets a good night's sleep.

The days pass slowly and uneventfully. With nothing to do, John gets bored. The voyage seems to take forever, certainly much longer than his previous trips across the Atlantic. The vast emptiness of the ocean that he used to enjoy watching from his private perch in the *White Lion's* crow's nest now feels oppressive.

To pass the time, he pays closer attention to the way the ship is run. The crew is a mix of veterans and greenhorns. The inexperience of the novice sailors leads to frequent miscommunications and delays. John smiles when he hears the old sea dogs barking their orders repeatedly in frustration when things take too long. One of the cabin boys, a mere stripling, often gets cuffed and yelled at by the more experienced tars, who are as rough as any of the privateers John sailed with. He remembers getting hazed aplenty himself, but he also had Captain Jope and Gareth looking out for him.

One afternoon John notices the youngster hiding in a cranny behind two large canvas-covered bales to escape from the taunts. He is trying to repair a frayed rope. John moves closer and, when the startled boy tries to bolt, holds him back.

"What is your name, lad?" he asks quietly.

"Henry," says the boy, his eyes darting nervously back and forth.

Hunkering down next to him, John takes the rope and says, "Here, let me show you how."

He demonstrates how to interlace the raveled ends and wrap them with heavy thread. Then he hands the mended rope to Henry and says, "Good as new."

Amazed, the youngster says, "Thank you, sir. I'm much obliged to you."

John smiles to himself. No one has ever called him "sir" before. He considers showing him how to tie a special knot when the boy's grateful countenance takes on a sly expression.

"You've been to sea before, haven't you, sir?" he asks. Before John can protest, he adds, "You walk like a sailor, not like a landlubber."

Surprised at how observant the boy is, John bends toward him and whispers conspiratorially, "You're right, Henry, but we'll let that be our little secret, won't we?" and is rewarded with an eager, cunning nod.

From that moment on, John is on alert, worrying that perhaps others on board also have realized that he is traveling under false pretenses and isn't a Dutch laborer at all. He tries to adjust his gait and watches the other sailors more carefully. Except for giving him an occasional glance, most don't pay much attention to him.

The next afternoon, however, John catches a brawny deckhand looking up at him as he passes by, eyeing him with a predatory expression. When he notices John staring back, he quickly looks away.

Henry, swabbing the deck farther on, whispers, "Watch out for him. Barnard and his mate are up to no good."

John smiles at him and says, "Thank you for the warning."

After supper that evening, John goes to sleep in his cabin with a feeling of unease. In the middle of the night he wakes all of a sudden. He wants to sit bolt upright, but a beefy hand clamps over his mouth and his arms feel immobilized. In the pale moonlight coming in the window, he recognizes the thick-set deckhand from earlier that day looming over him, wheezing, and smells his fetid breath.

Another voice rasps, "Be still, lad, and nothing will happen to you. We just want to have a look inside that travel chest of yours."

Realizing there are two of them, John wills himself to relax. The brute on top of him slackens his grip and reaches for the key around John's neck. He pulls hard, but the leather thong is too strong and won't break. Irritated, he lets go of one of John's arms to use both hands. When he yanks at the strap, John reaches for the dagger he's hidden by his side and slashes it across the face of his assailant. Howling in pain, the thug rears back.

In a flash John slips from the grip of the other attacker, rolls off the bunk, comes up next to him, and shoves the knife against his neck. He thrusts the point just a bit farther, enough to draw blood, and growls, "Leave now and I won't speak of this to the captain. Come back at me again, and I will slit both your throats. Understand?"

The man he slashed has both of his hands pressed to his bleeding cheek. He nods vigorously and backs away. The other follows carefully as John keeps the dagger at his throat. When they are gone, he closes the cabin door behind them. He does not think they will come back, but he is too wound up to go back to sleep. Smiling grimly, he thinks, *Captain Jope would be proud. He has taught me well!*

The next morning, Henry grins and gives him thumbs up when he sees John come on deck to go to breakfast. Some of the other sailors look at him doubtfully, and a few nod to him with admiration and respect. He does not see either of his assailants, but the following day he comes across Barnard, the stocky sailor. A dark red line runs underneath his black and purple eye. His partner wears a scarf around his neck. Both avoid looking at him.

John takes to wearing his dagger prominently at his belt, and no one bothers him for the rest of the voyage.

Still, he is relieved when they finally sight land. Surrounded by terns and seagulls, the *Saker* travels along the coast. One morning, it enters the Chesapeake Bay and arrives at Point Comfort before noon. The captain seems to be a regular trader with the colony because the harbormaster treats him like a familiar visitor and clears the ship to head to Jamestown in no time.

With each mile they sail upriver, the air becomes warmer—more humid and less salty. John stands in the bow, nervous and excited. He holds onto the beakhead and looks for natural formations he might recognize from before. The banks on either side are covered in dark green forest, making it difficult to get his bearings, but as the ship rounds the tip of Hogg Island, he remembers the place where he and Captain Jope met Margaret.

Ahead in the distance on the starboard side, he sees tiny houses—Jamestown—and the afternoon's golden sun above the landscape beyond. He expects to head in that direction and is surprised that the *Saker* continues to turn and sail toward the southern shore. Soon a large wooden dock comes into view up ahead with a small pinnace anchored at its side.

Henry comes up from behind, clears his throat, and says, "The captain asked me to tell you to collect your belongings and get ready to go ashore."

It takes John just a few moments to gather his blanket and get his travel chest. By the time he emerges on deck, the ship has slowed almost to a halt, and Captain Saker is waiting for him at the railing.

Gesturing toward shore he says, "That's College Land there. I will tell William Ewen that you arrived safely. Good luck to you."

John nods his thanks and climbs down the rope ladder on the side of the ship into a waiting rowboat. Someone hands his chest down to him, and two sailors take him to the dock. They wait just long enough for him to scramble onto the wooden platform before casting off and returning to the ship.

By then, a small crowd has gathered. The men and women, dressed in dark brown breeches, tan work shirts, and simple dresses, look at him with curiosity. They look well fed and healthy. One of the men, slightly older than the rest, is wearing a simple doublet.

John walks up to him and says, "My name is John Gowen. I am looking for Thomas Goodman."

The man looks at him in surprise and says, "That would be me. I'm the overseer here. How can I help you?"

"I have a letter for you from William Ewen that will explain my presence here."

John pulls a folded piece of parchment from his coat and hands it over. Goodman looks at the dark red seal, nods in recognition, and says, "Come to the house. We'll discuss this further there."

He turns and strides up the path. Before John follows him, he looks back at the *Saker*. Sailors are pulling the rowboat up on deck and making fast sails to catch the late afternoon breeze and head across the river to Jamestown. He smiles at the men and women on the dock, picks up his chest, and follows Goodman.

The house is a large, two-story, wood-frame building, big enough to accommodate Ewen in style and comfort on his occasional visits. There are rugs on the floor and expensive furnishings, as well as a slightly moldy smell. When Goodman ushers John into the study filled with shelves of books and documents, John's eyes light up. The library is bigger than the one at Jope's brother's estate.

Goodman sits down at a large table near a window, breaks the seal, and unfolds the letter. John remains standing and studies the plantation manager. The man is in his thirties with a well-trimmed beard. His face is open and without guile. If he is surprised by the contents of the missive, he does not show it at first. But when he comes to the paragraph that grants John free access to the library, he looks up startled to give John a questioning glance. John knows what it says since Ewen read it to him and Jope before he signed and sealed it. He takes out the contract of indenture and slides it across the table.

After Goodman finishes reading it, he stands and comes around to John's side of the table. He shakes his hand and says, "Well, John Gowen, welcome to College Land. We can always use another hard-working hand."

John likes his firm grip and friendly smile. "I am pleased to be here," he says.

"I imagine you haven't eaten in a while," Goodman says. "You can join us for supper and stay here tonight. I will find you a permanent place tomorrow after we get back from church and have one of the workers show you around."

It is a much warmer welcome than John expected. Pleased, he says, "That suits me fine. I am well content to be here."

26

REUNION

Hogg Island—Summer 1628

When Margaret rises early, the Sunday morning sky is cloudless and as blue as Captain Jope's eyes. By the time the inhabitants of Shepherd's Land, led by the lieutenant, hike to Lawne's Creek Church, it is already muggy, promising another sultry summer day. The tall oaks and hickory trees provide some shade along the way, and Margaret enjoys the damp smells rising from the sun-dappled forest floor and the nattering squirrels above acting like sentinels for their journey.

She looks forward to meeting up with the three Africans from College Land and is disappointed when she doesn't see them among the people crowding around the church entrance to greet one another. As Lieutenant Shepherd pays his respect to John Uty, his wife, and their young son, she considers that it is still early.

The air is humid inside the church, too, and several of the plantation owners' wives sitting up front are fanning themselves. Margaret moves to a pew several rows in back of them and kneels to pray in preparation for worship. As always, she prays for Captain Jope and John's safety and well-being, as well as for Emmanuel Driggers, Frances and Peter, and Anthony and Mary and their children. Then she sits, straightening her gown, and waits for the service to begin.

Margaret likes the informal quality of the Anglican service here better than in Jamestown. She certainly doesn't miss the punishing, Puritan fury of the Reverend Bennett's sermons at Warrosquoake. She doesn't mind references to life being brief as a candle and the need to work hard and make every hour count, but they don't need to come with frightening visions of hell and eternal damnation. She also appreciates the anticipatory silence, which allows her to gather her thoughts. But what she likes most of all is singing the hymns, which inspires her with a feeling of serenity and comfort.

As the church fills up, she looks back several times, hoping to see the contingent from College Land, but to no avail. Perhaps their pinnace sprung a leak.

John Uty, who is presiding over the worship service this day, steps up to the podium. He is not much older than her lieutenant, with similar chestnut-brown hair and beard, but he is pudgy in his face and midriff, where Shepherd is fit and lean. He looks over the congregation until everyone has settled and announces Margaret's favorite hymn. Everyone rises and, with Uty conducting, launches into "All People That on Earth Do Dwell."

Their voices swell in unison and fill the church. Margaret especially likes the last verse, an affirmation of the Creator's generosity and beneficence:

> The Lord our God is good;
> his mercy is forever sure;
> his truth at all times firmly stood,
> and shall from age to age endure.

With the last notes echoing from the rafters, the assembled worshippers sit back down. But before Uty can begin his reading from the Bible, there is a commotion at the entrance to the church. Everyone turns to look. It is the workers from College Land, arriving in the nick of time. They file in quickly, looking embarrassed and apologetic. Margaret knows that the manager, Thomas Goodman, can expect a dressing down from Uty afterward for being late.

As Margaret watches the three Africans—Michael, Katherine, and Matthew—enter, she is surprised to see another coming in behind them. Suddenly, her heart skips a beat and her hand flies to her mouth, stifling a cry. The young man looks very much like John. He is older and more mature than the youngster who came with Captain Jope two summers ago. Margaret can't believe her eyes. Surely, it can't be!

She quickly turns to the front, her heart pounding in her chest. A flurry of thoughts and questions rush through her mind. *Is it John? What is he doing here? Why is he with the College Land workers? Where is Captain Jope?*

Margaret goes through the rest of the service as if in a trance. She mouths the words of the hymns and registers the sermon and Bible readings, but she has no idea what was said. When it is over and she rises with the others, she feels almost weightless.

The usual bottleneck that forms at the entrance as people crowd to leave gives her the time to collect herself. By the time she gets outside, many of the attendees are dispersing, gathering in small groups, or taking a walk along one of the ravines.

At first, she doesn't see him and experiences a pang of fear—he can't have departed already. But when she steps down from the church porch, she notices him standing off to one side with others from College Land, listening to their animated conversations.

Margaret calls out softly, "John."

He doesn't respond. Perhaps he hasn't heard her or doesn't expect anyone else to address him.

Again she calls out, this time more forcefully, "John!"

He turns and for a moment stands there motionless, like a rock. Then a welter of emotions washes over his face in rapid succession—surprise, recognition, amazement, elation, joy.

"Margaret!"

He quickly walks over to her and is about to embrace her when he becomes aware that others, startled by his outburst, are watching. He stops, forces himself to be calm, and, hands at his side, bows. Realizing what he is doing, she curtsies in turn.

But then the words spill from her mouth. "What are you doing here? Where is Captain Jope? Is he all right?"

Giving her a warning glance, John says steadily, "It is good to see you, Margaret. Why don't we take a walk among the trees over there?"

As they move beyond the clearing, he glances around to make sure that the others are no longer paying attention to them. Out of sight of most of the churchgoers, they stop and face each other.

John says, almost shyly, "Let me look at you."

He examines her from head to toe in silence, taking in her slender neck, her soft, round curves, her calloused hands. He ends up looking back at her face, the face he has tried to imagine for so long. Margaret marvels at how much he has grown since the last time. He is a handsome young man. Then their glowing eyes meet, and they burst into laughter together, unable to hide their joy any longer. John takes her hand, and they both feel a jolt, like a spark passing between them.

For the next few minutes, words tumble from their mouths. John shares how he decided to come to Virginia and Ewen's plantation, and Margaret tells him how she left Chew's and where she is now. They have a host of questions and acknowledge that there are too many to answer in the brief time available.

All too soon, Matthew from College Land finds them and calls out, "John, we're leaving."

Squeezing Margaret's hand, John says, "I will see you next week again. When I am settled, I will come to Shepherd's Land for an afternoon so we can spend more time."

Then he leaves. Margaret looks after him in a daze. But as she returns to the group from Shepherd's Land, she experiences a sense of happiness and freedom she hasn't felt for a long time.

On the way back, the lieutenant asks her, "Who was that young man?"

"Someone I've known for some time who has come to work at College Land," she says carefully. She is pleased when he nods and accepts her explanation without further questioning.

Over the next few days Margaret feels all aglow. For the first time in many years, she has someone to look forward to seeing soon, someone she can count on, someone she has cared for longer than she can remember.

EPILOGUE

London—Fall 1628

eaning on a ceremonial walking stick, the other arm resting proudly on his hip, the Earl of Warwick looks like a statuesque figure. He does his best to stand perfectly still, but the smell of turpentine and pine resins assail him, and he has to resist the impulse to itch his nose. Light pours in from the window facing the courtyard of his London townhome, catching his features from the side.

At his wife's behest, he is having his portrait done by Daniel Mytens, the Dutch painter who is currently all the rage in London. Ever since King Charles himself declared that Mytens would be his "picture drawer" for life, the Dutchman has had England's nobles line up at his doorstep. So it was quite a coup when Warwick was able to engage him and have him set up a studio in his residence. Except for the King, Mytens normally requires his clients to come to him in his workshop in St. Martin's Lane.

The earl has been enduring these sessions for over a week. The things one does for posterity! Standing still for so long would be easier if he didn't have so much on his mind and so much to do.

It has been a trying year of small victories and bitter defeats. After much work behind the scenes, he and his cousin Nathaniel finally succeeded in getting a new charter from the King for the Massachusetts Bay Colony approved, assuring a permanent home for the Puritan settlers whose faith and well-being are so close to his heart. But power struggles with a founding member of the Council

for New England, of which Rich is currently president, have reared
their ugly head of late. It is almost a repeat of what happened with
George Sandys and the Virginia Company.

The itching is finally too much for Warwick. His hand flies to
his nose, and he scratches it vigorously, ruining his pose.

Behind his easel Daniel Mytens rolls his eyes and sighs. His apprentice, who is preparing red pigment, tries not to smirk. It is only
the fifth time that the earl has shifted his position in the past quarter
hour.

Mytens puts his brush and palette down on the small table next
to him. "Perhaps this is a good time to take a break, m'Lord," he
says, resigned.

"No!" Rich exclaims. "Let's get this session over and done with.
I don't have all afternoon."

Just then there is a loud knock at the door. Alfred appears and
whispers in Warwick's ear. The earl immediately steps down from
the raised platform. He turns to Mytens and says languidly, "I am
sorry, Daniel. Something has come up that can't wait. We will have
to postpone after all."

The painter knows better than to express his frustration. He
bows deeply and says, "Of course, m'Lord. I will return tomorrow."

Warwick waves his hand in his general direction and stomps out.
He rushes to his study, stops at the door, gathers himself, and makes
a dignified entrance. Captain Daniel Elfrith is waiting in the middle
of the study with Bullard at his side. The corpulent mariner executes
a deep bow. His stocky companion does the same but with less flair.

For a moment Rich wonders if the scowl is permanently etched
in the younger man's face. Then he cannot contain himself any longer. "You have news!" he bursts out.

Elfrith clears his throat and breaks out into a big grin. His cunning eyes almost disappear in his pudgy face. Then he says, impor-
tantly, "I do, m'Lord. By Charles's prickly knob, I do."

Warwick plops into his armchair. As he moves a pillow to the
side, Alfred hands him a glass of red wine. Rich gulps it down and

extends it to the butler to refill it. He takes a more moderate sip and holds the glass toward Elfrith and Bullard with a questioning look.

"Thank you, m'Lord. Don't mind if we do," says Elfrith. He nods to Bullard, then settles his massive bulk on the sofa opposite Warwick and scratches his scruffy chin.

Bullard stands uncomfortably off to the side. He accepts a glass of wine from Alfred and swigs it down as if it were a cup of rum.

Elfrith takes more time with his, savoring his first nip and smacking his lips in appreciation. Then he asks, "Would your Lordship like to hear the bad news first, or should I start with the good tidings?"

Rich doesn't dither. "Give me the good news first. It has been a dismal week, and I can use some cheering up."

Elfrith's plump cheeks seem to grow as a beatific smile blossoms on his face. "I have found the perfect spot for a new colony," he announces. "Two uninhabited islands off the coast of South America that, to my knowledge, do not appear on any map."

For a moment Rich is speechless. Then he leans forward eagerly and says, "That is most excellent intelligence, indeed. You must tell me all about it." He takes another sip of wine and continues, "But the bad news?"

Elfrith's face darkens, and his jaw tightens. As he hesitates, Bullard steps forward and growls, "The Flying Dutchman is up to his old tricks, privateering in concert with your Lordship's frigates and absconding with all the treasure hoard."

Warwick suddenly feels tired. Then a wave of fury rises inside him. "Bugger all," he shouts, leaping from his chair. "How many?"

Elfrith sighs. "Three of our ships."

"Three?"

"Aye, he's been busy as a barnacle, has our Flying Dutchman."

Warwick's face contorts into a mask of murderous malevolence. He fixes his black eyes first on Elfrith, then on Bullard, and with a feral sneer says, "Then I guess we'd better clip his wings!"

CPSIA information can be obtained
at www.ICGtesting.com
Printed in the USA
FSHW010910130519
58050FS